Investing In Dividend Growth Stocks

ABOUT THE AUTHOR

Shane Forbes is a retired investment actuary and former Fellow of the
Society of Actuaries. He holds an Honors Bachelor's degree, First Class,
in Mathematics and Physics from Dalhousie University and a Master's
degree in Mathematics from the University of Toronto. *Investing in
Dividend Growth Stocks* is his first book. He lives in Florida.

Investing In Dividend Growth Stocks

A Safer More Realistic Path To Financial Freedom

Shane Forbes

NeoCadence LLC

December 2015

NeoCadence LLC
Web: www.neocadence.com
Email: publishing@neocadence.com
Mail: PO Box 338, Gotha FL 34734

First edition published December 2015. Most copies are printed on demand and may include the printing date and location on the last page.

ISBN 978-0-9822870-0-2

In memory of my parents, Arlene and Russel Forbes.

IMPORTANT: Investment opinion is not investment advice. This book reflects the Author's opinion. It is not investment advice. The Author and Publisher are not financial advisors. Please speak to a financial advisor or other appropriate professional who understands your situation before investing in the instruments mentioned in this book. Investing in the financial markets, including the stock market, and in particular the instruments mentioned in this book, entails risk. Be mindful of the risks involved. The Author and Publisher are not responsible for any losses that may be incurred and in particular expressly disclaim any liability that may be incurred from investing in the investments mentioned in this book or from following the methods in this book. This book primarily pertains to U.S. securities and U.S. markets. It may not be relevant to other securities and other markets. This book provides links to sites on the web, retrieved as of mid-2015. The Author and Publisher are not responsible if the addresses of these sites change and are not responsible for the content of these sites. This book includes a link to an Excel 2007 spreadsheet. The spreadsheet comes with no warranties, implied or otherwise. The Author and Publisher are not responsible for any losses that may be incurred, and in particular expressly disclaim any liability that may be incurred, on using this spreadsheet. Use at your own risk.

Contents

List of Figures

List of Tables

Part I

Essentials

"You do things when the opportunities come along. I've had periods in my life when I've had a bundle of ideas come along, and I've had long dry spells. If I get an idea next week, I'll do something. If not, I won't do a damn thing."

Warren Buffett

Chapter 1

They're Back

"Old fashions please me best." Shakespeare

D IVIDENDS. During the bull market of the late 1990s, they were ridiculed as old-fashioned. Scorned. It was the New Economy. Dividends were ignored. They were just a dinosaur of the Old Economy. Of past importance. Now, irrelevant.

During the Crash of 2008, desperate investors just wanted their money back. Everything that could be sold was sold. Dividends did not matter. Dividend growth did not matter.

Yet, when we fast-forward a scant few years later, a funny thing has happened to these get-no-respect Rodney Dangerfield dividend growth companies. Nothing. While the Crash of 2008's Lehman and other overleveraged financials have transmogrified into the New Economy's Pets.com and other Dot Com darlings that have long since melted away, high-quality dividend growth companies are still around. Their businesses have recovered; their stock prices have recovered. They are still paying their dividends. They are still growing their dividends.

And while investors in riskier stocks are monetarily shell-shocked, investors in dividend growth stocks are doing nothing different. Safely and quietly, they are becoming rich.

3

Success

"If a man does not keep pace with his companions, perhaps it is because he hears a different drummer. Let him step to the music which he hears, however measured or far away." Henry David Thoreau

To succeed as a dividend growth investor, we need:

- Patience;

- Time; and

- High-quality dividend growth stocks,

  - growing at stable, moderate, and sustainable rates and

  - selling at reasonable valuations or better.

Patience is the cornerstone of investing success. Great investors buy great companies selling at reasonable valuations or better – then, quite simply, they wait. ***Over the long term, great companies grow at rates few investors can match.*** Impatience destroys this opportunity. Warren Buffett has said that, "lethargy, bordering on sloth should remain the cornerstone of an investment style." Likewise, most of the time, leave your (high-quality) stocks alone.

On the other hand, if we choose to trade, we will find that compounded over many years, even though we may occasionally do better than the market, overall, we will do worse – and sometimes much worse. Investors in 401(k) plans who time the market perform worse than those who do nothing. They also perform worse than the funds themselves. As a trader, we need (1) the right mindset; and (2) the right resources. But few of us have the right mindset. For instance, we have to accept losses, but few of us accept losses; few of us accept failure. Likewise, we cannot match the resources of professionals. From Bloomberg terminals to research to execution, professionals have the upper hand. We will find it difficult to win in an extended game against a stronger foe.

Realize, however, that when we do not trade, there will be times when the market tests our resolve. Our stocks stagnate – or fall – while others, usually speculative stocks, soar. Like sirens, they bid us to buy. Be careful. At best, take measured bets. Most speculative stories end poorly – with individual investors left holding the bag.

Time allows us to reap the benefits of dividend growth, dividend reinvestment, and compounding returns. Given enough time, our wealth and dividend income will soar.

High-quality stocks are the foundation of all long-term portfolios. High-quality businesses generate strong internal returns, *internal returns forming the basis of shareholder returns*. With high-quality stocks, the businesses get bigger and stronger. By contrast, over time, businesses with poor internal returns get smaller and weaker. Some even fail.

Dividend growth stocks are companies at a particular stage of their life cycle. They are well beyond the earliest stages, when a company depends on outside funds to survive and grow; and beyond even the later stages when the company begins to fund itself. At the dividend growth stage, not only does the company fund itself, but it generates so much extra cash it can afford to pay dividends.

Stable growth is always more valuable than fluctuating growth. Given equal average annual returns, we end up wealthier with stable growth compared to fluctuating growth. For instance, consider two stocks with average annual gains of ten percent. One gains seventy percent the first year then loses fifty percent the next (the average of 70 and *minus* 50 is ten). The second gains ten percent each year (the average of two tens is, wait for it, ten). With the first stock, wealth drops fifteen percent in two years. With the second stock, wealth rises twenty-one percent in two years. Stable growth makes us richer. Dividend growth stocks are stable stocks. *It is the low volatility of returns that is a subtle but substantial benefit of investing in dividend growth stocks.*

For long-term investors, neither the slow limp of survival of slow-growth companies nor the rapid chaos of cash burn of high-growth companies will do. Slow-growth companies are just battling it out to stay alive, battling it out to avoid becoming just another footnote in history. Dividend increases are mediocre – often well below the rate of inflation. High-growth companies burn through their cash rapidly. They continually need more. Many fail. They cannot afford to pay dividends, or, at most, they pay just a token dividend.

Slow growth never amounts to much. High growth usually fizzles out. *Instead, it is moderate growth that works. Over the long term, it is the only growth that can be sustained; it is the only growth that produces sound long-term returns.*

Ultimately, dividend growth arises from earnings per share growth. For our purposes, earnings per share growth averages 8-12 percent a year for large-caps and 8-16 percent a year for midcaps. Most of our dividend growth stocks are large-caps.

After we have found our high-quality dividend growth stocks, we value them properly. We buy only if our stocks sell at reasonable valuations or better. If we don't, it will not matter how our companies perform. Over the long term, our portfolio underperforms. Paying too much is the death knell of investing success.

The Business

"I am a better investor because I am a businessman, and a better business-man because I am an investor." Warren Buffett

Trust us. That's what Lehman's CEO, Board of Directors, and management effectively said to the markets and Lehman's shareholders in early 2008.

What shareholders received, instead, was disaster. Lehman had taken on too much risk. When credit markets froze, the company was trapped. On 15 September 2008, Lehman declared bankruptcy. Shareholders lost everything. A few months earlier, Lehman had even raised its dividend.

Stories such as Lehman's are not uncommon. A few more:

- Fannie Mae and Freddie Mac – both with stellar long-term records – once paid growing dividends. Yet, in 2008, with systemic risks looming, the government took them over. As of mid-2015, both remain in conservatorship.

- By the late 1990s, Nortel was a star. In 1998, it had even started paying a dividend. But the company underestimated the Dot Com downturn. Today, it is a shadow of itself.

- Winn-Dixie, a grocery chain in the Southeast, was a dividend growth dynamo. It had paid dividends for more than sixty years and had raised dividends for more than fifty. Yet, in 2005, the company declared bankruptcy. (Later, it emerged from bankruptcy. It did not pay a dividend. It was taken private in 2012.)

Are dividends not silver bullets? No, unfortunately, they are not:

- A history of dividends does not guarantee future dividends or dividend growth.

- A dividend from a terrible or weakened business cannot stop its shares from falling to zero.

- Investment success is not guaranteed even when a company has raised its dividend for decades.

Dividends are not a panacea. Do not look at dividends independently of the business. *It is not the dividend as such, but the ability of the business to pay a dividend that matters most, the vitality of the business ultimately steering the dividend, its sustainability, and its growth.*

Return

"What is algebra, exactly? Is it those three-cornered things?" J. M. Barrie

When you invest in a share of stock, you earn an *annual* return equal to dividend yield plus growth rate in share price:[1]

---

[1]The formulas in this section apply when dividends are paid at the end of a year. Dividends paid at intermediate points can be reinvested – or even invested in something else. The complete formula – incorporating dividend reinvestment – is on page 73, in Chapter 5.

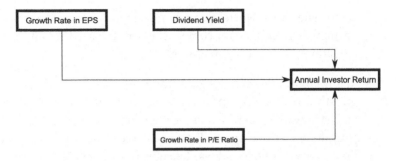

Figure 1.1. Dividend yield, growth rate in earnings per share, and growth rate in P/E ratio as contributors to annual (investor) return.

$$Annual\ Return\ =\ Dividend\ Yield$$
$$+\ Growth\ Rate\ in\ Share\ Price$$

You can use this formula to calculate a stock's expected annual return. For instance, suppose you invest in a share of stock at $100. You expect the stock to reach $110 in a year. You also expect to receive $3 a share in dividends. What is the stock's expected annual return? Dividend yield is 3 / 100 or 3 percent. Growth rate in share price is (110 - 100) / 100 or 10 / 100 or 10 percent. Expected annual return is, therefore, 3 + 10 percent, or 13 percent.

With a bit of algebra, not one of those three-cornered things, we expand growth rate in share price to derive the following equivalent formula:

$$Annual\ Return\ =\ Dividend\ Yield$$
$$+\ Growth\ Rate\ in\ Earnings\ Per\ Share$$
$$+\ Growth\ Rate\ in\ P/E\ Ratio$$
$$+\ (\ \ Growth\ Rate\ in\ Earnings\ Per\ Share$$
$$*\ Growth\ Rate\ in\ P/E\ Ratio\ \ )$$

We generally ignore the term in parentheses because it is comparatively tiny. After discarding this term, the formula becomes approximate and the sum of the remaining three terms (Figure 1.1):

$$Annual\ Return\ =\ Dividend\ Yield$$
$$+\ Growth\ Rate\ in\ Earnings\ Per\ Share$$
$$+\ Growth\ Rate\ in\ P/E\ Ratio$$

This is a general result that applies to any stock. As an example, suppose a stock yields 3 percent with expected growth rate in earnings per share of 10 percent. If P/E ratio does not change, we expect the stock to return 10 + 3 percent, or 13 percent. If P/E ratio rises, (say) from 15 to 18, a 20 percent increase, we expect the stock to return 13 + 20 percent, or 33 percent. If P/E ratio falls, (say) from 15 to 12, a 20 percent decrease, we expect the stock to return 13 - 20 percent, or -7 percent.

This last calculation highlights one of the dangers of holding stocks with potentially rapid drops in P/E ratio, a particularly thorny problem when P/E ratio is high: *Even with rapid growth in earnings per share, a big drop in P/E ratio can decimate your returns faster than Carl Icahn can say Gangnam Style.* When you buy a stock with a high P/E ratio, you must be certain business momentum can be maintained – or even accelerate.

Use this formula and data from sites such as Yahoo! Finance to estimate returns. Consider IBM. As of mid-2015, IBM's dividend yield is 3.5 percent and expected growth rate in earnings per share is 6.5 percent. Using our formula, if P/E ratio does not change, we expect the stock to return 3.5 + 6.5 percent, or 10.0 percent. What if P/E ratio changes? We cannot know how much it will change. We have to consider what-ifs. For instance, if P/E ratio falls 5 percent, the stock will return 10.0 - 5.0 percent, or 5.0 percent. By contrast, if P/E ratio rises 5 percent, the stock will return 10.0 + 5.0 percent, or 15.0 percent. Though admittedly a broad range, and notwithstanding IBM's recent problems, it is not unreasonable to say that – *if earnings come out as expected and expectations do not change too drastically* – we expect IBM to return between 5.0 percent and 15.0 percent the next twelve months.

In these formulas, annual return is dividend yield plus something else. We call this something else, the contribution from capital changes: When this contribution is positive, we say we have a *capital gain*; when this contribution is negative, we say we have a *capital loss*. When we hold on to our stock, our gain or loss is *unrealized*. When we sell our stock, our gain or loss is *realized*.

Dividend yield has historically produced about one-third of market returns; capital gains, about two-thirds. Moreover, of the contribution from capital gains, almost all has come from growth rate in earnings per share. That is, **over long periods, growth rate in P/E ratio has contributed nothing**. Sometimes, it has added. At other times, it has subtracted. Net, it has produced nothing.

As a broad rule, buy stocks when the market's P/E ratio is reasonable or low. Likewise, buy stable stocks, such as high-quality dividend growth stocks, when their P/E ratios are reasonable or low. A reasonable or low P/E ratio gives you some hope that P/E ratio will rise and add to your returns; or, at least, that P/E ratio does not fall too much and subtract from your returns.

You can generally count on receiving your dividends, especially your dividends from high-quality stocks. Capital gains are another matter. *Capital gains are inherently unstable and fleeting.* A skeptic would say that you cannot collect capital gains without the help of a Greater Fool. That is, someone has to step forward and pay more for your shares. Though this notion is widely accepted, it is perhaps a bit untrue. As the last formula shows, contribution from capital changes is growth rate in earnings per share plus growth rate in P/E ratio. It seems reasonable that someone will pay for the former because a company typically adds to its value when it grows earnings per share. It is in the latter, however, that the Theory of the Greater Fool has merit. Growth rate in P/E ratio is volatile because it has underpinnings in random things such as psychology and expectations; and random events such as weather and war.

*With taxes, **after-tax** return is simply **after-tax** dividend yield plus growth rate in earnings per share and growth rate in P/E ratio.* Dividends are taxed; the other two terms are not. This assumes you hold on to your stock. By contrast, if you sell with a capital gain, you pay taxes on the capital gain; if you sell with a capital loss, you are (naturally) not taxed on the loss, and in fact can use the loss to offset certain other taxes and thus reduce your total tax, in effect, the government subsidizing part of your loss.

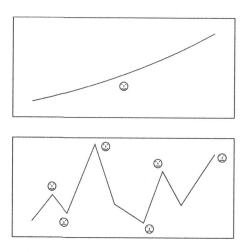

Figure 1.2. The stable emotions of steady growth versus the fluctuating emotions of whipsawed growth.

Risk

"Annndd, it's gone." Bank employee, South Park Bank Savings and Loans (South Park)

A savings account has one attractive feature: If you do not make any withdrawals, your balance *steadily* grows. As an investor, not only is steady growth good for its own sake, it removes emotion.

By contrast, whipsawed growth kindles trouble. Investors go through a range of emotions (Figure 1.2), emotions that very often get the best of them. They react to whatever makes them most comfortable. They sell after the market has been falling (and they cannot take it any longer). They buy after the market has been rising (and they feel left out).

The comfort of a savings account comes at a steep price, however: Returns are low.

To overcome the shackles of low returns, investors lean on risk. As one way, they invest in stocks. Over time, stocks have produced higher returns than savings accounts.

But there is a catch: Investors now forgo the prospect of steadily rising account balances. Instead, balances whipsaw in concordance with the crises of bear markets and the euphoria of bull markets. In effect, investors exchange the prospect of safe and steadily rising account balances for risk – and the prospect of much higher account balances in the future.

By convention, risk is defined as volatility of returns.[2] Just as jumping around with a Pogo stick is riskier than walking, something that varies more is riskier than something that varies less. Likewise, stocks that fluctuate more are riskier than stocks that fluctuate less, and, therefore, as a collection of broad rules, smaller stocks are riskier than larger stocks, stocks at lower prices are riskier than stocks at higher prices, and stocks with higher leverage are riskier than stocks with lower leverage. Although some have rightly challenged this definition of risk, it remains in wide use.

Often, when we buy stocks, the upside seduces us. The downside gets short shrift. Do not fall into this trap. Realize that large gains go hand in hand with large losses. *If you chase extraordinary gains, be prepared for extraordinary losses. With too much risk, if enough positions move against you – like watching a sorry ending to a bad movie – your time is wasted, your portfolio ruined.*

Investing fads exemplify the kinds of dangers that investors face when they take on the wrong kind of risk or too much risk. Dreams of large and faddish gains can be intoxicating, but, like bell-bottoms and dance crazes, fads do eventually fade. And when they do, investors get punished. *Perhaps for every one-hundred investors in faddish stocks, eighty lose money, fifteen break even, and five do well.* These are Vegas odds. The history of faddish stocks is littered with the corpses of expectations, unrealistic and unmet.

---

[2] More precisely, and in turn, volatility of returns is defined as the *standard deviation* of returns. Standard deviation measures how much a series varies about its average. The series {0.05, 0.10, 0.15} has a standard deviation half that of the standard deviation of the series {0.10, 0.20, 0.30}. The second series varies more widely. If these series are stock returns, we say the first stock is half as risky as the second stock.

Drop	To get back to even	
	Percentage increase needed	Years needed at returns of ten percent a year
10%	11%	1.1
20%	25%	2.3
30%	43%	3.7
50%	100%	7.3
70%	233%	12.6
90%	900%	24.2
95%	1900%	31.4
97%	3233%	36.8
99%	9900%	48.3
100%	Complete loss	Not happening

Table 1.1. Drops in stock prices and how much and how long are needed (at returns of ten percent a year) to get back to even. Ten percent is an illustration. Risky stocks can recover much faster than ten percent a year. But we cannot count on this. They do not always recover. Some remain in the dustbin of penny stock perdition forever. Others declare bankruptcy.

Dividends do seem to reduce volatility. When the price of a dividend-paying stock drops, its dividend yield rises. The higher dividend yield attracts traders and investors. They step in. Their buying lends support, lowering the volatility of the stock. In effect, the dividend acts as a *floor*.

In all cases, the company paying the dividend must be sound. Buying Lehman in 2008 – as its share price cratered and its dividend yield soared – would have been a mistake. Buying high-quality businesses, such as Starbucks and Emerson Electric, would have been wise.

Because the dividend acts as a floor, losses in high-quality dividend stocks are often muted. Consequently, *these stocks do not have to repeatedly recover from large losses in the past*. Such recoveries can take a long time. For instance, suppose a stock loses fifty percent. It then needs to gain one-hundred percent to get back to even. If the stock returns ten percent a year, it needs more than seven years to recover. By contrast, if a stock loses twenty percent, it needs a little more than two. Table 1.1 shows how much and how long are needed (at returns of ten percent a year) to get back to even. *Note that the bigger the drop, the **exponentially longer** that it takes for the stock price to recover – and, because of this, the far less likely you are to eventually becoming rich. To become rich, you must avoid large losses **at all costs**.*

The performance of the S&P 500[®] Dividend Aristocrats[®] attests to the strength of dividend growth stocks. Dividend Aristocrats are stocks in the S&P 500 that have raised their dividends twenty-five consecutive years. In terms of wealth accumulation over long periods (the only thing that matters, really), they have beaten the market and have done so with lower volatility (risk). For instance, according to Standard & Poor's, in the ten years ending 30 September 2015, they returned 10.0 percent a year compared to 6.8 percent a year for the S&P 500. Their volatility of 13.8 percent was lower than the 14.9 percent volatility of the S&P 500.

Thinking about risk and return in the broadest of terms, we do have a reasonable basis to expect dividend growth stocks to outperform with lower risk:

- Dividend growth companies are stable businesses. This means lower business vulnerabilities, thus a more stable stock price and lower risk.

- Because of the stable stock price, investors, both old and new, buy and hold – thus further bolstering stock price stability and lowering risk.

- Because the dividend acts as a floor, sharp losses are often muted, thus further lowering risk.

- Typically, these companies do not experience the kind of catastrophic failure implied in *crushingly* poor returns. For instance, few become penny stocks; few declare bankruptcy.

- Dividend growth companies grow at a stable, moderate, and sustainable pace. *Over the long term, moderate growth is the only growth that can be maintained – and still make you rich.* Slow growth never amounts to much. High growth usually fizzles out.

- Returns of dividend growth stocks do not suffer from high volatility. *It is a mathematical truism that, given equal average returns, volatility reduces the accumulation of wealth, high volatility resulting in much lower accumulation of wealth than low or moderate volatility.* For instance, a stock with an expected annual return of ten percent and annual volatility of twenty percent can be expected to increase wealth roughly eight percent a year. Double that volatility to forty percent and wealth takes an unmistakable drubbing – it increases just two percent a year. *It is the low volatility of returns that is a subtle but substantial benefit of investing in dividend growth stocks.* It is probably why, mathematically, when combined with moderate returns, the S&P 500 Dividend Aristocrats have produced so much accumulated wealth over long periods. Boring is not just safe. Boring makes you richer.

With dividend growth stocks, risk is low and returns are moderate. On a risk-adjusted basis, the stocks outperform.

Inflation

"Consequences, shmonsequences, as long as I'm rich." Daffy Duck

"Money is always there, but the pockets change." Gertrude Stein

Over the long term, income must rise faster than inflation. If not, buying power whittles away. Retirees who invest conservatively learn this lesson the hard way. At first, little is out of reach. A few years later, what was affordable becomes a luxury. Later still, paying for basic necessities becomes difficult.

Gold, real estate, and commodities such as oil, nickel, and copper respond quickly to inflation. Gold responds when uncertainty emerges.

Real estate holds its value. And, because commodities such as oil, nickel, and copper are used by, or in, so many things they surge when inflation accelerates.

Financial assets react differently to inflation. Cash has barely kept pace with inflation; (long-term) bonds have slightly outpaced inflation; and stocks have returned far more than inflation.

These returns reflect risk. The safety and liquidity of cash means it cannot return much more than inflation. Against the backdrop of the 2008 Financial Crisis, as of mid-2015, cash has returned almost nothing since 2009. Bonds are riskier than cash. Risks to bonds include falling market values, illiquidity, default risk, and low reinvestment rates. Stocks are the riskiest. In addition to company-specific risks – competition, regulations, leverage, fraud, and so on – returns depend on psychology, valuation, economic forecasts, and sector and industry risk.

In the long run, stocks beat inflation because of what the underlying companies create and sell and the risks that they take, both financial and otherwise. In the short run, however, most stocks are poor hedges against inflation. When inflation surges, most companies cannot raise prices fast enough to offset inflation. Earnings suffer. Dividend growth suffers. Only those few stocks that directly relate to commodities keep pace with surging inflation. Like springs, their selling prices, thus sales and earnings, respond quickly to inflation. Other stocks, and especially those that use commodities as raw materials, fail miserably.

Within the universe of stocks, high-quality dividend growth stocks play a unique role. Because of underlying business stability – and stable, moderate, and sustainable growth – they offer the safety of current income and the inflation-beating power of income growth. Many high-quality dividend growth stocks have raised dividends 8-12 percent a year for decades, well ahead of the roughly three percent rate of long-term inflation.

Many investors are too cautious. Chastened by the stock market's history of stomach-churning drops, they overplay the dangers of investing in stocks and, consequently, hold too much in bonds and cash, thus squeezing their long-term buying power.

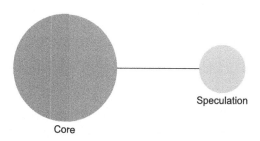

Speculation

Core

Figure 1.3. Portfolio barbell.

Portfolios

"My mother always phones me and asks, Is everything all wrong?" Richard Lewis

Core holdings are investments that you make to pay for serious long-term financial goals such as retirement and college. Because these investments have to match important debts far into the future, core holdings must have a high likelihood of success.

At the other end of the investment spectrum, speculative holdings are investments that you can afford to lose. Speculative investments are play money, long shots. They have three features in common:

- They have a low likelihood of long-term success.

- They have a high likelihood of *complete* long-term failure.

- They are *not* buy-and-hold stocks. They are trades.

Speculative stocks include stocks such as Jones Soda. It has had its run. It is still around. Others such as Pets.com have faded into the dustbin of history.

In general, consider any stock selling below $10 a *rank* speculative stock. There are exceptions, of course. For instance, during bear markets, share prices of even good companies fall below $10. Nevertheless, as a general observation: Below $10, be careful; preferably, don't buy.

Penny stocks take speculation to another level. Never buy penny stocks. You throw your money away.

The intelligent investor holds a large core position with some speculation, like an unbalanced barbell with the large end as the core and the small end as speculation (Figure 1.3). *This allocates the majority of assets to safety and return and wraps a tight band around risk.*

Unfortunately, most investors indulge in the opposite. Guided by hope, rather than by reality, they hold a flipped version of the unbalanced barbell. They hold a large speculative position and a small core position. They binge on speculation.

How large of a core position should the intelligent investor hold? The answer depends on factors such as risk tolerance and the timing and size of long-term financial goals. Nevertheless, as a broad guideline, the conservative investor holds at least ninety percent in the core, the typical investor at least eighty percent, and the risk-chasing multimillionaire-or-bust investor at least seventy percent. Unless you know what you are doing, are risk-seeking, are young or rich or single with no obligations, are new to investing and want to learn the wrong lessons, willing to take punishing losses and most likely experiencing permanent losses to your capital, do not hold less than fifty percent in the core. In other words, for almost all reasonable investors, core exceeds speculation. The potential extra gain from excess speculation is worth neither the headache nor the heartache.

We have classes between core and speculation. In general, think of your portfolio as a pyramid with core as a broad and robust base, stocks other than core and speculation in the middle, and a smattering of speculation at the top (Figure 1.4). In the previous paragraph's guidelines, you can shrink speculation by some appropriate amount and replace that amount with stocks in the "other" category. Stocks in the "other" category include slow-growth large-cap stocks with generous dividends, cyclical large-cap stocks, many midcaps, and even conservative small-caps – anything that does not naturally group into core or speculation.

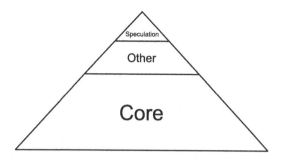

Figure 1.4. Portfolio pyramid.

Especially when held over long periods, most core holdings trounce most speculative holdings. Core holdings avoid the sharp losses that sculpt wanton speculation. *Core holdings march relentlessly up and to the right, the steady long-term compounding of stable, moderate, and sustainable gains resulting in robust gains in long-term wealth.* You may strike it rich with a speculative pick; but you are more likely to underperform or lose it all. If you choose speculation, spread your bets: Buy several speculative stocks or even a mutual fund or ETF that focuses on such things. With core stocks, you can get away with owning a few positions; with speculative stocks, you cannot. You need many more speculative stocks because some crash and many do just about nothing – you want the occasional big winner to offset the many poor performers. During the stock market's usually once-in-a-generation speculative bubble, when some change promises to transform society – such as the popularization of the Internet and the World Wide Web in the late 1990s – speculative stocks in such areas explode. It pays to take advantage of such manias when you can – because the gains can be astronomical; but even then do not overextend, and know when to fold and go home – because the culmination of such manias always ends in a crash.

You can hold funds (mutual funds and ETFs) or individual stocks in the core. A balanced fund exemplifies the kind of fund that belongs in the core. Balanced funds normally hold 55-65 percent of their portfolios in stocks, 30-40 percent in bonds, and the rest in cash. In bull markets, these funds do not rise as much as the market. In bear markets, they do not fall as much. *Their stronger relative returns during bear markets more than compensate for their weaker relative returns during bull markets.* These funds typically avoid large losses. Long term, they march quietly up and to the right. Started in 1929, Vanguard Wellington fund (Investor Shares, VWELX), the country's oldest balanced fund, has returned 8.2 percent a year since inception with lower-than-average risk.

A portfolio of reasonably valued high-quality dividend growth stocks fits squarely in the core. Like a balanced fund, this portfolio gets a reasonable portion of its return from income with a larger portion from growth. Admittedly, and importantly, unlike a balanced fund, the *sources* of income and growth are not distinct. Still, at least there is income – and a focus on the importance of income; and there is growth – and a focus on the importance of growth. In addition, just like a balanced fund, this portfolio rises less than the market during bull markets and falls less than the market during bear markets. The latter more than makes up for the former. These stocks march to the beat of a different drummer – but a very sensible one.

A reasonable core portfolio strategy uses:

- balanced funds in employee retirement accounts, where stocks and specialized funds are generally not available; and

- dividend growth stocks, dividend growth funds, and balanced funds in other accounts.

In the next chapter, we turn to dividends. ♣

CHAPTER 2

Dividends

"Many solutions were suggested for this problem, but most of these were largely concerned with the movements of small green pieces of paper, which is odd because on the whole it wasn't the small green pieces of paper that were unhappy." Douglas Adams (The Hitchhiker's Guide to the Galaxy)

D IVIDENDS are distributions that companies make to their shareholders, typically in cash. The source of a company's dividends is its profits.[1] Most U.S. companies pay quarterly dividends.

A company's Board of Directors must approve every dividend. The board has to meet, make an assessment, and declare each dividend payable. Once a company declares a dividend, it is legally obligated to pay it.

Nothing prevents a board from adjusting every dividend. For instance, P. F. Chang's, which has since gone private, used to pay forty-five

---

[1] In certain cases, up to some limit, companies can return to shareholders part of what shareholders *invested* in the company. Confusingly, these payments are also called "dividends." In this book, I do not consider these dividends. I consider dividends as arising from profits. This makes dividends a component of return. By contrast, getting back part of what you invested is not a component of return.

percent of each quarter's earnings – as a matter of policy – as dividends. Nevertheless, most companies do not adjust their dividends more frequently than annually.

The Board of Directors must consider these dividend adjustments carefully. A company makes a huge mistake when it raises its dividend – only to unceremoniously cut it later. Typically, the stock market pummels a company that lowers or ends its dividend. Some companies should never have initiated a dividend in the first place. (Think Nortel.)

Some claim a dividend is a sign of weakness. This view is extreme. It is not without criticism:

- First, without a dividend, investors have to believe in the sanctity (and accuracy) of stock prices. But the stock market makes no guarantees here – especially over the short term – as stock prices gyrate for all sorts of reasons, some having nothing to do with how the company performs.

- Second, without a dividend, income-oriented investors have to continually sell a portion of their shares to replicate or "manufacture" a so-called homemade dividend. This constant selling has trading costs. Moreover, many find it psychologically difficult to do.

- Third, for *companies* to profitably invest what they pay out as dividends they have to find opportunities to invest and management has to be infallible. But profitable opportunities are far from plentiful and management is not infallible. Better to pay a dividend now than fritter away the money later.

- Fourth, there comes a stage in a company's *life cycle* when it generates so much extra cash it cannot invest it all. When this happens, it has to buy back shares, pay dividends, or do both.

- Fifth, and directly, investors *want* their dividends. In 2012, Apple resumed its dividend because shareholders wanted at least part of the cash it was continually accumulating. They did not want the cash to idle. (With its iMojo on life support at the time, Apple ended its first foray into dividends in 1995.)

- Sixth, and philosophically, *the ultimate objective of any stock is to pay dividends.* Investing is not charitable giving. Investors do not part with their money for fun. At some point, dividends must begin.

A better view of a dividend accepts that it is a cost that companies must bear. A dividend to shareholders is not that different from interest to bondholders or taxes to the government. Each party gets its share. Long-term shareholders are partners in a company's journey. A dividend is their portion of a company's success. A *reasonable* dividend policy is not an admission of defeat. *It is a reasonable allocation of success.*

Dividend Yield

Dividend yield is equivalent annual dividend divided by current stock price:

$$Dividend\ Yield\ =\ \frac{Equivalent\ Annual\ Dividend}{Current\ Stock\ Price}$$

For quarterly dividends, equivalent annual dividend is quarterly dividend times four. For monthly dividends, equivalent annual dividend is monthly dividend times twelve. For semiannual dividends, the multiplier is two. For annual dividends, the multiplier is one.

As I write this, mid-2015, IBM trades at $148.85. With a quarterly dividend of $1.30, its equivalent annual dividend is 1.30 * 4 or $5.20. IBM's dividend yield is therefore 5.20 / 148.85 or 3.49 percent.

Implicitly, this formula assumes dividends do not change in the next year. But good companies raise their dividends annually. Thus, the numerator understates dividends for these companies – *and calculated dividend yield understates true dividend yield*. Consider IBM again. IBM typically raises its quarterly dividend in May. Suppose IBM raises its quarterly dividend to $1.45 in May 2016. Dividends in the next year are thus $1.30, $1.30, $1.45, and $1.45, for a total of $5.50. True dividend yield is thus 5.50 / 148.85 or 3.70 percent.

A natural question to ask about this discrepancy is, "What is the adjustment?" Clearly, there is no universal answer because the adjustment varies depending on the time between when we calculate the stock's dividend yield and when the company raises its dividend but *on "average," for the typical case – a company that pays quarterly dividends and raises its dividend once a year – the adjustment is 0.625 times the dividend growth rate, expressed in percentage points*. For instance, if a company pays quarterly dividends and raises its dividend ten percent once a year, a not atypical combination for a high-quality dividend growth stock, the average adjustment is 0.625 * 10 percent or 6.25 percent. In this case, true dividend yield is on average 1.0625 times calculated dividend yield and a company with a calculated dividend yield of (say) 3.50 percent has a true dividend yield on average of 1.0625 * 3.50 or 3.72 percent. Make this rough mental adjustment to dividend yield on financial websites that use calculated dividend yield. With good companies, you receive more than the going rate. You have to estimate the dividend growth rate.

Instead of using equivalent annual dividend in the formula, investors sometimes use variations:

- They use *estimated* dividends per share.

- They use *history*. That is, they use dividends per share paid during the previous twelve months.

- They use history *and* they do not use per share values. Instead, they use dividends paid during the year divided by the company's market value, that is, its market capitalization, calculated as share price times number of shares outstanding.

None of these definitions, including our original one, is mathematically precise. Nevertheless, they are good enough.

A company's dividend yield often depends on the maturity of the industry it operates in. Companies in young industries – with typically good growth prospects – invest heavily in their businesses to grow. They cannot pay dividends; or, at best, they pay token dividends. By contrast, companies in older industries with limited growth prospects have nothing to invest in. They return as much as they want. Some pay hefty dividends.

Investors unwittingly compare dividends from corporations to distributions from non-corporations such as REITs and MLPs – but that compares chess and checkers. REITs and MLPs play by special rules that generally distort their yields:

- REITs have to distribute ninety percent of their taxable income to shareholders. Because they are partnerships, MLPs have to distribute all their income. Corporations have no such rules. They typically distribute much less.

- Because they distribute so much, REITs and MLPs have to continually raise funds. If they raise funds in the debt market, risk increases. If they raise funds in the stock market, dilution of existing holders follows, negating some of the benefits of the distributions.

- Tax rates on distributions from REITs and MLPs are usually higher than tax rates on dividends from corporations.

Dividend yield rises when equivalent annual dividend rises or stock price falls. Generally, a rising equivalent annual dividend is a good thing. When stock price falls, however, a higher dividend yield can and usually does suggest a more attractive valuation, but not always. With stable businesses, the conclusion of a more attractive valuation is right. (Of course, if the company was overvalued at the start, a more attractive valuation does not mean much.) But exercise care otherwise. The market may be warning of deteriorating business conditions. Like a plague, these conditions can persist for years. Such was the case with drug stocks in the 2000s as the market understood the implication of wave after wave of patent expirations.

Do not be tempted by the Cassandra of *absurdly* high dividend yields. An absurdly high dividend yield signals distress. It suggests a dividend cut or imminent bankruptcy. For instance, in April 2009, General Growth Properties' dividend yield soared to *several hundred* percent. It meant nothing. The company declared bankruptcy. (It has since emerged from bankruptcy.)

Besides regular dividends, companies sometimes pay another type of dividend called a *special dividend*. A special dividend is usually larger and nonrecurring. For instance, in 2004, Graco paid a special dividend of $1.50, amounting to *seven years* of regular dividends. Special dividends provide companies with flexibility. As business conditions warrant, companies boost their regular dividends with special dividends.

Other companies have expanded the meaning of special dividends. They pay an extra dividend *regularly* – but perhaps less frequently than a regular dividend, (say) annually versus quarterly – but vary the amount based on business performance. For instance, except for 2009, Paccar has declared a special dividend every year since 1992. In December 2014, the company declared a special dividend of $1.00. This was in addition to its regular quarterly dividend of 22¢.

Special dividends paid regularly should be included in dividend yield calculations. This might not be so easy prospectively – with widely fluctuating special dividends, it is virtually impossible – but certainly can be done historically. Stock-screening software is not always so careful.

Yield on Cost

"For today we will finally learn once and for all the plain and simple answer to all these nagging little problems of Life, the Universe, and Everything!"
Douglas Adams (The Hitchhiker's Guide to the Galaxy)

A dividend measure of another kind is *yield on cost* (Figure 2.1):

$$Yield\ on\ Cost = \frac{Equivalent\ Annual\ Dividend}{Original\ Stock\ Price}$$

For instance, suppose you own shares of IBM. You paid $85 a share many years ago. As of mid-2015, IBM's equivalent annual dividend is $5.20. Your yield on cost is thus 5.20 / 85.00 or 6.12 percent. This yield on cost is unique to you and anyone else who bought IBM at $85 a share. IBM's 3.49 percent calculated dividend yield, derived in the previous section, is a market measure. Yield on cost equals dividend yield when you first buy a stock. After that, they typically diverge.

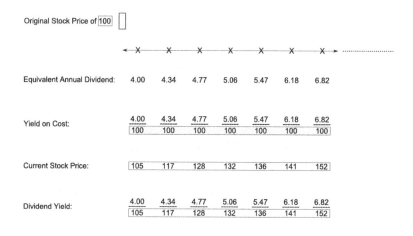

Figure 2.1. Difference between yield on cost and dividend yield. Yield on cost uses original stock price. Dividend yield uses current stock price.

Some confuse yield on cost with returns. For at least three reasons, yield on cost has little to do with returns. First, yield on cost does not use capital gains or losses. Second, to calculate an annual return, the denominator must be the stock price from a year ago, not the stock price, potentially, from many years ago. Third, regarding multiyear returns, yield on cost uses dividends for one year whereas multiyear returns use dividends for *all* years.

At best, yield on cost measures *part* of this multiyear return. For instance, suppose you own a stock that you bought at the end of 2008 for $100 a share. Dividends of $6 a share are expected in 2015. Ignoring dividend reinvestment, or anything else you could have done with your dividends – including (say) the intangible benefit of buying a waffle-maker – your 7-year return is the sum of dividends from 2009 through 2015 plus the change in price by the end of 2015 all divided by $100. Your yield on cost for 2015, 6 percent (6 / 100), is part of this return.

So what good is yield on cost? At best, to communicate income growth. Income growth shows up readily as a rising yield on cost.

Figure 2.2. Chronology of the four dividend-related dates. D: Declaration Date. E: Ex-Dividend Date. R: Record Date. P: Payment Date.

The Mechanics of Dividend Payments

"That may be the mistake in the translation." Sir John Vanbrugh

Four dates are relevant to the payment of dividends:

- *Declaration Date.* The Board of Directors declares the dividend payable on the declaration date. Companies establish this date when, for instance, they issue a press release detailing the payment of the dividend.

- *Record Date.* Not everyone who buys the stock after the declaration date gets the dividend. Shareholders need to be on the company's books by another date, the record date.

- *Ex-dividend Date.* To add to the confusion, because it takes a few days after shares are bought for funds to transfer and shares recorded, shares need to be bought before yet another date, the ex-dividend date. The company does not set the ex-dividend date. Instead, it is set by the stock exchanges or the National Association of Security Dealers (NASD). *Currently, the ex-dividend date is two **business** days before the record date. If shares are bought **on or after** the ex-dividend date, the buyer does **not** get the dividend declared on those shares. Instead, the dividend goes to the previous owner.*

- *Payment Date.* The payment date follows the record date, usually by a few weeks. The dividend is paid on the payment date.

Figure 2.2 shows the chronological sequence: DERP, rhymes with slurp. The declaration date is first. The ex-dividend date is second. The record date is third. The payment date is fourth.

For instance, on 13 August 2015, T. Rowe Price issued a press release declaring its September 2015 quarterly dividend:

> T. Rowe Price Group, Inc. (NASDAQ-GS: TROW) announced today that its Board of Directors has declared a quarterly dividend of $0.52 per share payable September 29, 2015 to stockholders of record as of the close of business on September 15, 2015. ...

In this case, the declaration date is the date of the press release, 13 August 2015. The payment date is 29 September 2015. The record date is 15 September 2015. The press release does not specify the market-controlled ex-dividend date. In this case, the ex-dividend date is 11 September 2015, a Friday, two *business* days before the record date, a Tuesday. Buyers on or after 11 September 2015 are fashionably late – they do not get the dividend. Instead, the dividend goes to the previous owner.

The Fall in Share Price

"That's what she said." Michael Scott (*The Office*)

Consider a world with no taxes. A company has $100 in cash and nothing else. It has no other business plan other than to pay $5 a share in annual dividends. Suppose the company has exactly one share outstanding. Its share price must be $100. Consider the alternatives: (1) If the share price were more than $100, everyone stays away. They would pay more than $100 for something worth $100. The reduced demand causes the share price to fall to $100. (2) Conversely, if the share price were less than $100, everyone clamors to buy – the sale's on. They would pay less than $100 for something worth $100. The extra demand causes the share price to rise to $100. Now, consider what happens when the company pays the $5 dividend. It is left with $95 in cash. The one shareholder has $5

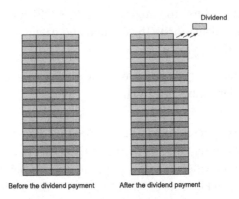

Figure 2.3. Dividend payments and value in a world with no taxes. After a company pays a dividend, its share price falls by the value of the dividend. Value after the dividend payment (that is, share price plus dividend) equals value before the dividend payment (share price only). The dividend does not represent extra value.

because he or she does not have to pay taxes on the dividend. Similar to the argument that the share price must be $100 before the dividend payment, the share price must be $95 after the dividend payment. In other words, *in a world with no taxes, the share price falls by precisely the value of the dividend*. Furthermore, the dividend does not change anything: *What benefits the shareholder on the one hand, the dividend, is offset by a cost on the other, the fall in share price*. The shareholder had $100 before (one share worth $100). The shareholder has $100 after (one share worth $95 plus the dividend worth $5). The dividend does not represent extra value (Figure 2.3). As with most (fair) exchanges, immediately after the exchange, no change in value takes place.

In a world with taxes, our world, things get more complicated, but the argument is essentially the same. In our world, the share price falls not by the value of the dividend, but by the *after-tax* value of the dividend (Figure 2.4). We have two cases depending on the interplay between the shareholder's dividend tax rate for the stock and the tax rate implied by the fall in share price, the so-called market dividend tax rate for the stock:

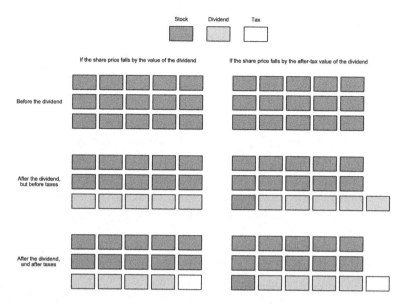

Figure 2.4. In a world with taxes, if the share price falls by the value of the dividend, shareholders lose out. By contrast, if the share price falls by the **after-tax** value of the dividend, shareholders are made whole. Suppose a stock is worth $15 before paying a large dividend of $5. If the share price falls by the value of the dividend, the share price falls to $10. After the dividend, but before taxes, the shareholder has $15 (10 + 5). With a twenty percent dividend tax rate, the shareholder has to pay $1 in taxes. Thus, after the dividend, and after taxes, the shareholder has $14 (10 + 5 - 1), poorer by $1. If this were how things worked, shareholders would not want their dividends. By contrast, if the share price falls by the *after-tax* value of the dividend, investors are not shortchanged. As before, suppose a stock is worth $15 before paying a large dividend of $5. If the share price falls by the after-tax value of the dividend, with a twenty percent dividend tax rate, the share price is worth $11 (15 - 0.8 * 5). After the dividend, but before taxes, the shareholder has $16 (11 + 5). But the shareholder has to pay $1 in taxes. Thus, after the dividend, and after taxes, the shareholder has $15 (11 + 5 - 1). The shareholder is made whole. Markets price in what they know. To ignore information is strange. The bond market, for instance, sets yields of tax-free bonds lower than yields of otherwise equivalent taxable bonds. This also means the bond market understands taxes. Likewise, I believe the stock market prices in what it knows, understands taxes, and the share price falls by the after-tax value of the dividend – if not, and you have to pay dividend taxes, never ask your companies to pay dividends again.

- For the shareholder paying the market dividend tax rate, the result is a wash. The stock falls by the after-tax value of the dividend. The shareholder pays the equivalent taxes on the dividend. The shareholder is right back where he or she started, just as in the no-tax world.

- For the shareholder paying a different tax rate from the market dividend tax rate, the result is not a wash. If the shareholder pays a lower tax rate than the market dividend tax rate, the shareholder benefits by the difference in tax rates. Conversely, if the shareholder pays a higher tax rate than the market dividend tax rate, the shareholder loses by the difference in tax rates.

Because most dividends are small in relation to the share price, the fall in share price after a dividend payment is difficult to detect. For instance, with a quarterly dividend and a dividend yield of four percent, the quarterly dividend is one percent of the share price. Many stocks fluctuate more than one percent during the trading day. This makes it difficult to detect the effect of the dividend.

By contrast, the fall in share price is easier to detect when the company pays a large dividend, typically a large special dividend. For instance, on 20 July 2004, Microsoft announced a $3 special dividend:

> The company will also pay a one-time special dividend of $3 per share... The special dividend will be payable on Dec. 2, 2004, to shareholders of record on Nov. 17, 2004, conditioned upon shareholder approval of amendments to the employee stock plans at the annual shareholders meeting currently planned for Nov. 9, 2004.
>
> Because the company's employee stock plans did not contemplate a one-time special dividend, the board has approved adjustments, subject to shareholder approval, that will protect employees *as the share price declines due to the one-time special dividend* [emphasis added]. *Mathematically, after a company makes a large one-time distribution, the overall value of the company declines by the amount of*

the distribution, which in turn reduces the stock price by a similar amount [emphasis added].

On Friday, 12 November 2004, the last business day before the ex-dividend date, Microsoft closed at $29.97. On the following Monday, it opened at $27.34. The lower price reflected: (a) the $3 special dividend; (b) the 8¢ quarterly dividend; (c) a tax adjustment; and (d) a small timing adjustment, which we ignore. In its press release, Microsoft did not mention taxes and timing.

How did shareholders benefit? They received cash. They did not have to sell their shares. In this sense, the dividend benefited them – and they naturally felt richer. But this understandably Pavlovian reaction was unwarranted. In fact, in some ways, the entire episode was a financial charade. Looking at overall value, except for a possible tax benefit, nothing changed.

If you held one share of Microsoft at the close on 12 November 2004, you had the equivalent of $29.97. Immediately after the stock went ex-dividend, the following Monday, you had one share worth $27.34 and were entitled to dividends of $3.08, for a combined value of $30.42. On the face of it, you benefited by $0.45 (30.42 - 29.97). But this does not include taxes. The net benefit depends on how much you paid in taxes:

- Suppose your dividend tax rate was fifteen percent, the maximum dividend tax rate at the time. The result was a wash. Your 15 percent * 3.08, or $0.46, in taxes wiped out the purported $0.45 benefit. The dividend did not represent extra value. (The $0.01 difference may have reflected a random move or other tiny effects.)

- Suppose your dividend tax rate was zero percent. The result was not a wash. You benefited by the $0.45.

Many investors believe that interest – from (say) a savings account – and dividends are similar. They believe that dividends, like interest, are somehow "extra." But dividends are paid out of a company's coffers. *The share price must fall to reflect the company's lower value (with tax adjustments).* **Unlike interest, except for any possible tax-related benefit, dividends are not extra.**

Bonds as Competition

Bonds and stocks are in a perpetual state of tug-of-war. When bond yields are high, new money gravitates toward bonds. When bond yields are low, *some fraction* of new money gravitates toward stocks – but not all. Investors understand stocks are riskier than bonds. Even when bond yields are low, some prefer bonds.

Not all bonds are safe. Though Treasuries have never defaulted and bonds from highly rated companies are reasonably safe, the bond market is vast. Many bonds are risky. For instance, bonds issued by tiny companies and bonds issued by companies and nations with questionable finances are not safe. Do not be fooled by higher yields on bonds such as these. Often, the emperor wears no clothes.

Higher yields seduce investors – who often look at yield and little else. This is a mistake. One of the tragedies that precipitated the Crash of 2008 was the harm caused by the insatiable thirst for yield. Investors did not understand the risks that they were taking (and some were surely duped). A properly functioning bond market demands higher yields to compensate for higher risks. Many esoteric securities with higher yields had higher risks – which played out in the worst possible way.

In another sense, however, almost all bonds are never safe. The culprit is inflation. Inflation eats away at the nominal values inherent in bonds. You lose buying power. For instance, because of inflation, the principal that you invest in (say) a 30-year Treasury bond loses perhaps sixty percent of its buying power when you get back your principal in thirty years. Likewise, the coupons that you receive from most bonds are not indexed to inflation.

You need enough growth to overcome the corrosive effect of inflation – the unrelenting damage that inflation does to your buying power. Stocks generally have it. Bonds generally don't. Growth rescues the buying power of your investments. If, instead of receiving a fixed coupon every six months and a fixed redemption value when the bond matures, you receive sufficiently growing coupons and a sufficiently large redemption value, your buying power stays the same, or even better, increases. Of course, the nature of these requirements makes this an unusual "bond."

Instead, this pattern is essentially that of a stock. The coupons become dividends; the redemption value, the final selling price of your stock. Of course, unlike the stipulations of a bond, you do not know what these future values will be. In effect, you take on another type of risk: You exchange the certainty of lower values with bonds for the prospect and uncertainty of higher values – values that beat inflation – with stocks.

The exchange here is one of knowledge, as well. With bonds, you know how much you will receive in coupons and you know how much you will receive when the bond matures – assuming no default. With stocks, you do not know what the stock price will be at any point in the future. That's the risk with stocks. That's always the risk with stocks. This risk is real and a potentially huge one – though much less of a risk with higher-quality stocks such as dividend growth stocks than with lower-quality stocks such as speculative stocks.

Investors often compare dividend yields to yields on bonds and other bond-like investments. For short time horizons, they compare dividend yields to yields on savings accounts and short-term CDs. For longer time horizons, they compare dividend yields to yields on ten-year Treasuries and ten-year corporate bonds.

Comparisons such as these can be misleading. Investments carry different risks and, while dividends from stocks typically grow, coupons from bonds typically do not. *Besides, what ultimately matters are **returns** – not merely yields.* Return equals yield *plus* contribution from capital changes. If the latter is poor, returns suffer. For instance, a yield of six percent does little good if investment value falls eight percent. What you gain from yield, you lose in value. What goes in one pocket, you lose – and then some – from the other. Counting gains in one pocket while not accounting for losses in the other is a mistake. Both pockets count.

Instead, think of these comparisons as *heuristics*. They might work, but only when the difference is large, (say) five or more percentage points, a large difference (hopefully) removing any chance of being wrong. Even then, appreciate the difference in risk. A junk bond with a yield of eight percent differs from a AAA bond with a yield of five percent and a dividend growth stock with a dividend yield of three percent and a dividend growth rate of nine percent.

Taxes

"Certainty?... In this world nothing is certain but death and taxes." Benjamin Franklin

The IRS recognizes three basic types of investment income: interest, dividends, and capital gains.[2] As of mid-2015:

- Interest is taxed like ordinary income.

- Dividends are either qualified or not. Qualified dividends meet certain criteria, including a specified holding period. Your 1099-DIV tax forms will help you identify which of your dividends are qualified and which are not. Taxes on qualified dividends are capped at twenty percent. Non-qualified dividends are taxed like ordinary income.

- Taxes on capital gains depend on how long the investment is held before it is sold. Gains (and losses) on investments held one year or less are classified as *short-term*. Short-term capital gains are taxed like ordinary income. Gains (and losses) on investments held longer than one year are classified as *long-term*. Taxes on long-term capital gains are capped at twenty percent. Naturally, losses, both short- and long-term, are not taxed. Losses offset gains. You can use any remaining losses, up to $3,000 each year, to offset other taxable income. Additional losses are carried over to later years.

In addition, the 2010 Affordable Care Act imposes a 3.8 percent surtax on certain high-income taxpayers.

---

[2] Taxes in this section refer to *regular* federal income taxes. You may have to pay other types of taxes. I just cover the basics. Taxes are complicated and ever-changing. They have many conditions and what-ifs, which I do not cover here. You may want to check with a tax professional. The IRS has many useful publications, including Publication 550, Investment Income and Expenses (Including Capital Gains and Losses).

You can use tax-advantaged accounts such as Health Savings Accounts (HSAs) and Individual Retirement Arrangements (IRAs) to defer, or even avoid, paying taxes.[3] (Regular) HSAs are a free lunch:

- Contributions are deductible. This means you can offset taxable income with contributions to an HSA.

- Earnings accumulate tax-free.

- You pay no taxes when you take out funds for allowed health-related purposes.

IRAs come in two flavors for individual taxpayers, namely, traditional IRAs and Roth IRAs. For traditional IRAs:

- Contributions are either deductible or nondeductible.

- Earnings accumulate tax-free.

- You pay taxes on distributions, except for that portion of your distributions that originates from nondeductible contributions. Your nondeductible contributions were taxed once – you do not pay taxes on them again.

For Roth IRAs:

- Contributions are nondeductible.

- Earnings accumulate tax-free.

- Distributions are tax-free.

The best tax-advantaged account is the HSA, followed by, for most, the Roth IRA, then the traditional IRA. Figure 2.5 summarizes the tax implications of HSAs and IRAs. For comparison, the figure also includes a taxable account.

---

[3]However, these accounts have constraints that limit their broad appeal. Examples of constraints include eligibility requirements, restrictions on use, and limits on contributions.

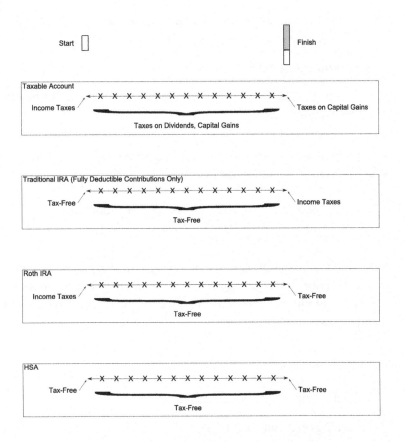

Figure 2.5. Federal income taxes that apply to various investment accounts. For the traditional IRA, only fully deductible contributions are considered. You can also make nondeductible contributions. For the IRAs and HSA, only the tax implications of "normal" distributions are shown. If you remove funds for other purposes, you may have to pay additional taxes, penalties, or both.

If you work for an employer that provides a savings plan, such as a 401(k) plan, you can, and typically should, make deductible contributions to the plan. This reduces your current taxes. Moreover, you capture any employer matching contributions. If you are self-employed, you can create and contribute to savings plans such as SEP IRAs, SIMPLE IRAs, and individual 401(k)s.

Two caveats apply to the advantages of tax-advantaged accounts over taxable accounts:

- You typically cannot gain access to your funds early unless you pay a penalty, a penalty that can negate the tax advantages.

- If income tax rates eventually rise, you may be better off paying taxes sooner rather than later. As a result, deductible contributions lose some of their luster.

Taxes and Dividend-Paying Stocks

"Take nothing on its looks; take everything on evidence. There's no better rule." Charles Dickens

Experts chastise dividend-paying companies for three reasons related to taxes:

- Double taxation. Dividends are taxed twice. At the corporate level, dividends arise from earnings – which are already taxed. At the recipient level, unless dividends are tax-sheltered, investors pay taxes on the dividends that they receive.

- Unfavorable tax rates. Long-term capital gains are generally taxed more favorably than dividends, though, currently, mid-2015, they are taxed identically.

- No tax deferral. Dividends are taxed annually. Dividend investors have no choice in the matter. Investors in non-dividend-paying stocks defer taxes to whenever they sell.

Do taxes change the dividend investment equation? Perhaps, but the arguments are subtle. There are tradeoffs:

- Because stock prices fall after dividends are paid, all else equal, stock prices of dividend-paying stocks do not rise as much as stock prices of equivalent non-dividend-paying stocks. Capital gains are thus lower for dividend-paying stocks. This, at least partially, offsets the higher current dividend taxation.

- Dividend-paying stocks are typically not as risky as their non-dividend-paying counterparts. Dividend-paying companies are generally older. Their businesses are more stable and their stock prices are not as volatile (risky). After adjusting for this lower risk, after-tax returns may be fair, or indeed, even better.

- Investors hold more in mutual funds than individual stocks. Mutual fund turnover averages more than one-hundred percent. As a result, investors in mutual funds often pay taxes at unfavorable short-term capital gains tax rates.

- Investors in individual stocks decide *when* to sell their stocks, potentially for the highest after-tax return. With mutual funds, though you still decide when to sell *your* shares, portfolio managers decide when to sell the fund's stocks. You can time your selling, but the portfolio managers time theirs. This cannot be optimal for everyone. This will rarely be optimal for you.

- When a stock pays a dividend, it falls by the after-tax value of the dividend. Because tax rates vary, you benefit if the tax rate you pay on dividends is lower than the tax rate implied by the fall in share price, the so-called market dividend tax rate for the stock in question. For instance, suppose you own a $100 stock that pays a $1 dividend. Let the market dividend tax rate for the stock be 20 percent. If your tax rate on dividends is lower, (say) 15 percent, after the dividend, you have $100.05, 5¢ above market. This corresponds to an extra return, a freebie. In a tax-advantaged account, you have $100.20, corresponding to an even larger freebie.

- Chapter 5 will show that the income growth rate from investing in a dividend growth stock and reinvesting dividends is roughly dividend growth rate plus *after-tax* dividend yield. The reduction in income growth rate for dividend growth stocks because of taxes is not that large. For instance, suppose you own a stock with a dividend growth rate of 10 percent and a dividend yield of 3.5 percent. Without taxes, your income growth rate is roughly 13.5 percent a year. With taxes, (say) a 15 percent tax rate on dividends, your income growth rate is roughly 13.0 percent a year. Although not irrelevant, especially over long periods, this drop in income growth rate is not that large.

In the final analysis, your after-tax return is what matters most. Your after-tax return includes all relevant taxes at all points in time. For instance, for taxable accounts, it includes – federal and, potentially, state – income taxes on dividends and capital gains. As another example, for traditional IRAs, with fully deductible contributions, it includes – federal and again, potentially, state – income taxes when you take your money out.

Suppose you own a dividend-paying stock in a traditional IRA. True, you do not pay current taxes on your dividends, but you do pay income taxes when you withdraw your money. If, instead of the traditional IRA, you hold your dividend-paying stock in a taxable account you pay taxes on dividends and, when you sell, taxes on capital gains. Like cuisines, all these tax rates differ – and, moreover, can change. Thus there is no guarantee one option is universally better than the other.

In addition, because the tax rate on bond interest is typically higher than the tax rate on dividends, if you hold bonds, you may want to keep your bonds in tax-advantaged accounts. Consequently, you may not have enough room in your tax-advantaged accounts for all your dividend-paying stocks. You may have no choice but to let some of them fall into your taxable accounts.

Still, because of the benefit of tax deferral, and the always tasty prospect of a lower current tax bill, for many investors, it makes sense to simplify and shelter dividends from current taxes by keeping dividend-paying stocks

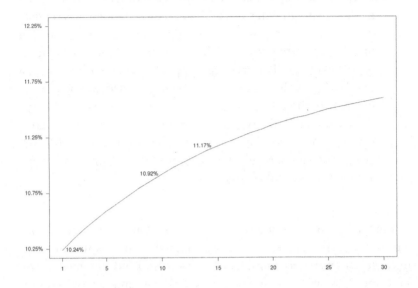

Figure 2.6. The benefit of tax deferral - I. Annual after-tax return versus holding period. The stock earns an annual pre-tax return of 12.24 percent. It does not change. The investor earns the annual after-tax return indicated if she sells her stock at the end of the holding period. For instance, if she sells her stock at the end of ten years, she earns an annual after-tax return of 10.92 percent. In this figure, the investor pays taxes on dividends and only capital gains are deferred.

in tax-advantaged accounts. The larger the dividend, the greater the (current) benefit.

Tax deferral is important. ***When you defer taxes you leave more of your money to work. This benefits you directly in a higher after-tax return***. And it is not just through lower dividend taxes. More important, even for dividend growth stocks, is the deferral of capital gains taxes. Figure 2.6 shows the typical pattern of an investor's return if she sells her stock at the end of each of the next thirty years. In the figure, the stock earns an annual pre-tax return of 12.24 percent. It does not change. Yet, annual after-tax return rises the longer she holds her stock. The rate of improvement is large early then tapers off. If she somehow holds the

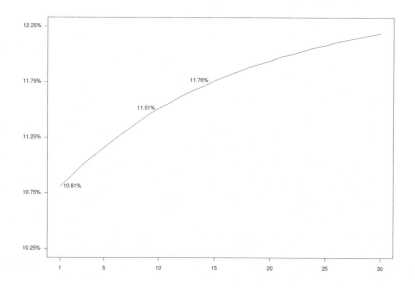

Figure 2.7. The benefit of tax deferral - II. Annual after-tax return versus holding period. The stock earns an annual pre-tax return of 12.24 percent. It does not change. The investor earns the annual after-tax return indicated if she sells her stock at the end of the holding period. For instance, if she sells her stock at the end of ten years, she earns an annual after-tax return of 11.51 percent. In this figure, the investor does not pay taxes on dividends and capital gains are deferred.

stock forever, she realizes the 12.24 percent. As we will see in Chapter 4, even a small difference in long-term annual returns results in a big difference in long-term wealth. Ironically, our investor gains the extra return by being lazy, by doing nothing.

You eviscerate your long-term returns when you sell your high-quality stocks too freely. It is not just that you have to pay taxes. More important is that you leave less of your money to work. This removal of capital destroys your long-term after-tax returns. Just because you can sell, or it is cheap to sell, does not mean you should sell.

Figure 2.7 takes the previous figure and discards taxes on dividends as well. This leaves more of the investor's money to work. Not surprisingly, the returns in this figure exceed the returns in the previous figure.

The moral: Watch for *anything* that removes funds from your investment. It can be taxes; as we will see in Chapter 4, it can be not reinvesting your dividends. All else equal, the greater the amount removed, the lower your long-term after-tax returns. It sounds frighteningly obvious when stated this way, yet many continue to sell too soon, trade recklessly, and happily pay taxes freely.

Warren Buffett does not sell his stocks for this reason. The naive interpretation is that he does not sell to avoid paying taxes. The more thorough explanation is that by not selling he does not remove funds from his investment, thus leaving more of his money to work. As he is such a long-term holder of high-quality stocks, it would not surprise me if this act alone results in a one or two percentage point increase in his long-term annual after-tax returns. And one or two percentage points is the difference between genius and average.

In the next chapter, we cover share buybacks, in many ways just a different cut of dividend, a discretionary type of dividend. ♣

CHAPTER 3

Share Buybacks

"After all is said and done, more is said than done." Anonymous

W HEN a company undertakes a share buyback, it uses cash or debt to buy back its shares over a stated period. A company usually buys back its shares on the open market, though some companies buy back their shares privately or through other means.

If a company funds its buyback with cash earned through its business activities, I consider the buyback similar to a dividend in many important ways. By contrast, if a company funds its buyback with cash raised in the stock market or debt market, I do not consider the buyback similar to a dividend.

Both types of buybacks result in changes in the shape of a company's assets, a rearrangement between what shareholders own (equity) and what others own (debt).

Prior to the SEC passing Rule 10b-18 in 1982, share buybacks were unpopular. Companies that undertook them risked running afoul of the SEC because of the potential for price manipulation. Rule 10b-18 specified guidelines, a so-called safe harbor, so that the SEC would then not view share buybacks that abided by those guidelines as manipulative. Quoting from the SEC's website:

> In 1982, the Commission adopted Rule 10b-18, which provides that an issuer will not be deemed to have violated Sections 9(a)(2) and 10(b) of the Exchange Act, and Rule 10b-5 under the Exchange Act, *solely* by reason of the manner, timing, price, or volume of its repurchases, if the issuer repurchases its common stock in the market in accordance with the safe harbor conditions. Rule 10b-18's safe harbor conditions are designed to minimize the market impact of the issuer's repurchases, thereby allowing the market to establish a security's price based on independent market forces without undue influence by the issuer.

In other words, and quite reasonably, a company can undertake a share buyback as long as it does not influence the market's independent price-finding mechanism too much.

Share buybacks have several advantages over dividends:

- The cash used for buybacks is not taxed twice because investors are not taxed on the money used.

- Remaining shareholders automatically own a greater proportion of the company's shares. For instance, suppose a shareholder owns one percent of a company's shares before a buyback and the shareholder does not sell any of her shares in the buyback. If the company buys back twenty percent of its shares, the shareholder now owns 1.25 percent of the company's shares.

- Buybacks can *directly* support a stock price, as, for instance, when a company vacuums all shares available at a particular price.

- Buybacks are discretionary. The company chooses if and when to buy back its shares. If business conditions weaken, or if the stock price looks expensive, the company can choose to suspend – or even end – its buyback.

But share buybacks have several disadvantages over dividends as well:

- Unlike dividends, buybacks are not a legal commitment. Companies can renege. Many do.

- U.S. companies view dividends as a shareholder commitment. They operate as if they *have* to pay their dividends. In turn, this imposes a welcome dose of responsible behavior. The discretionary nature of buybacks imposes no such responsibility.

- Investors view dividends as something *real*. They do not view buybacks in much the same way.

- Companies typically implement buybacks when they are flush with cash, often, when times are good and the economy is robust. But this is also when stock prices are high. Thus, companies buy high.

- Conversely, during economic downturns, companies go into ostrich mode. Even as stock prices fall, they preserve their cash, reluctant to buy back their shares. This is a "don't buy low" strategy.

- During bear markets, dividend yield functions as a stock price floor. With one exception during the depths of a bear market – when a widely respected company announces a large and immediate buyback – buybacks do not function so explicitly as a stock price floor.

- We cannot know how much a company *will* spend on buybacks each year. A company can twist from buying five percent of shares one year to buying nothing the next.

A share buyback is an **exchange** between a company and its shareholders. When a company buys back its shares, it exchanges its cash for shares from its shareholders. As with most (fair) exchanges, after a share buyback, no *immediate* change in value takes place, either for the company or its shareholders. For the company, its remaining value plus the value of the shares it buys back equals its value before. For shareholders,

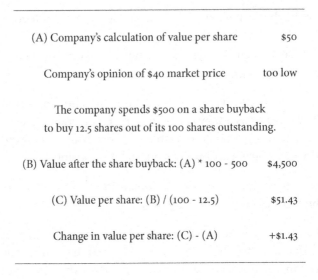

(A) Company's calculation of value per share	$50
Company's opinion of $40 market price	too low
The company spends $500 on a share buyback to buy 12.5 shares out of its 100 shares outstanding.	
(B) Value after the share buyback: (A) * 100 - 500	$4,500
(C) Value per share: (B) / (100 - 12.5)	$51.43
Change in value per share: (C) - (A)	+$1.43

Table 3.1. Effect of a buyback when a company believes its shares are undervalued: Value per share is created.

the value of their remaining shares plus the cash they receive from the company equals the value they had before.

Although no immediate change in value takes place with a share buyback, *longer term*, remaining shareholders (that is, shareholders who still own shares after the buyback) can benefit if the company buys back its shares at a reasonable price. A share buyback is an *investment* in the company's shares to the exclusion of everything else – business development, acquisitions, reducing debt, and so on. When a company announces a share buyback, it signals to the market that it considers the share buyback the best way to raise company value. Quite simply, if this investment earns a high enough return, remaining shareholders benefit. But if the money could have been put to better use, remaining shareholders lose.

In particular, all else equal, this says the company considers its shares undervalued – because *buying undervalued shares creates value; buying fairly priced shares does not change value; and buying overpriced shares destroys value.* See Tables 3.1, 3.2, and 3.3, respectively.

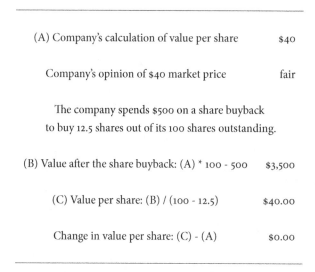

(A) Company's calculation of value per share	$40
Company's opinion of $40 market price	fair
The company spends $500 on a share buyback to buy 12.5 shares out of its 100 shares outstanding.	
(B) Value after the share buyback: (A) * 100 - 500	$3,500
(C) Value per share: (B) / (100 - 12.5)	$40.00
Change in value per share: (C) - (A)	$0.00

Table 3.2. Effect of a buyback when a company believes its shares are fairly valued: Value per share is unchanged.

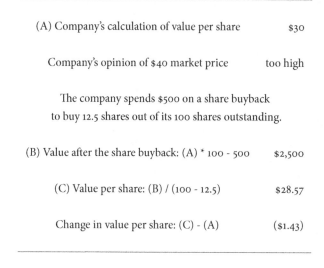

(A) Company's calculation of value per share	$30
Company's opinion of $40 market price	too high
The company spends $500 on a share buyback to buy 12.5 shares out of its 100 shares outstanding.	
(B) Value after the share buyback: (A) * 100 - 500	$2,500
(C) Value per share: (B) / (100 - 12.5)	$28.57
Change in value per share: (C) - (A)	($1.43)

Table 3.3. Effect of a buyback when a company believes its shares are overvalued: Value per share is destroyed.

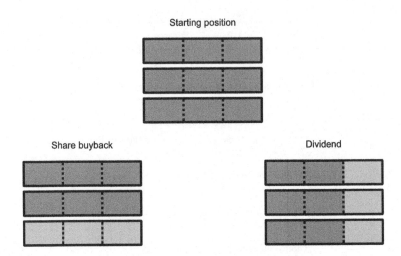

Figure 3.1. Share buybacks and dividends as different rearrangements of blocks. In both cases, shareholders are left with six blocks. The blocks are just rearranged differently. The figure assumes no taxes on dividends.

Different Rearrangements of Blocks

Imagine that a company's shares are made up of blocks (Figure 3.1). Let us first assume a world with no taxes on dividends. Stack these shares – made up of blocks – in a column. Share buybacks and dividends are nothing more than different rearrangements of these blocks, with the company taking away some blocks for cash, exactly how many depending on the value of the share buyback or dividend. With a share buyback, this taking away is explicit – the shareholder ends up with fewer shares; with a dividend, this taking away is implicit – the value of each share falls. *Think of a share buyback as nothing more than taking away some blocks horizontally; and a dividend as nothing more than slicing away some blocks vertically*. In each case, the company gives shareholders cash for the blocks that it takes away. Figure 3.1 shows this for a company with three shares, each share made up of three blocks. With a share buyback, where the company buys back one-third of its market value, thus one of its shares, the company takes away one share, or three blocks, horizontally. With a dividend, where the company pays the equivalent

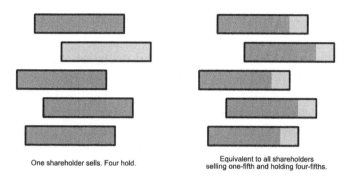

One shareholder sells. Four hold.   Equivalent to all shareholders
                                                   selling one-fifth and holding four-fifths.

Figure 3.2. With a share buyback, instead of thinking of *some* shareholders as selling some (or all) of their shares and others holding, think of *all* shareholders as selling a fraction of their shares.

amount as a dividend, thus a large one-third of its market value as the dividend, the company takes away one block from each share, in effect, vertically slicing off one block from each share. Thus, with the share buyback, shareholders are left with two rows of three blocks; and with a dividend of the same amount, shareholders are left with two columns of three blocks. In each case, shareholders are left with six blocks. The blocks are just rearranged differently.

You may ask if this argument breaks down for shareholders who do not sell. After all, they do not end up with fewer shares. It does not. With a share buyback, instead of thinking of *some* shareholders as selling some (or all) of their shares and others holding, think of *all* shareholders as selling a fraction of their shares. For instance, suppose a company has exactly five shares, each share held by one shareholder (Figure 3.2). In a share buyback, the company buys back one share from one of its shareholders. The remaining four shareholders hold. From a total economic perspective, this result is identical to one in which *all* shareholders sell one-fifth of their shares and hold four-fifths. After all, one-fifth of five is one, equal to the number of shares sold; and four-fifths of five is four, equal to the number of shares held.

In a world with taxes on dividends, our world, share buybacks and dividends are still just different rearrangements of blocks. Moreover, because share buybacks do not involve taxes, everything about share buybacks remains unchanged. What changes with dividends is the size of the blocks. With dividends, larger blocks remain because the share price falls not by the value of the dividend, but by the after-tax value of the dividend. Offsetting this is the dividend tax that shareholders have to pay. In theory, overall, this should net out as the market dividend tax rate matches the average shareholder dividend tax rate. However, particular shareholders may benefit if their dividend tax rates are lower than the market dividend tax rate; and others, if their dividend tax rates are higher than the market dividend tax rate, may look heavenward and clench their fists screaming, "Why! Why me!"

Thus, *once a given amount of cash leaves a company's coffers and makes its way to shareholders, how it gets split, whether by dividends or share buybacks or indeed a mix, does not matter*. Admittedly, with dividends, because of differing dividend tax rates, any particular shareholder may see a slight additional benefit or cost – but, overall, that is it.

Long-Term Returns

We've seen that, after a share buyback, as with most (fair) exchanges, no immediate change in value takes place. We've also seen that, viewed as an investment, if a share buyback earns a high enough return, remaining shareholders benefit. This is worth pursuing in another way. The question is: Longer term, do share buybacks boost returns?

When a company uses its existing cash to buy back shares, interest income falls and, thus, so do earnings. Likewise, when a company takes on debt to buy back shares, earnings fall because interest expense rises. In both cases, offsetting lower earnings (a negative factor) is a lower share count (a positive factor). Often, earnings *per share* rises because the lower share count more than offsets the lower earnings. Therefore, because growth rate in earnings per share is a component of return, a reasonable conclusion is that returns should rise.

It's not that simple, however. Returns also depend on growth rate in P/E ratio – and P/E ratio may fall. In fact, a company gets riskier after a share buyback because it has more debt relative to equity. Because investors demand compensation for risk, P/E ratio can fall. The fall in P/E ratio may be large enough to more than offset growth rate in earnings per share. When this happens, long-term returns do not rise.

Not surprisingly, the price at which a company buys back its shares does matter to long-term returns. If a company has the discipline to buy back its shares at low multiples, thus not spending as much to buy back a given number of shares, debt does not rise as much relative to equity, the fall in P/E ratio is less severe, and returns tend to rise. Conversely, if a company has the tendency to buy back its shares at high multiples, returns tend to suffer.

We can introduce other possibilities into these arguments. For instance, one of the advantages of share buybacks is that companies part with their cash. Many investors argue that long-term returns suffer when companies fritter away their cash, for instance, on grandiose buildings, expensive acquisitions, and toga parties in the Greek Isles. Thus, the argument goes, long-term returns after share buybacks are higher than they otherwise would be.

We can raise the same overall question about dividends: Do dividends boost long-term returns? As the previous section showed, excluding the tax grab, dividends and share buybacks are essentially the same. Thus, if share buybacks do not necessarily boost long-term returns, neither do dividends.

Giant Share Buybacks

Sometimes, underleveraged companies – to take advantage of the tax benefits of debt – or companies that believe the market undervalues their stock use cash or issue debt to fund a giant onetime share buyback. When this happens, the financial topology of the company changes dramatically. Though all share buybacks increase debt relative to assets, with giant share buybacks the difference is one of scale, the difference between tearing down walls and rearranging furniture.

For example, in 2007, Linear Technology used $3 billion in cash and debt to buy back 83.3 million shares, about 27 percent of its shares then outstanding. Share buybacks of this size signal a vote of confidence. In announcing the buyback, Robert H. Swanson, the company's founder and Executive Chairman, said:

> Over the last twenty-five years we have built a strong profitable analog franchise. During this period we have grown entirely organically without any Company acquisitions and have accumulated roughly $2.0 billion in cash. We believe that our best investment continues to be ourselves, Linear Technology Corporation. Accordingly, we plan to purchase $3.0 billion of Linear stock in this transaction.

Unfortunately, and with the benefit of eight years of hindsight, Linear overpaid. As of mid-2015, its stock trades at $44, not much higher – taking into account the passage of time – than the roughly $36 per share it doled out in 2007. An argument can be made that an acquisition would have been a better use of the money. Moreover, Linear's value was not boosted by the resulting higher earnings per share because the stock's P/E ratio adjusted. Such is life – and the world of finance.

Shareholder Yield

To account for share buybacks, we tweak the formula for dividend yield. We do this in two steps. First, we include cash spent on share buybacks. This gives us *gross shareholder yield*:

$$\textit{Gross Shareholder Yield} = \frac{\textit{Dividends} + \textit{Cash Spent on Share Buybacks}}{\textit{Market Capitalization}}$$

Second, we *also* subtract cash received from shares issued. This gives us *net shareholder yield*:[1]

---

[1] In calculating cash received from shares issued, there are complicating factors, for

Net Shareholder Yield

$$= \frac{Dividends \ + \ Cash \ Spent \ on \ Share \ Buybacks}{Market \ Capitalization}$$

$$- \frac{Cash \ Received \ From \ Shares \ Issued}{Market \ Capitalization}$$

Market capitalization is the value of the company in the stock market, calculated as share price times number of shares outstanding.

Table 3.4 compares dividend yield and shareholder yields for the TJX Companies. Here, dividend yield is total dividends paid divided by market capitalization. As the table shows, dividend yield paints an inaccurate picture of TJX's commitment to shareholders. The company's gross and net shareholder yields are much higher. In fact, they are so much higher – and the company is still growing robustly, among other things that we will later see – the company becomes a strong candidate for dividend growth investing.

The best gauge of yield is net shareholder yield. Unlike dividend yield, it includes buybacks. Unlike gross shareholder yield, it paints a more accurate picture of the size of those buybacks.

Nevertheless, these ratios are not perfect:

- They can change significantly from one year to the next.

- Companies can buy back shares with cash that was once raised in the stock market or the debt market. This is not the kind of buyback that returns *excess* cash to shareholders. This is not the kind of buyback that is similar to dividends. Rationally, we have to change our formulas – but this quickly gets complicated. Companies may not disclose how much additional debt, if any, went

---

instance, potential tax effects related to stock options. These are potentially complex and perhaps not always clear. For many years, companies did not even disclose them. In general, for simplicity and comparability, I ignore these complications. However, the impact can sometimes be significant. You may choose to include them. The idea is to account for *all* cash that the company receives as a result of issuing shares.

Fiscal Year	Dividend Yield	Gross Shareholder Yield	Net Shareholder Yield
2010	1.3	7.5	6.4
2011	1.4	8.6	7.5
2012	1.3	7.6	6.6
2013	1.0	5.1	4.7
2014	1.0	4.9	4.5

Table 3.4. Dividend and shareholder yields for the TJX Companies. Values are calculated as of the middle of the fiscal year. Dividend yield paints an inaccurate picture of TJX's commitment to shareholders. The company's gross and net shareholder yields are much higher.

toward share buybacks and in any case cash is fungible. Just be aware of the possibility.

Dividends are the first leg of a three-legged dividend stool. Share buybacks and dividends are different rearrangements of blocks. In the next chapter, we turn to dividend reinvestment, the second leg of our three-legged dividend stool. ♣

CHAPTER 4

Dividend Reinvestment

"Now the general who wins a battle makes many calculations in his temple ere the battle is fought." Sun-tzu

Y ou can do three things with a dividend: (1) Spend it. (2) Set it aside, waiting for the right time to invest it – and most likely investing it in something else. (3) Or reinvest it.

When you spend a dividend, (say) on a waffle-maker, your invested wealth must fall. Dividends are not extra. What you gain from the dividend, you lose with a lower stock price. You might see a small tax benefit, but that is all.

Most professionals opt for the second choice. For most individual investors, this is complicating and unnecessary. It causes second-guessing and paralysis: What do I buy? When do I buy?

Of the three choices, the simplest is to reinvest. With the right account, it costs you nothing. You do not need to decide what to buy and when to buy. Moreover, as you reinvest, the number of shares that you own continually – and reassuringly – increases.

Simple and Compound Interest

"The most powerful force in the universe is compound interest." Albert
Einstein

Suppose you invest in a stock that, on every payment date, pays the same
dividend. If you do not reinvest, then, not surprisingly, your income
never changes. Your income depends on your initial investment – and
nothing else.

If you reinvest, however, things change. Your income increases
every payment date. Your income depends on your initial investment
– *and* the additional shares that you earn through reinvestment. Over
long enough periods, even at reasonable dividend yields, your income
increases dramatically.[1]

At the heart of this apparent magic is the difference between simple
interest and compound interest. With simple interest, only the initial
investment earns interest. Nothing else contributes (Figure 4.1). With
compound interest, every dollar earns its keep. The initial investment
earns interest. The accumulated interest earns interest (Figure 4.2).

Simple interest is similar in form to not reinvesting your dividends.
Only the initial dollars (shares) generate interest (dividends). **Compound interest is similar in form to reinvesting your dividends**. All
dollars (shares) – whether they be the initial dollars (shares) or later
dollars (shares) – generate interest (dividends).

Given enough time, even at reasonable interest rates, you will have
dramatically higher income with compound interest compared to simple interest. Likewise, given enough time, even at reasonable dividend
yields, you will have dramatically higher income when you reinvest your
dividends than when you don't.

---

[1]Your increase in income is independent of the company growing *its* dividends.
That dividend growth only accelerates your growth in income. With one small exception,
this chapter does not deal with dividend growth. Chapter 5 covers dividend growth.
Patience, grasshopper.

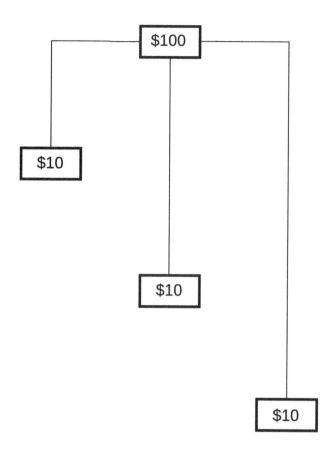

Figure 4.1. Simple interest – the staircase pattern. The interest rate is ten percent a year. At the end of the first year, the $100 investment earns $10. At the end of the second year, it earns another $10. At the end of the third year, it earns yet another $10. In three years, total interest earned is $30. With simple interest, only the initial investment earns interest. Nothing else contributes.

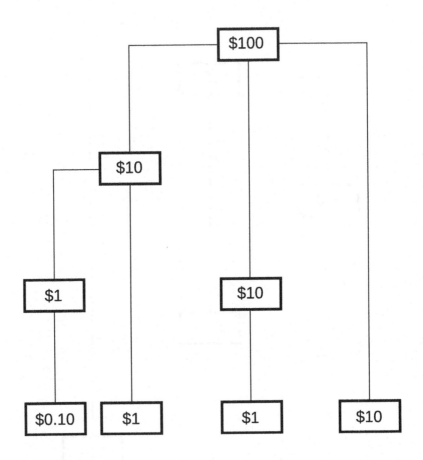

Figure 4.2. Compound interest – the octopus pattern. The interest rate is ten percent a year. At the end of the first year, the $100 investment earns $10. At the end of the second year, the $10 from the first year earns $1 and the original $100 earns another $10. Interest earned at the end of the second year is $11, the sum of the values in the third row of boxes. At the end of the third year, the $1 from the second year earns $0.10, the $10 from the first year earns $1, the $10 from the second year earns $1, and the original $100 earns another $10. Interest earned at the end of the third year is $12.10, the sum of the values in the fourth row of boxes. In three years, total interest earned is $33.10. With compound interest, every dollar earns its keep. The initial investment earns interest. The accumulated interest earns interest.

| Interest | Years | | | | | | |
Rate	1	5	10	15	20	25	30
1%	1,010	1,051	1,105	1,161	1,220	1,282	1,348
2%	1,020	1,104	1,219	1,346	1,486	1,641	1,811
3%	1,030	1,159	1,344	1,558	1,806	2,094	2,427
4%	1,040	1,217	1,480	1,801	2,191	2,666	3,243
5%	1,050	1,276	1,629	2,079	2,653	3,386	4,322
6%	1,060	1,338	1,791	2,397	3,207	4,292	5,743
7%	1,070	1,403	1,967	2,759	3,870	5,427	7,612
10%	1,100	**1,611**	**2,594**	**4,177**	**6,727**	**10,835**	**17,449**

Table 4.1. Future values of $1,000 invested at a variety of interest rates and over a variety of horizons.

The formula for compound interest is what makes it, as Einstein notes, "[t]he most powerful force in the universe:"

$$Future\ Value\ =\ Current\ Value\ *\ (1+i)^{n}$$

In this formula, i is the interest rate *per period* and n is the number of periods. For instance, $1,000 earning ten percent a year for five years has a future value of 1000 * (1 + 0.10)^5 or $1,611. Table 4.1 compares future values of $1,000 invested at a variety of interest rates and over a variety of horizons.

In this formula, the placement of that innocuous little n makes this ***exponential growth***. Exponential growth creates extraordinarily large future values given reasonably big enough combinations of n and i. ***The magic arises because every dollar contributes at every point. Percentage changes are equal over equal periods, implying dollar changes – and dollar amounts – explode.*** For instance, from Table 4.1, when i is ten percent, the percentage change every 5-year period is 61 percent. It stays the same. The dollar change every 5-year period, however, explodes: It is $611, from zero to five years; $983, from five to ten; $1,583, from ten to fifteen; $2,550, from fifteen to twenty; $4,108, from twenty to twenty-five;

and $6,614, from twenty-five to thirty. In the last period, for example, you made more than 10 times what you made in the first period. *To reap the benefits of exponential growth, you must give time a chance* – given enough time, your wealth will soar. *For investors, this truism is one of the most important concepts to appreciate*, just as important to investing as eating (a minimum of) five a day is to health. Our formula is more sensitive to n than i, though for reasonable values of i the sensitivity is roughly the same.

Our formula applies to more than just interest. In fact, *it applies to anything where everything contributes at every point*. In particular, it applies to returns and dividends:

- Compounding returns and wealth. Suppose you expect a $1,000 investment to compound ten percent a year for ten years. In ten years, your investment is worth $1000 * (1 + 0.10)^{10}$ or $2,594. This matches the $2,594 in the last row of Table 4.1. In fact, you can just as well interpret the interest rate in Table 4.1 as a return. Because n is at least as important as i in our formula, it does not take a necessarily massive i to reach a given level of wealth. You can just as well use a larger n. Given enough time, your wealth will soar. Thus, high returns are not the only way to reap the benefits of exponential growth. *You can just as well trade off a lower return for a longer time*. (This is important because higher returns mean higher risks – many things can go wrong. For instance, higher returns can rarely be maintained over long periods, (say) at least ten years.) Consider a horizon of thirty years and an investment of $25,000 growing at various compound annual returns. At a compound annual return of one percent, growth barely registers – the original investment of $25,000 becomes $33,696 in thirty years. At three percent, roughly the average rate of inflation, the original investment grows to $60,682. At five percent, equivalent to certain combinations of bonds, wealth reaches $108,049. Now consider what happens when the compound annual return approaches the long-term return of stocks. At nine percent, the long-term return of a good stock mutual fund minus one percentage point in expenses, wealth rises to a much improved $331,692. At ten percent, the long-term return of the stock market with no expenses, wealth soars to $436,235. At eleven percent, admittedly a challenging return to maintain over thirty years, wealth reaches $572,307. As another way of looking at these results, **over a long enough period, if you lose just a small portion of your return each year, you end up with much lower wealth.** *Thus, for instance, avoid taxes (legally) and keep expenses as a fraction of your return very low.* Finally, the proportionately lower your starting value, the proportionately lower your wealth. Thus, if you start with $10,000 instead of $25,000, you end up with 60 percent less wealth. You must save.

- Dividends, no reinvestment. Suppose a stock pays a $4 dividend. You expect the dividend to grow eight percent a year for ten years. What is the dividend in ten years? $4 * (1 + 0.08)^{10}$ or $8.64. You can just as well interpret Table 4.1 as the dividend income that arises from dividends, no reinvestment, assuming you currently receive $1,000 in dividends. The interest rate becomes the dividend growth rate. Compounding also applies to dividends, with reinvestment, but what compounds is not entirely clear. We look at this in the next section.

The Reinvestment Factor

"I used to work in a fire hydrant factory. You couldn't park anywhere near the place." Steven Wright

As you reinvest, the number of shares that you own continually increases. Because dividend reinvestment and compound interest are similar in form, the formula for the increase in shares because of dividend reinvestment involves dividend yield – but with a catch. As the dividend payment causes the share price to fall, the increase in shares is not just dividend yield, it is dividend yield *kicked up* by the lower share price.

To see how this formula develops, let us first assume a world with no taxes on dividends. In this world, once a dividend is paid, the share price falls by the value of the dividend. For instance, suppose the share price is $100 before the dividend is paid and the dividend is $1. After the dividend is paid, the share price falls to \$99. With dividend reinvestment, for every share that you own, the increase in shares through reinvestment is 1 / 99 or 0.0101. This equals 0.01 / (1 - 0.01), that is, dividend yield divided by, or kicked up by, (one minus dividend yield). The logic in the general case is identical. Thus, *in a world with no taxes on dividends, the increase in shares through reinvestment, for every share that you own, is given by:*[2]

$$\frac{Dividend\ Yield}{1\ -\ Dividend\ Yield}$$

Let us now return to the real world, where dividends are usually taxed, sadly. In this world, once a dividend is paid, the share price falls not by the value of the dividend, but by the *after-tax* value of the dividend. Moreover, you potentially have to pay taxes on the dividend. Combining these two facts, *in a world with taxes on dividends, the increase in shares through reinvestment, for every share that you own, is given by*:

$$\frac{(1\ -\ p)\ *\ Dividend\ Yield}{1\ -\ (1\ -\ m)\ *\ Dividend\ Yield}$$

Let us give this expression a fancy, okay, mundane name. Let us call it the *reinvestment factor*. Here m is the market dividend tax rate for the stock in question, something between zero and the maximum IRS dividend tax rate. (Another potential concern is tax rates other than federal tax rates. We ignore those.) It can vary from stock to stock because of clientele differences. For instance, some funds cannot own sin stocks. Others will not own stocks below \$5. The varying clientele impacts demand, and thus the market dividend tax rate for the stock in question. (To be fair, the market might arbitrage these differences away.) I believe many investors take m to be the maximum IRS dividend tax rate. The generality that we have here does no harm. *Besides, if you experiment with various values of m, you will find that the value of the expression does not change all that much. To a reasonable approximation, m is inconsequential.*

P is *your* (p as in "personal;" y as in "your" is too close to y as in dividend **y**ield) dividend tax rate for the stock in question. For instance,

---

[2] The expressions in this section do not include dividend growth. Chapter 5 covers dividend growth. Easy, grasshopper.

if you own the stock in an IRA, p is zero. If you own the stock in a taxable account, p can be as high as 23.8 percent for 2014.

As an example, with a quarterly dividend yield of 1 percent, a market dividend tax rate of 20 percent, and a personal dividend tax rate of 15 percent, the reinvestment factor is 0.00857. Thus, for every 100 shares that you own, you receive 0.857 extra shares through reinvestment. In a tax-advantaged account, you receive more. In a tax-advantaged account, p is zero and the reinvestment factor is 0.01008. In this case, you receive 1.008 extra shares for your 100 shares, an 18 percent improvement over the taxed case.

Using this formula in the real world raises four objections:

- First, the reinvestment factor applies to the moment immediately after a dividend payment is made. In the real world, the dividend is paid a few weeks after the ex-dividend date, the day the stock drops to reflect the upcoming dividend payment.

- Second, dividend yield on the payment date usually differs from dividend yield on the ex-dividend date.

- Third, with quarterly dividend payments, we have to compound values during the year.

- Fourth, again with quarterly dividend payments, we have to deal with changing dividend yields during the year.

All these things are nuisances. Ultimately, we are interested in *estimates* – and nuances such as these are not our biggest concerns. We take a few liberties. We assume the dividend is paid immediately after the stock goes ex-dividend. We apply the formula to annual dividend yield. Our usage becomes approximate. It remains useful for estimates.

We can apply our compound interest formula to dividends, with reinvestment. Simply let i be the value of the above expression. For instance, with our earlier example of a (quarterly) reinvestment factor of 0.01008, in ten years, we end up with $(1 + 0.01008)^{40}$ shares, or 49 percent more. You earn bonus points if the 40 in this expression did

Date	Share price	Dividends per share	Dividends received	Extra shares	Shares
1/31/2013					100.000
3/29/2013	59.65	0.17	17.00	0.285	100.285
6/28/2013	65.58	0.17	17.05	0.260	100.545
9/30/2013	72.11	0.17	17.09	0.237	100.782
12/31/2013	74.48	0.17	17.13	0.230	101.012

Table 4.2. Dividend reinvestment (without taxes) in Ross Stores.

not cause a twitch. It is 40 because the dividend is paid quarterly for ten years: 4 * 10 is 40. If the company does not grow its dividend – the assumption we generally use in this chapter – in ten years, we end up with 49 percent more dividend income.

Real-World Dividend Reinvestment

"If only God would give me some clear sign! Like making a large deposit in my name at a Swiss bank." Woody Allen

Table 4.2 shows how dividend reinvestment works in the real world. During 2013, Ross Stores paid a quarterly dividend of 17¢ per share. Suppose you owned 100 shares of Ross Stores on 31 January 2013 in a tax-advantaged account and you remained invested throughout 2013. If you did not reinvest, you received $17.00 every payment date. If you did reinvest, your income grew. By the last payment date, you received $17.13, yes a whopping 13¢ more.

In fact, *if companies do not lower their dividends, as is typically the case with high-quality dividend growth stocks, then much like an inflating balloon, when you reinvest, your income always grows.* Each reinvested dividend leads to an increase in shares. Each increase in shares leads to an increase in dividends. The connection looks like a feedback

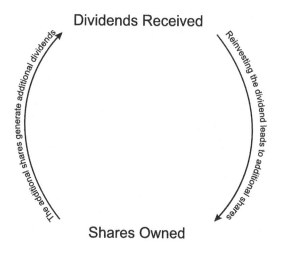

Figure 4.3. The feedback loop of dividend reinvestment: Shares generate dividends. Reinvested dividends lead to additional shares.

loop, with shares generating dividends and reinvested dividends leading to additional shares (Figure 4.3).

To be fair, however, if you do not reinvest, you must do *something* with your dividends. For instance, if you keep your dividends in cash, the interest earned on that cash must be included in a fair comparison. Even if you spend the dividends, some argument can be made for the pleasure gained – if you bought a waffle-maker, for instance, the taste of homemade waffles – offset by a drop in value, over time, of whatever was bought.

Dividend reinvestment is not alchemy. It is a form of savings. Instead of spending the dividend, you buy shares. The sacrifice pays off. You end up with higher income later.

However, one caution with dividend reinvestment must be pointed out: Because you build a larger and larger position in the underlying company – and without selling have taken nothing out – if the company ever were to fail, not only have you lost everything but you've earned nothing in the interim – and have paid taxes on your dividends as well.

So, ultimately, it's a disaster. Thus you must invest in the right company. It must have long-term staying power. (As an aside, in this regard, of most importance, the business must be simple to understand. Never invest for the long term in a complex business, the likes of Enron. Few understood it. Investors lost everything.)

Next, we look at the third and final leg of our three-legged dividend stool, dividend growth. ♣

CHAPTER 5

Dividend Growth

"Why stay we on the earth except to grow?" Robert Browning

W ITH dividend reinvestment and dividend growth, for every share that you own, your income is made up of four parts by the next dividend payment date (Figure 5.1):

- The original dividend on your original share.

- The growth in the dividend on your original share.

- The original dividend on the extra shares earned through reinvestment.

- The growth in the dividend on those extra shares.

The second through fourth parts contribute to your *income growth rate*. We have the following expression for the income growth rate:

> *Dividend Growth Rate*
> *+ Extra Shares * (1 + Dividend Growth Rate)*

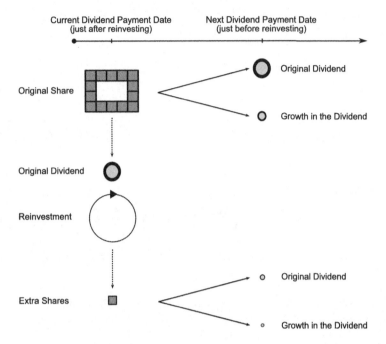

Figure 5.1. Sources of income by the next dividend payment date after dividend reinvestment and dividend growth. Income is made up of the four parts on the right.

The extra shares correspond to the reinvestment factor from Chapter 4. As a check, when you do not reinvest, the extra shares are zero and your income grows at the dividend growth rate. Likewise, when the dividend does not grow, the dividend growth rate is zero, and your income growth is, as we saw in the last chapter, entirely because of the extra shares earned through reinvestment. Finally, when the dividend does not grow *and* you do not reinvest, the dividend growth rate is zero, the extra shares earned through reinvestment are zero, and your income does not grow. Sad, but true.

Suppose you own shares of Clorox in an IRA. Because your shares are in an IRA, your dividends are not currently taxed. You expect dividends to grow 9 percent this year. The stock yields 3.5 percent. Assume a market dividend tax rate for Clorox of 20 percent. Then, from Chapter 4, the reinvestment factor is 0.036. Thus, your income growth rate is 0.09 + 0.036 * (1 + 0.09) or 12.9 percent. Of this, the growth in the dividend on your original shares contributes 9.0 percentage points; the original dividend on the extra shares contributes (0.036 * 1) or 3.6 percentage points; and the growth in the dividend on the extra shares contributes (0.036 * 0.09) or 0.3 percentage points.

For dividend growth stocks, the ordering of these contributions is typical: The growth in the dividend on the original shares contributes the most; the original dividend on the extra shares contributes less; the growth in the dividend on the extra shares contributes much less.

We can substitute the formula for the reinvestment factor into the above expression and simplify it to derive a general expression for the income growth rate. The result is messier than a doctor's handwriting.

Instead, we take two shortcuts. First, because the growth in the dividend on the extra shares makes such a tiny contribution, we drop the dividend growth rate from the parentheses in the above expression. Second, in the formula for the reinvestment factor from Chapter 4, we set the denominator equal to one because it is close to one. When we make these changes, we get the following simplified but approximate expression for the income growth rate:

$$\textit{Dividend Growth Rate}$$
$$+ \; (1 - p) \; * \; \textit{Dividend Yield}$$

In other words, **as an approximation, with dividend reinvestment and dividend growth, income growth rate equals dividend growth rate plus after-tax dividend yield.** This expression is worth remembering. Here, as in the last chapter, p is (your) personal dividend tax rate for the stock in question.

Many investors emphasize dividend yield – almost to the exclusion of dividend growth. For dividend growth stocks, and indeed for most stocks with moderate to good dividend growth, this emphasis is incorrect. In fact, for the typical dividend growth stock – because dividend growth rate is comparatively larger and dividend yield is (potentially) taxed – dividend growth rate matters more than dividend yield. For instance, suppose you own a dividend growth stock with a dividend yield of

3.5 percent and a dividend growth rate of 9 percent. With a personal dividend tax rate of (say) 20 percent, your stock's after-tax dividend yield is (1 - 0.20) * 3.5 or 2.8 percent. Because 9 / 2.8 is 3.2, your stock's dividend growth rate is more than three times as important to your income growth rate as its dividend yield.

As another example, consider a high-yielding but slow-growth stock with a dividend yield of 6 percent and a dividend growth rate of 3 percent. With (say) a 15 percent personal dividend tax rate, your income growth rate is 0.03 + (1 - 0.15) * 0.06 or 8.1 percent. Now, consider a dividend growth stock with a lower dividend yield of 3.5 percent but a higher dividend growth rate of 10 percent. Your income growth rate is now 0.10 + (1 - 0.15) * 0.035 or 13.0 percent, almost five percentage points higher.

The moral of these examples: *Do not focus on dividend yield to the exclusion of dividend growth. What matters is not today's dividend but the timing and amount of dividends over the **lifetime** of your investment. And for that, dividend growth matters. Focus on dividend yield and dividend growth rate. Often, and especially over the long term, dividend growth rate matters more.*

We don't judge a racer by the first step he takes. We judge him based on the culmination of thousands of steps.

The Formula for the Return With Dividend Reinvestment

"It's a huge competitive advantage to be able to think long term..." Jeff Bezos

"It's actually much rarer than you think." Jeff Bezos

In Chapter 1, we saw that annual return is dividend yield plus contribution from capital changes, where capital changes involve growth rate in earnings per share and growth rate in P/E ratio. With dividend reinvestment, the direct contribution of dividend yield to annual return goes away. In its place, the investor has the extra shares earned through

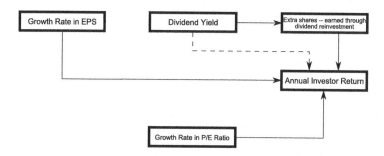

Figure 5.2. Contributors to annual (investor) return when investors reinvest their dividends. Dividend yield contributes indirectly.

dividend reinvestment (Figure 5.2). These extra shares generate a return identical to the contribution from capital changes in Chapter 1. Moreover, the original shares do the same. Thus, with dividend reinvestment, we have the following formula for annual return, where *extra shares* correspond to the reinvestment factor of Chapter 4:

$$Annual\ Return\ =\ G \\ +\ Extra\ Shares\ *\ (1\ +\ G)$$

Here, G is a complex growth rate identical to the contribution from capital changes expression in the second formula for the return in Chapter 1:

$$G\ =\ Growth\ Rate\ in\ Earnings\ Per\ Share \\ +\ Growth\ Rate\ in\ P/E\ Ratio \\ +\ (\ Growth\ Rate\ in\ Earnings\ Per\ Share \\ *\ Growth\ Rate\ in\ P/E\ Ratio\ )$$

As in Chapter 1, we generally ignore the term in parentheses because it is comparatively tiny. Also, as in Chapter 1, our formula for the return assumes we hold on to our stock. If we sell we potentially pay capital gains taxes.

The first formula in this section parallels the first formula in this chapter. The analogy is direct because the logic is similar.

Real Return

"Inflation is taxation without legislation." Milton Friedman

Returns that do not account for inflation are incomplete. Properly termed nominal returns, these are not the most important returns – especially over the long term. What is important is not how much paper wealth you control, but how much buying power that paper commands. Owning a wheelbarrow of cash does little good if all that wheelbarrow buys you is a loaf of bread.

Real returns remove the effects of inflation. Real returns gauge buying power. Real returns matter because real wealth matters; not the paper wealth measured by nominal returns.

When inflation is low, real return is, roughly, the difference between nominal return and inflation:[1]

$$Real\ Return\ =\ Nominal\ Return\ -\ Inflation$$

Long-term real stock market returns have averaged seven percent a year. This is the nominal long-term stock market return of ten percent a year minus long-term inflation of three percent a year. Thus, unfortunately, long-term investors in the stock market are not as rich as they think they are. What we noted in Chapter 4 about the long-term wealth-reducing effect of removing a portion of the return each year applies similarly here. Nevertheless, long-term investors in the stock market have fared better than most. For checking accounts, real returns have been close to zero. For cash-under-the-mattress accounts, real returns have been negative.

Zero and negative real returns should come with a warning that they are hazardous to your financial health. For instance, a nominal

---

[1]The exact formula is more complicated:

$$Real\ Return\ =\ \frac{(1\ +\ Nominal\ Return)}{(1\ +\ Inflation)}\ -\ 1$$

Nominal Return

Inflation	1	2	3	4	5	6	7	8	9	10	11	12	13	14	15
0	5	10	16	22	28	34	40	47	54	61	69	76	84	93	101
1	0	5	10	16	21	27	33	40	46	53	60	68	75	83	91
2	-5	0	5	10	16	21	27	33	39	46	53	60	67	74	82
3	-9	-5	0	5	10	15	21	27	33	39	45	52	59	66	74
4	-14	-9	-5	0	5	10	15	21	26	32	38	45	51	58	65
5	-18	-13	-9	-5	0	5	10	15	21	26	32	38	44	51	58
6	-21	-17	-13	-9	-5	0	5	10	15	20	26	32	38	44	50

Figure 5.3. Changes in cumulative five-year buying power, in percent, given inflation and a nominal return. High inflation and low nominal returns, the lower left corner, are especially destructive. This figure uses the exact formula from Footnote 1 on the facing page.

one-year return of two percent and inflation of four percent results in a real return of *minus* two percent, a sizable drop in buying power in just one year. If this pattern persists, the problem cascades. Figure 5.3 shows the cumulative effect over five years. In five years, a nominal return of two percent and inflation of four percent results in a cumulative drop in buying power of nine percent.

By contrast, positive real returns help. For instance, again from Figure 5.3, in five years, a nominal return of five percent and inflation of three percent results in a cumulative increase in buying power of ten percent. Not bad. Swap that five percent nominal return for a ten percent nominal return, the stock market's nominal long-term return, and cumulative five-year buying power jumps thirty-nine percent. Better than apple pie.

Your nominal returns must outpace inflation. Many investors are too cautious. They do not understand that *safety of principal is not safety of wealth*. Instead, they keep their long-term assets in "safe" "investments" such as cash. Steadily, their buying power whittles away.

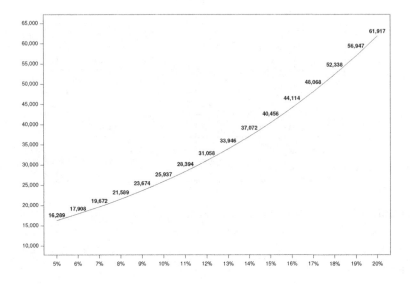

Figure 5.4. Wealth after ten years starting with $10,000 given a variety of average annual returns and *fixed* annual volatility of o percent.

Stable is Better

"Time discovers truth." Seneca

If you had to choose between (a) two years of returns at 10 percent a year and (b) a first-year return of o percent a year followed by a second-year return of 20 percent a year, which would you choose? Although the average of both choices is 10 percent a year (the average of two tens is 10 and the average of o and 20 is 10), the stable growth of the first choice results in more wealth. With the first choice, for every $100 that you invest, you end up with $121; with the second choice, for every $100 that you invest, you end up with $120. Yes, all of $1 less; but what counts is the general principle: *For a given average return, where the average is computed simply as the sum of the annual returns divided*

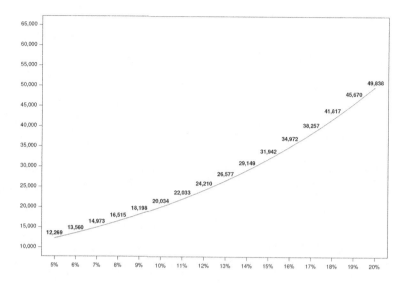

Figure 5.5. Wealth after ten years starting with $10,000 given a variety of average annual returns and *fixed* annual volatility of **25** percent.

by the number of years, stable growth is always more valuable than fluctuating growth.

What matters, always, is your eventual wealth – and for that, given identical average returns, the more stable the pattern of returns the better because volatility takes its toll. In fact, the closer to stability the better. Thus, a pattern of 7 percent one year and 13 percent the next is better than a more variable pattern of 0 percent one year and 20 percent the next. Each number in the first pattern is three points away from the average of ten (10 - 7 is 3 and 13 - 10 is 3); each number in the second pattern is ten points away (10 - 0 is 10 and 20 - 10 is 10). Likewise, both patterns are superior to a roller-coaster risky-stock pattern of 100 percent one year and *minus* 80 percent the next.

Figures 5.4 and 5.5 illustrate the destructive power of volatility. Figure 5.4 shows wealth after ten years starting with $10,000 given a variety of average annual returns and fixed annual volatility of 0 percent. Annual

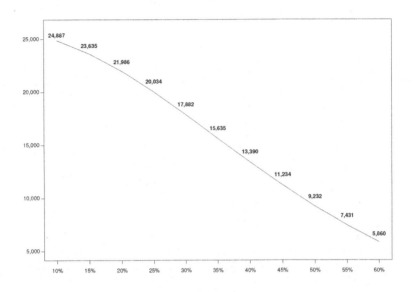

Figure 5.6. Wealth after ten years starting with $10,000 given a *fixed* average annual return of 10 percent with annual volatility varying between 10 percent and 60 percent. *High volatility is disastrous to long-term wealth. In fact, with very high volatilities, you actually end up poorer – you actually lose wealth.*

volatility of 0 percent means each year's return equals the average return. Because of this, our compound interest formula – applied to returns – applies. For instance, at an average return of 10 percent a year, $10,000 at 10 percent a year, over ten years, amounts to wealth of $10,000 * (1 + 0.10)^{10}$ or $25,937, as shown in the figure. *With non-zero volatility, however, things change. Wealth takes a turn for the worse.* Figure 5.5 uses the same assumptions as the previous figure's, except that annual volatility now ratchets up to 25 percent a year, a not unreasonable long-term value for the volatility of many large-caps and even certain more aggressive funds such as small-cap growth funds. *For any given return, wealth in this figure is lower than wealth in the previous figure.* For instance, at an average return of 10 percent a year, when annual volatility is 0 percent, wealth reaches $25,937; by contrast, when annual volatility is 25 percent, wealth reaches $20,034. In other words, given identical average returns, *higher volatility drags wealth down*, a general result. *As a long-term holder, volatility is not your friend.*

Figure 5.6 shows just how bad things get when volatility increases. The figure shows wealth after ten years starting with $10,000 given a fixed average annual return of 10 percent with annual volatility varying between 10 percent and 60 percent. As the figure shows, *high volatility is disastrous to long-term wealth. In fact, with very high volatilities, you actually end up poorer – you actually lose wealth.* For instance, from the figure, with annual volatility somewhere between 45 percent and 50 percent, in ten years, wealth drops below $10,000. In other words, in ten years, you end up with *less* than what you started with – *even with a positive average annual return.* Annual volatilities of 40 percent to 60 percent are not uncommon for riskier stocks – including many small-caps. To be fair, average annual returns for such stocks are higher – but I do not believe they are high enough to compensate *long*-term *holders.* I believe the majority of high-volatility stocks are trades. Only exceedingly rarely are they buy-and-holds. If you are attracted to high-volatility stocks, buy several stocks, or even better buy a fund, and never bet too much on just one stock.

What is true of returns is true of dividends. **Given identical average dividend growth rates, the more volatile the pattern of dividend growth rates, the lower the ultimate dividend.** A company that raises its dividend 10 percent a year for ten years raises its dividend a cumulative 159 percent (Figure 5.7). By contrast, a company that alternates raising its dividend a more volatile 0 percent one year and 20 percent the next raises its dividend a cumulative 149 percent (Figure 5.8).

Dividend growth stability mirrors business stability. But only a handful of businesses are stable. Coca-Cola is one. Its 2001-2014 annual dividend growth rates (ignoring decimals for clarity) are 6%, 11%, 10%, 14%, 12%, 11%, 10%, 12%, 8%, 7%, 7%, 9%, 10%, and 9%. Cumulative growth: 259 percent. Average annual growth: 10 percent. Though not every dividend growth rate equals ten percent, as a reflection of real-world business performance, they are close. Even without dividend reinvestment, an investor who collected $1,000 in dividends from Coca-Cola in 2000 collected $3,588 in dividends in 2014. That's dividend growth.

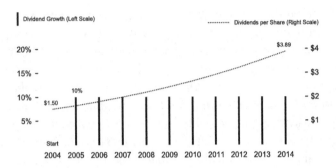

Figure 5.7. A stable dividend growth pattern of 10 percent a year results in cumulative ten-year dividend growth of 159 percent. In ten years, the dividend grows from $1.50 to $3.89.

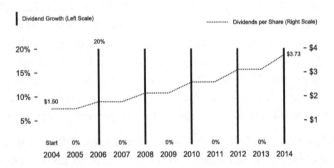

Figure 5.8. A fluctuating dividend growth pattern that alternates between 0 percent one year and 20 percent the next results in cumulative ten-year dividend growth of 149 percent. In ten years, the dividend grows from $1.50 to $3.73. Compare this to the $3.89 from the previous figure. Given identical average dividend growth rates, stable growth is always more valuable than fluctuating growth.

Cyclical businesses are the polar opposites of stable businesses. Cyclical businesses react violently to arcs in the economy. They print money when the economy does well. They bleed money when the economy does poorly. Alcoa, the giant aluminum company, is the canonical cyclical. Its dividend pattern shows it. Alcoa's 2001-2014 annual dividend growth rates (ignoring decimals for clarity) are 20%, 0%, 0%, 0%, 0%, 0%, 13%, 0%, *minus* 62%, *minus* 54%, 0%, 0%, 0%, and 0%. Cumulative growth: *minus* 76 percent. Average annual growth: *minus* 6 percent. An investor who collected $1,000 in dividends from Alcoa in 2000 collected $240 in dividends in 2014. Although only characters from "Dude, Where's my car?" invest in Alcoa for its dividends, a 76 percent reduction in dividends is not good.

Stability plays a crucial role in forecasting and valuation. When a business is stable, we are able to more accurately forecast earnings and dividends – and thus less likely to make a catastrophic mistake valuing the stock. *By contrast, with a volatile business, we are far less reliant on business history and, in many cases, are essentially guessing.*

Finally, taking into account investor behavior, over the long term, I believe investors holding stable stocks – stocks with low to moderate volatility – should realize higher returns than investors or traders holding or playing with more volatile stocks. *Holding volatile stocks over the long term will not work. They bounce around too much. Many fail. For holders, high volatility takes its toll on wealth.* Thus, the proper approach is to trade them successfully. But this is never easy. In addition to trading costs and taxes, you have to keep guessing right. You have to know when to buy and when to sell. Moreover, not being fully invested typically hurts. By contrast, *holding stable stocks over the long term will work.* These stocks are less likely to make sharp moves in most markets. You are thus less inclined to trade, less likely to panic during downturns, and more likely to hold over the long term. Trading costs and taxes are lower. You tend to remain fully invested. You do not need to continually know when to buy and when to sell. **By remaining in the game,** *with the right stocks, and not being our own worst enemy,* **realized** *returns with stable stocks should be higher than realized returns with more volatile stocks.* **Stability is a subtle but essential attribute for long-term investing success. Dividend growth stocks are stable stocks.**

Income Projections: How Much Income Will You Have?

"You pays your money and you takes your choice." Punch

How much income will you have after X years if you invest in a dividend-paying stock today? We can use what we have learned to calculate this. In the examples that follow, I use ten years as the time frame. To communicate how much you will have, I use an after-tax yield on cost.

In addition to time frame, the answer depends on these factors:

- Your (personal) dividend tax rate.

- The stock's dividend yield.

- The stock's dividend growth rate.

- The market dividend tax rate for the stock.

- Dividend reinvestment.

- Changes in the stock's dividend yield.

The results are in Tables 5.1, 5.2, 5.3, 5.4, and 5.5. The tables list ten-year after-tax yields on cost. Personal dividend tax rates are 0, 15, 18.8, 20, and 23.8 percent respectively. In these tables, the stock's dividend yield ranges from 1 percent to 6 percent in half-point increments and the stock's dividend growth rate ranges from 6 percent to 12 percent in one-point increments. Each table includes results for no dividend reinvestment and full dividend reinvestment.

Additionally, these tables include the following assumptions:

- The market dividend tax rate for the stock is 20 percent. That said, changing the market dividend tax rate does not change the results all that much.

| Ten-year after-tax yield on cost (**personal dividend tax rate of 0 percent**) | | | | | | | |
| Dividend yield | Dividend growth | | | | | | |
	6%	7%	8%	9%	10%	11%	12%
			No dividend reinvestment				
1.0%	1.8%	2.0%	2.2%	2.4%	2.6%	2.8%	3.1%
1.5%	2.7%	3.0%	3.2%	3.6%	3.9%	4.3%	4.7%
2.0%	3.6%	3.9%	4.3%	4.7%	5.2%	5.7%	6.2%
2.5%	4.5%	4.9%	5.4%	5.9%	6.5%	7.1%	7.8%
3.0%	5.4%	5.9%	6.5%	7.1%	7.8%	8.5%	9.3%
3.5%	6.3%	6.9%	7.6%	8.3%	9.1%	9.9%	10.9%
4.0%	7.2%	7.9%	8.6%	9.5%	10.4%	11.4%	12.4%
4.5%	8.1%	8.9%	9.7%	10.7%	11.7%	12.8%	14.0%
5.0%	9.0%	9.8%	10.8%	11.8%	13.0%	14.2%	15.5%
5.5%	9.8%	10.8%	11.9%	13.0%	14.3%	15.6%	17.1%
6.0%	10.7%	11.8%	13.0%	14.2%	15.6%	17.0%	18.6%
			Full dividend reinvestment				
1.0%	2.0%	2.2%	2.4%	2.6%	2.9%	3.1%	3.4%
1.5%	3.1%	3.4%	3.8%	4.1%	4.5%	5.0%	5.4%
2.0%	4.4%	4.8%	5.3%	5.8%	6.3%	6.9%	7.6%
2.5%	5.8%	6.3%	6.9%	7.6%	8.3%	9.1%	10.0%
3.0%	7.3%	8.0%	8.8%	9.6%	10.5%	11.5%	12.6%
3.5%	8.9%	9.8%	10.8%	11.8%	12.9%	14.2%	15.5%
4.0%	10.7%	11.8%	12.9%	14.2%	15.6%	17.0%	18.6%
4.5%	12.7%	14.0%	15.3%	16.8%	18.4%	20.2%	22.1%
5.0%	14.9%	16.3%	17.9%	19.7%	21.5%	23.6%	25.8%
5.5%	17.2%	18.9%	20.8%	22.8%	25.0%	27.3%	29.9%
6.0%	19.8%	21.7%	23.9%	26.2%	28.7%	31.4%	34.3%

Table 5.1. Ten-year after-tax yield on cost given a starting dividend yield and dividend growth rate. The personal dividend tax rate for the stock is **0 percent**. (The market dividend tax rate for the stock is 20 percent. Changing the market dividend tax rate does not change the results all that much.) The jagged line separates after-tax yields on cost of less than 10 percent from after-tax yields on cost of 10 percent or more.

Ten-year after-tax yield on cost (**personal dividend tax rate of 15 percent**)							
Dividend	Dividend growth						
yield	6%	7%	8%	9%	10%	11%	12%

No dividend reinvestment

	6%	7%	8%	9%	10%	11%	12%
1.0%	1.5%	1.7%	1.8%	2.0%	2.2%	2.4%	2.6%
1.5%	2.3%	2.5%	2.8%	3.0%	3.3%	3.6%	4.0%
2.0%	3.0%	3.3%	3.7%	4.0%	4.4%	4.8%	5.3%
2.5%	3.8%	4.2%	4.6%	5.0%	5.5%	6.0%	6.6%
3.0%	4.6%	5.0%	5.5%	6.0%	6.6%	7.2%	7.9%
3.5%	5.3%	5.9%	6.4%	7.0%	7.7%	8.4%	9.2%
4.0%	6.1%	6.7%	7.3%	8.0%	8.8%	9.7%	10.6%
4.5%	6.8%	7.5%	8.3%	9.1%	9.9%	10.9%	11.9%
5.0%	7.6%	8.4%	9.2%	10.1%	11.0%	12.1%	13.2%
5.5%	8.4%	9.2%	10.1%	11.1%	12.1%	13.3%	14.5%
6.0%	9.1%	10.0%	11.0%	12.1%	13.2%	14.5%	15.8%

Full dividend reinvestment

	6%	7%	8%	9%	10%	11%	12%
1.0%	1.7%	1.8%	2.0%	2.2%	2.4%	2.6%	2.9%
1.5%	2.6%	2.9%	3.1%	3.4%	3.8%	4.1%	4.5%
2.0%	3.6%	4.0%	4.4%	4.8%	5.2%	5.7%	6.3%
2.5%	4.7%	5.2%	5.7%	6.2%	6.8%	7.5%	8.2%
3.0%	5.9%	6.5%	7.1%	7.8%	**8.6%**	9.4%	10.3%
3.5%	7.2%	7.9%	8.7%	9.5%	10.4%	11.4%	12.5%
4.0%	8.6%	9.4%	10.4%	11.4%	12.5%	13.6%	14.9%
4.5%	10.1%	11.1%	12.2%	13.4%	14.6%	16.0%	17.5%
5.0%	11.7%	12.9%	14.2%	15.5%	17.0%	18.6%	20.4%
5.5%	13.5%	14.8%	16.3%	17.8%	19.5%	21.4%	23.4%
6.0%	15.4%	16.9%	18.6%	20.3%	22.3%	24.4%	26.7%

Table 5.2. Ten-year after-tax yield on cost given a starting dividend yield and dividend growth rate. The personal dividend tax rate for the stock is **15 percent**. (The market dividend tax rate for the stock is 20 percent. Changing the market dividend tax rate does not change the results all that much.) The jagged line separates after-tax yields on cost of less than 10 percent from after-tax yields on cost of 10 percent or more.

Dividend yield	Ten-year after-tax yield on cost (**personal dividend tax rate of 18.8 percent**) Dividend growth						
	6%	7%	8%	9%	10%	11%	12%
No dividend reinvestment							
1.0%	1.5%	1.6%	1.8%	1.9%	2.1%	2.3%	2.5%
1.5%	2.2%	2.4%	2.6%	2.9%	3.2%	3.5%	3.8%
2.0%	2.9%	3.2%	3.5%	3.8%	4.2%	4.6%	5.0%
2.5%	3.6%	4.0%	4.4%	4.8%	5.3%	5.8%	6.3%
3.0%	4.4%	4.8%	5.3%	5.8%	6.3%	6.9%	7.6%
3.5%	5.1%	5.6%	6.1%	6.7%	7.4%	8.1%	8.8%
4.0%	5.8%	6.4%	7.0%	7.7%	8.4%	9.2%	10.1%
4.5%	6.5%	7.2%	7.9%	8.7%	9.5%	10.4%	11.3%
5.0%	7.3%	8.0%	8.8%	9.6%	10.5%	11.5%	12.6%
5.5%	8.0%	8.8%	9.6%	10.6%	11.6%	12.7%	13.9%
6.0%	8.7%	9.6%	10.5%	11.5%	12.6%	13.8%	15.1%
Full dividend reinvestment							
1.0%	1.6%	1.7%	1.9%	2.1%	2.3%	2.5%	2.7%
1.5%	2.5%	2.7%	3.0%	3.3%	3.6%	3.9%	4.3%
2.0%	3.4%	3.8%	4.1%	4.5%	5.0%	5.4%	5.9%
2.5%	4.5%	4.9%	5.4%	5.9%	6.5%	7.1%	7.7%
3.0%	5.6%	6.1%	6.7%	7.4%	8.1%	8.9%	9.7%
3.5%	6.8%	7.5%	8.2%	9.0%	9.8%	10.8%	11.8%
4.0%	8.1%	8.9%	9.8%	10.7%	11.7%	12.8%	14.0%
4.5%	9.5%	10.4%	11.4%	12.5%	13.7%	15.1%	16.5%
5.0%	11.0%	12.1%	13.3%	14.5%	15.9%	17.4%	19.1%
5.5%	12.6%	13.9%	15.2%	16.7%	18.3%	20.0%	21.9%
6.0%	14.4%	15.8%	17.3%	19.0%	20.8%	22.8%	24.9%

Table 5.3. Ten-year after-tax yield on cost given a starting dividend yield and dividend growth rate. The personal dividend tax rate for the stock is **18.8 percent**. (The market dividend tax rate for the stock is 20 percent. Changing the market dividend tax rate does not change the results all that much.) The jagged line separates after-tax yields on cost of less than 10 percent from after-tax yields on cost of 10 percent or more.

Ten-year after-tax yield on cost (**personal dividend tax rate of 20 percent**)							
Dividend	Dividend growth						
yield	6%	7%	8%	9%	10%	11%	12%
			No dividend reinvestment				
1.0%	1.4%	1.6%	1.7%	1.9%	2.1%	2.3%	2.5%
1.5%	2.1%	2.4%	2.6%	2.8%	3.1%	3.4%	3.7%
2.0%	2.9%	3.1%	3.5%	3.8%	4.1%	4.5%	5.0%
2.5%	3.6%	3.9%	4.3%	4.7%	5.2%	5.7%	6.2%
3.0%	4.3%	4.7%	5.2%	5.7%	6.2%	6.8%	7.5%
3.5%	5.0%	5.5%	6.0%	6.6%	**7.3%**	8.0%	8.7%
4.0%	5.7%	6.3%	6.9%	7.6%	8.3%	9.1%	9.9%
4.5%	6.4%	7.1%	7.8%	8.5%	9.3%	10.2%	11.2%
5.0%	7.2%	7.9%	8.6%	9.5%	10.4%	11.4%	12.4%
5.5%	7.9%	8.7%	9.5%	10.4%	11.4%	12.5%	13.7%
6.0%	8.6%	9.4%	10.4%	11.4%	12.4%	13.6%	14.9%
			Full dividend reinvestment				
1.0%	1.6%	1.7%	1.9%	2.1%	2.2%	2.5%	2.7%
1.5%	2.4%	2.7%	2.9%	3.2%	3.5%	3.8%	4.2%
2.0%	3.4%	3.7%	4.1%	4.5%	4.9%	5.3%	5.8%
2.5%	4.4%	4.8%	5.3%	5.8%	6.3%	7.0%	7.6%
3.0%	5.5%	6.0%	6.6%	7.2%	7.9%	8.7%	9.5%
3.5%	6.7%	7.3%	8.0%	8.8%	**9.6%**	10.6%	11.6%
4.0%	7.9%	8.7%	9.6%	10.5%	11.5%	12.6%	13.8%
4.5%	9.3%	10.2%	11.2%	12.3%	13.5%	14.7%	16.1%
5.0%	10.8%	11.8%	13.0%	14.2%	15.6%	17.1%	18.7%
5.5%	12.4%	13.6%	14.9%	16.3%	17.9%	19.6%	21.4%
6.0%	14.1%	15.4%	16.9%	18.6%	20.4%	22.3%	24.4%

Table 5.4. Ten-year after-tax yield on cost given a starting dividend yield and dividend growth rate. The personal dividend tax rate for the stock is **20 percent**. (The market dividend tax rate for the stock is 20 percent. Changing the market dividend tax rate does not change the results all that much.) The jagged line separates after-tax yields on cost of less than 10 percent from after-tax yields on cost of 10 percent or more.

Ten-year after-tax yield on cost (**personal dividend tax rate of 23.8 percent**)

Dividend yield	Dividend growth						
	6%	7%	8%	9%	10%	11%	12%

No dividend reinvestment

Dividend yield	6%	7%	8%	9%	10%	11%	12%
1.0%	1.4%	1.5%	1.6%	1.8%	2.0%	2.2%	2.4%
1.5%	2.0%	2.2%	2.5%	2.7%	3.0%	3.2%	3.5%
2.0%	2.7%	3.0%	3.3%	3.6%	4.0%	4.3%	4.7%
2.5%	3.4%	3.7%	4.1%	4.5%	4.9%	5.4%	5.9%
3.0%	4.1%	4.5%	4.9%	5.4%	5.9%	6.5%	7.1%
3.5%	4.8%	5.2%	5.8%	6.3%	6.9%	7.6%	8.3%
4.0%	5.5%	6.0%	6.6%	7.2%	7.9%	8.7%	9.5%
4.5%	6.1%	6.7%	7.4%	8.1%	8.9%	9.7%	10.6%
5.0%	6.8%	7.5%	8.2%	9.0%	9.9%	10.8%	11.8%
5.5%	7.5%	8.2%	9.0%	9.9%	10.9%	11.9%	13.0%
6.0%	8.2%	9.0%	9.9%	10.8%	11.9%	13.0%	14.2%

Full dividend reinvestment

Dividend yield	6%	7%	8%	9%	10%	11%	12%
1.0%	1.5%	1.6%	1.8%	1.9%	2.1%	2.3%	2.6%
1.5%	2.3%	2.5%	2.8%	3.0%	3.3%	3.6%	4.0%
2.0%	3.2%	3.5%	3.8%	4.2%	4.6%	5.0%	5.5%
2.5%	4.1%	4.5%	5.0%	5.5%	6.0%	6.6%	7.2%
3.0%	5.2%	5.7%	6.2%	6.8%	7.5%	8.2%	8.9%
3.5%	6.3%	6.9%	7.5%	8.3%	9.1%	9.9%	10.9%
4.0%	7.4%	8.2%	9.0%	9.8%	10.8%	11.8%	12.9%
4.5%	8.7%	9.6%	10.5%	11.5%	12.6%	13.8%	15.1%
5.0%	10.1%	11.1%	12.1%	13.3%	14.6%	16.0%	17.5%
5.5%	11.5%	12.7%	13.9%	15.2%	16.7%	18.3%	20.0%
6.0%	13.1%	14.4%	15.8%	17.3%	19.0%	20.8%	22.7%

Table 5.5. Ten-year after-tax yield on cost given a starting dividend yield and dividend growth rate. The personal dividend tax rate for the stock is **23.8 percent**. (The market dividend tax rate for the stock is 20 percent. Changing the market dividend tax rate does not change the results all that much.) The jagged line separates after-tax yields on cost of less than 10 percent from after-tax yields on cost of 10 percent or more.

- The dividend yield remains constant. Changes in dividend yield are difficult to forecast.

- Dividends are paid annually. This keeps things simple. With quarterly dividends, all else equal, you get slightly better results because dividends compound more frequently.

The jagged lines in the tables separate after-tax yields on cost of less than 10 percent from after-tax yields on cost of 10 percent or more.

Here's how to calculate each full dividend reinvestment entry in these tables:

1. Calculate the reinvestment factor from Chapter 4.

2. Calculate the income growth rate using the first formula in this chapter.

3. Use the compound interest formula from Chapter 4 to get the future value after ten years. You now have your (pre-tax) yield on cost.

4. Calculate the after-tax yield on cost. We have to do this because the final dividend has not been taxed.

Here's an example. From Table 5.4, with a personal dividend tax rate of 20 percent, full dividend reinvestment, a dividend yield of 3.5 percent, and a dividend growth rate of 10 percent, the ten-year after-tax yield on cost is 9.6 percent. Here's how to calculate it:

1. Calculate the reinvestment factor from Chapter 4. The reinvestment factor is $(1 - 0.20) * 0.035 / (1 - (1 - 0.20) * 0.035)$ or 0.02881. Here, the first 0.20 is your (personal) dividend tax rate and the second 0.20 is the market dividend tax rate for the stock.

2. Calculate the income growth rate using the first formula in this chapter. The income growth rate is $0.10 + 0.02881 * (1 + 0.10)$ or 0.1317.

3. Use the compound interest formula from Chapter 4 to get the future value after ten years. The future value is $0.035 * (1 + 0.1317)^{10}$ or 0.1206. You now have your (pre-tax) yield on cost.

4. Calculate the after-tax yield on cost. The after-tax yield on cost is $(1 - 0.20) * 0.1206$ or 0.096 or 9.6 percent. Here, 0.20 is your (personal) dividend tax rate.

If you are willing to forgo a bit of accuracy, you can take a shortcut by combining Steps 1 and 2 using the approximate formula for the income growth rate, the second formula in this chapter.

Calculating the no dividend reinvestment entry in these tables is simpler. The reinvestment factor from Step 1 is zero and the income growth rate from Step 2 is the dividend growth rate. In effect, therefore, you start from Step 3 with the dividend growth rate as what compounds. For instance, from Table 5.4, with a personal dividend tax rate of 20 percent, no dividend reinvestment, a dividend yield of 3.5 percent, and a dividend growth rate of 10 percent, the ten-year after-tax yield on cost is 7.3 percent. Here's how to calculate it. From Step 3, the future value is $0.035 * (1 + 0.10)^{10}$ or 0.0908. From Step 4, the after-tax yield on cost is $(1 - 0.20) * 0.0908$ or 0.073 or 7.3 percent.

Not surprisingly, income rises with a higher dividend yield, a higher dividend growth rate, a lower personal dividend tax rate, and full dividend reinvestment. *The first factor depends on the **market**, the second factor depends on the **company**, and the last two factors depend on **you**.* All else equal, minimize dividend taxes and reinvest.

Here's an example of how to *use* these tables. Suppose a stock trades at $50. It has a 3.0 percent dividend yield. You expect 10.0 percent dividend growth the next ten years. Your (personal) dividend tax rate is 15 percent. Assume the market dividend rate for the stock is 20 percent. You reinvest your dividends. How much income will you have in ten years? According to Table 5.2, your ten-year after-tax yield on cost is 8.6 percent. You will therefore have $0.086 * 50$, or $4.30 in income, after taxes, in ten years. If you start with more than one share, multiply this result by your starting number of shares. Thus, if you start with 100 shares, you will have 4.30 * 100, or $430 in income, after taxes, in ten years.

Two caveats:

- Changes in dividend yield change the result; but changes in dividend yield, like changes in P/E ratio, are difficult to forecast. (We will see later that, for well-established companies, changes in dividend yield and changes in P/E ratio are, essentially, two faces of the same coin.)

- You do not know whether your stock is overvalued. This matters because what you gain in income you can lose in capital changes. In Chapter 9, we look at the important concept of valuation and develop a model to value our dividend growth stocks.

Trading vs. Investing

"Speculation is a hard and trying business, and a speculator must be on the job all the time or he'll soon have no job to be on." Edwin Lefèvre

"[O]nce a stock has been properly selected and has borne the test of time, it is only occasionally that there is any reason for selling it at all." Philip A. Fisher

Trading can humble the arrogant and bankrupt the genius. Instead of making a hard decision just a few times (which high-quality stock do I buy?), traders juggle. Exiting a stock or the stock market is only one part of trading. The other part is knowing when to get back in. And in many cases when traders get back in they are under-invested. Much of their portfolio sits in cash – waiting for just the right moment. Traders do not learn until it is too late that it is not easy to keep guessing right. Eventually, to make up for lost time, or lost opportunity, they bet heavily on the "sure one." It is usually not the right one. It is usually late in the bull market. The market is a brutal – and painfully expensive – place to learn.

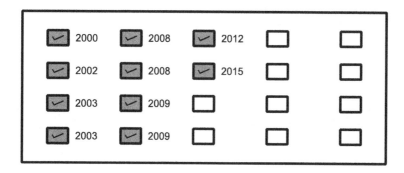

Figure 5.9. Punch card of decisions.

While a trader chooses to make many decisions, an investor chooses to make (a careful) few. Too much selling can be hazardous to your financial health. The proper long-term investing approach, instead, is to give your companies time to grow, time to let their earnings – and your dividends – compound. If you sell too soon, you lacerate this benefit of time.

Warren Buffett has remarked that you should invest as if you own a punch card with twenty slots. Each time you invest in something new, punch a slot (Figure 5.9). Once you punch twenty slots, the clock strikes midnight. You are done. You do not lose a glass slipper – but you cannot make any new investments.

Buffett's point is not that there is innate magic in the number twenty. There isn't. It is not as if twenty is forty-two, the answer to Life, the Universe, and Everything. Instead, Buffett wants you to focus on making just a few decisions, each decision weighed with the utmost of care. Care and caution become the key attributes of the decision-making process. ***Your key decision, repeated just a few times, becomes, "Which high-quality stock do I buy?"***

For the most part, that's it. Yes, an overheated market is a serious problem. And, yes, so is an overheated stock. But, by and large, once you've picked your high-quality stocks there's little else to do. Owning high-quality stocks gives you that freedom. Owning lower-quality stocks never does.

Conservatively Aggressive

"Good news, everyone." Professor Farnsworth (Futurama)

Three ducks, none of whom can fly, must make it to the warm springs before winter arrives. To do so, they must cross twenty roads. The first duck, an extremely careful one, waits until she cannot see cars as far as the horizon before she crosses each road. She crosses six roads before it gets too dark to see. She rests for the night under a tree. A fox seeing the sleeping duck kills her. When the second duck hears of the death of the first duck, she decides to cross each road quickly. As soon as she spots an opening, she darts across. She makes good time but she gets overconfident. She takes bigger and bigger risks. Crossing the eleventh road, she waltzes across. She does not see the speeding car as it hits her and kills her. Realizing what happened to the first two ducks, the third duck acts prudently. She crosses each road carefully but quickly. She looks both ways and crosses when she can. She neither is too careful nor too aggressive. She crosses the twenty roads in good time. She makes it to the warm springs. She lives happily after.

Conservative investors embrace income – unwittingly, to the exclusion of growth. As a result, inflation gnaws away at their real wealth. On the other hand, aggressive investors chase growth. More often than not, impatience destroys their wealth. They underperform over long periods.

Over the long term, neither conservative investing nor aggressive investing will do. The better investing approach is to combine the best of both. The better investing approach is to be conservatively aggressive. Dividend growth investing is conservatively aggressive. ***The dividend provides an element of conservatism; dividend growth, the right amount of aggressiveness.*** ♣ ♣

A Summary: Part I

"Whoever said money can't buy happiness did not know where to shop."
Anonymous

Here are the more important points from this part of the book:

- To succeed as a dividend growth investor, you need patience, time, and high-quality dividend growth stocks growing at stable, moderate, and sustainable rates and selling at reasonable valuations or better.

- Over the long term, great companies grow at rates few investors can match.

- Dividends are not a panacea. Do not look at dividends independently of the business.

- When you invest in a share of stock, you earn an annual return equal to, roughly:

$$\begin{aligned}
\textit{Annual Return} &= \textit{Dividend Yield} \\
&+ \textit{Growth Rate in Earnings Per Share} \\
&+ \textit{Growth Rate in P/E Ratio}
\end{aligned}$$

- Holding stocks with potentially rapid drops in P/E ratio can be dangerous, a particularly thorny problem when P/E ratio is high: Even with rapid growth in earnings per share, a big drop in P/E ratio can decimate your returns.

- Over long periods, growth rate in P/E ratio has contributed nothing to returns.

- By convention, risk is defined as volatility of returns.

- If you chase extraordinary gains, be prepared for extraordinary losses.

- To become rich, you must avoid large losses at all costs.

- Over the long term, moderate growth is the only growth that can be maintained – and still make you rich. Slow growth never amounts to much. High growth usually fizzles out.

- It is a mathematical truism that, given equal average returns, volatility reduces the accumulation of wealth, high volatility resulting in much lower accumulation of wealth than low or moderate volatility.

- Returns of dividend growth stocks do not suffer from high volatility. It is the low volatility of returns that is a subtle but substantial benefit of investing in dividend growth stocks.

- With dividend growth stocks, risk is low and returns are moderate. On a risk-adjusted basis, the stocks outperform.

- In the long run, stocks beat inflation because of what the underlying companies create and sell and the risks that they take, both financial and otherwise. In the short run, however, most stocks are poor hedges against inflation.

- Core holdings are investments that you make to pay for serious long-term financial goals.

- The intelligent investor holds a large core position with some speculation, like an unbalanced barbell with the large end as the core and the small end as speculation.

- A portfolio of reasonably valued high-quality dividend growth stocks fits squarely in the core.

- For good companies, calculated dividend yield understates true dividend yield. On "average," for a company that pays quarterly dividends and raises its dividend ten percent once a year, true dividend yield is 1.0625 times calculated dividend yield.

- Do not confuse yield on cost with returns. Yield on cost has little to do with returns.

- The four dates relevant to dividend payments are the declaration date, the ex-dividend date, the record date, and the payment date.

- Immediately after a dividend, the share price falls by the after-tax value of the dividend.

- Unlike interest, except for any possible tax-related benefit, dividends are not extra.

- You need enough growth to overcome the corrosive effect of inflation. Stocks generally have it. Bonds generally don't.

- The best tax-advantaged account is the HSA, followed by, for most, the Roth IRA, then the traditional IRA.

- When you defer taxes you leave more of your money to work. This benefits you directly in a higher after-tax return.

- A share buyback is an investment in the company's shares. If this investment earns a high enough return, remaining shareholders benefit.

- Share buybacks and dividends are different rearrangements of blocks.

- Once a given amount of cash leaves a company's coffers and makes its way to shareholders, how it gets split, whether by dividends or share buybacks or indeed a mix, does not matter.

- Neither share buybacks nor dividend payments necessarily boost long-term returns.

- The best gauge of yield is net shareholder yield. Net shareholder yield adds to dividends cash spent on buybacks and subtracts cash received from shares issued.

- Simple interest is similar in form to not reinvesting your dividends. Compound interest is similar in form to reinvesting your dividends.

- With compound interest, growth is exponential. With exponential growth, percentage changes are equal over equal periods, implying dollar changes – and dollar amounts – explode.

- High returns are not the only way to reap the benefits of exponential growth. You can just as well trade off a lower return for a longer time. This is important because higher returns mean higher risks – many things can go wrong. For instance, higher returns can rarely be maintained over long periods, (say) at least ten years.

- Over a long enough period, if you lose just a small portion of your return each year, you end up with much lower wealth. Thus, for instance, avoid taxes (legally) and keep expenses as a fraction of your return very low.

- If companies do not lower their dividends, as is typically the case with high-quality dividend growth stocks, then much like an inflating balloon, when you reinvest, your income always grows. Each reinvested dividend leads to an increase in shares. Each increase in shares leads to an increase in dividends.

- One caution with dividend reinvestment: Because you build a larger and larger position in the underlying company – and without selling have taken nothing out – if the company ever were to fail, not only have you lost everything but you've earned nothing in the interim – and have paid taxes on your dividends as well. So, ultimately, it's a disaster. Thus you must invest in the right company. It must have long-term staying power. In this regard, of most importance, the business must be simple to understand.

- When you invest in a dividend growth stock and reinvest the dividends, your income growth rate is given by, roughly (here p is your personal tax rate):

$$Dividend\ Growth\ Rate$$
$$+ (1 - p) * Dividend\ Yield$$

- Do not focus on dividend yield to the exclusion of dividend growth. Often, and especially over the long term, dividend growth rate matters more.

- With dividend reinvestment, we have the following formula for the annual return, where *extra shares* correspond to the reinvestment factor from Chapter 4:

$$Annual\ Return\ =\ G$$
$$+ Extra\ Shares\ *\ (1 + G)$$

Here, G is a complex growth rate:

$$G\ =\ Growth\ Rate\ in\ Earnings\ Per\ Share$$
$$+ Growth\ Rate\ in\ P/E\ Ratio$$
$$+ (\ Growth\ Rate\ in\ Earnings\ Per\ Share$$
$$*\ Growth\ Rate\ in\ P/E\ Ratio\ )$$

In this expression, we generally ignore the term in parentheses.

- Your nominal returns must outpace inflation. Many investors are too cautious. They do not understand that safety of principal is not safety of wealth.

- For a given average return, where the average is computed simply as the sum of the annual returns divided by the number of years, stable growth is always more valuable than fluctuating growth. Given identical average returns, higher volatility drags wealth down. As a long-term holder, volatility is not your friend.

- Moreover, high volatility is disastrous to long-term wealth. In fact, with very high volatilities, you actually end up poorer – you actually lose wealth.

- What is true of returns is true of dividends. Given identical average dividend growth rates, the more volatile the pattern of dividend growth rates, the lower the ultimate dividend.

- Dividend growth stability mirrors business stability.

- With stable stocks, we are less inclined to trade, less likely to panic during downturns, and more likely to hold over the long term. By remaining in the game, with the right stocks, and not being our own worst enemy, realized returns with stable stocks should be higher than realized returns with more volatile stocks. Stability is a subtle but essential attribute for long-term investing success. Dividend growth stocks are stable stocks.

- To calculate projected income from a dividend-paying stock, calculate, in order, the reinvestment factor, the income growth rate, the future value using the compound interest formula, and finally the after-tax future value. This is an estimate. Many things can change.

- Trading can humble the arrogant and bankrupt the genius. The market is a brutal – and painfully expensive – place to learn.

- As an investor in high-quality stocks, your key decision, repeated just a few times, becomes, "Which high-quality stock do I buy?" By and large, once you've picked your high-quality stocks there's little else to do. Owning high-quality stocks gives you that freedom. Owning lower-quality stocks never does.

- Dividend growth investing is conservatively aggressive. The dividend provides an element of conservatism; dividend growth, the right amount of aggressiveness.

***

This concludes the first part of the book. We studied dividends. We studied share buybacks. We saw that dividends and share dividends are different rearrangements of blocks. We looked at dividend reinvestment, a form of savings and important to the growth of your wealth, and dividend growth, which for most dividend growth stocks matters more than dividend yield – and thus dividend reinvestment – because it is larger and not currently taxed.

But dividend growth investing does not exist in a vacuum. Success depends on the underlying investment. Thus far, however, we have paid scant attention to the underlying investment. We have assumed, with little or no thought, that we know what the future will bring. In particular, we have assumed that we know how fast the dividend will grow. That's unrealistic. Any old dividend from any old stock will not do. The dividend may not be sustainable. The dividend may be cut. The dividend may not grow fast enough. Finally, we have focused almost entirely on income and have paid little attention to what ultimately matters, returns.

This leads us to the second part of the book, where we put the spotlight on the underlying investments, the *companies*, and explore the *criteria* to find high-quality dividend growth stocks. The underlying *business* and *valuation* take precedence. We answer questions such as these: What business traits do these long-term success stories share? What numerical signposts do we look for? What returns should we expect? ♣ ♣ ♣

Part II

Criteria

"Before everything else, getting ready is the secret of success."

Henry Ford

CHAPTER 6

The Business

"My own business always bores me to death; I prefer other people's." Oscar
Wilde

THE long and dazzling dividend histories of companies such as
Fannie Mae and Freddie Mac led many an investor astray. They
believed that these businesses would endure. They believed
that dividends and dividend growth would continue.

Yet, up against an economic maelstrom in 2008, these businesses
were tested and put to the sword. These – and others like them – collapsed. Dividends were reduced. Dividends were obliterated. Even today,
mid-2015, many remain just a pale shadow of what they once were.

In the meantime, in the midst of market pandemonium and fear,
other companies continued to prosper. On 12 September 2008, Abbott
announced its 339th consecutive dividend. Thirteen days later, McDonald's announced a 33 percent increase in its dividend.

For companies such as Abbott and McDonald's, *the vitality of divi-*
dends springs from the vigor of fortress-like businesses, businesses that
through the economy's ups and downs generate the strong and steady
profits that support rich and rising dividends.

Over time, strong businesses persist; weak businesses fade away.

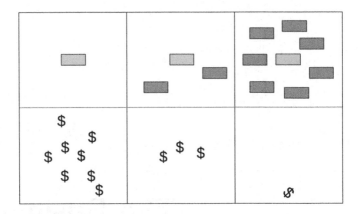

Figure 6.1. Extreme competition leads to collapsing profits.

Competition

"Competition is a sin." John D. Rockefeller

What is the competition? Ask that first of all your long-term invest-ments. Competition erodes the vitality of a business. Without compe-tition, investing would be easy. Companies would act like monopolies. Shareholders would reap their dividends.

Yet, few companies enjoy the comfort of none or limited competition. On the contrary, most face a Darwinian struggle to survive. Though a company may experience little competition at first, as new competition emerges, sales growth starts to weaken and profit growth starts to slow. When competition is extreme, profits collapse (Figure 6.1).

Recently, the solar industry felt the slap of brutal competition that wipes companies off the face of the map. First Solar, one of the industry's bigger players, surged more than one-thousand percent in its first year and a half as a public company. In May 2008, the stock reached an all-time high. Later, as subsidies fell and competition grew, pricing collapsed and profitability cratered. By June 2012, First Solar was in the clearance aisle, the stock selling at ninety-six percent below its all-time high. In four years, not only had all the heady gains vanished, but the stock was selling for less than its 2006 IPO price. (The times they are a-changin' though. First Solar is revamping its business model. Moreover, given enough time – and this is true of any industry – once competition kills the weaker players, the survivors get a lifeline. As of mid-2015, First Solar has risen more than three-hundred percent off its 2012 low.)

New competition brings in new technology and a different way of doing things. Established companies are often set in their ways. Instead of adapting to change, they often persist in denial. Blockbuster faced years of growing competition from Netflix – and years of denial – before the reality of its fate set in. The company declared bankruptcy in 2010. It survives today as a crust of its former self. As of mid-2015, all its corporate U.S. stores are closed. Only a few franchised U.S. stores remain.

As they age, even formerly strong industries can witness the withering sting of unrelenting competition. In the last few years, pharmaceuticals have experienced difficulties. Companies such as Pfizer and Merck have faced new competition – and slowing sales – as patents have expired and generic competition has emerged. (However, as with First Solar, wait long enough and things can change. Pfizer and Merck are awakening from their decade-long comas.)

High profits attract competition. When profits are high, new competition emerges. In time, the market becomes oversupplied. Pricing becomes irrational. Profits collapse.

High growth attracts competition. During the Internet boom of the late 1990s, competition bubbled. Virtually everyone wanted in. With extreme competition, however, the market broke. Profits tumbled and companies collapsed. Even for the survivors, the road back has been long. And painful. Lucent, now part of Alcatel-Lucent, has never recovered. Sun was acquired by Oracle. Cisco has tried to adapt – but it will take years before it broaches its 2000 high, if ever.

In general, *avoid investing in companies that face rising competition*. With rising competition, a company sees declining internal returns and, in time, your returns will do the same. In general, *you will do your portfolio an immense amount of good when you invest in companies that face stable or falling competition*. With stable competition, if the company's internal returns are already high, they are more likely to remain that way – at least. With falling competition, the company's internal returns are more likely to increase – and your returns will do the same.

Ideally, a high-quality established business – the type of business exemplified by the typical dividend growth stock – shares the following overriding competitive traits, traits that not surprisingly suggest stable or falling competition:

- The company has few competitors and competitors act rationally. In a perfect world (for its shareholders), the company dominates its markets, for instance, by virtue of its size.

- The business produces profits that are good but not necessarily obscene. Obscene profits attract competition.

- The business grows at a pace that isn't hurried (but also isn't soporific). High growth attracts competition. In the early 2000s, internet-related companies found this out the hard way.

Business Stability

"Financial genius is before the fall." John Kenneth Galbraith.

Stable modestly growing profits form the basis of dividend growth. Profits should not vary wildly, like a yo-yo, from year to year. A company with wildly varying profits cannot hope to pay a dividend, let alone a growing dividend. Ideally, profits grow modestly from year to year and never fluctuate wildly.

The consumer staples sector exemplifies the kind of stability we hope to see with our dividend growth stocks. Because businesses in the consumer staples sector sell inexpensive and recurring products, demand does not collapse when the economy slows. Demand growth is steady.

By contrast, unless they have offsets such as a strong brand or a dominant market position, companies that sell expensive things (for instance, houses) or occasional things (for instance, fads) can never be good dividend-paying stocks. Profits fluctuate too widely (houses) or eventually flop (fads).

Diversification aids stability – a full range of coloring pencils is better than one or two. Diversification reduces business risks and helps control costs. For instance, a company with operations in many countries faces reduced currency risks. Likewise, a company with many suppliers pays less for its raw materials.

Generally, large companies are more stable than small companies:

- They have more pricing power.

- They can more easily influence their suppliers.

- They can market widely, persistently, and aggressively.

- They can raise funds more easily – and at better prices.

- They can more readily absorb legal and other business risks.

- They are less likely to lose money when business stalls because they more readily cover their fixed costs.[1] By contrast, when business stalls, many small companies quickly go into the red.

Stability helps companies survive. Stable businesses have a reasonable idea of what the next quarter and next year will bring. Growth is neither excessive nor negative. ***Stable companies persist, an essential trait of any investment if you want to be a long-term owner***. Nestlé, the consumer staples giant, has been around since 1866. Valspar, the paint and coatings manufacturer, has been around since 1806.

---

[1] Businesses face two types of costs: fixed costs and variable costs. Fixed costs do not vary with the number of items produced; variable costs do. Rent is a fixed cost; the cost of raw materials to produce what a business sells is a variable cost. Because companies typically do not lower their dividends, *dividends share some of the characteristics of fixed costs.*

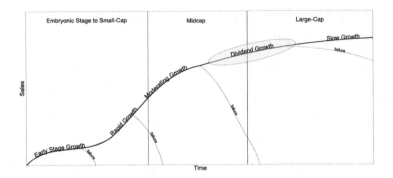

Figure 6.2. Stages of company growth. The growth rate changes as the company ages. Failure is a possibility at every stage.

Growth

"You've got to do your own growing, no matter how tall your grandfather was." Irish Saying

As companies age, they travel along a well-cobbled path (Figure 6.2). The successful company grows from embryonic stage to small-cap to midcap to large-cap.[2] Sales grow slowly, then rapidly, then moderate, then crawl. Earnings can vary dramatically because companies differ widely in how they control costs. Nevertheless, over a successful company's lifetime, it should have minted its early investors fortunes.

The investment path mirrors the growth path. The successful company progresses from speculative stock to aggressive growth stock to growth stock to dividend growth stock to conservative stock, where, by conservative stock, I mean the company finds few areas to invest, therefore grows slowly, but compensates shareholders with a high dividend payout.

The dividend growth stage differs from the earlier stages by how much cash the company generates. During the earliest stages, the com-

---

[2] Investors often make finer distinctions. They subdivide small-caps into small-caps, microcaps, and nanocaps. They subdivide large-caps into large-caps and megacaps. We do not subdivide small-caps in this book; and, with the exception of Chapters 11 and 13, we do not subdivide large-caps into large-caps and megacaps.

Expected five-year	Company size		
earnings per share growth rate	Small	Midsize	Large
Below 0%	Value	Value	Value
0-4%	Value	Value	Conservative
4-8%	Value	Conservative	Conservative
8-12%	Growth	Growth, Div Gr	Growth, Div Gr
12-16%	Growth	Growth, Div Gr	Aggr Growth
16-20%	Aggr Gr	Aggr Growth	Speculative
Above 20%	Speculative	Speculative	Speculative

Table 6.1. Investing styles by expected five-year earnings per share growth rate and company size. Aggr Gr stands for Aggressive Growth; Div Gr stands for Dividend Growth. For any company that sits on an overlapping expected five-year earnings per share growth rate boundary, place the company in the slot you deem fit.

pany depends on outside funds to grow. It does not grow so rapidly otherwise. As the company gets larger, growth begins to slow. At some point, the company begins to generate cash. Eventually, the company funds itself. *At the dividend growth stage, not only does the company fund itself, but it generates so much extra cash it can afford to pay dividends.*

This happy trajectory marks the successful company. But what of the company that is unsuccessful, either temporarily, or otherwise? Or, for that matter, what of the company that is temporarily too successful? Table 6.1 uses two variables, expected five-year earnings per share growth rate and company size, to delineate, *roughly – this can never be perfect as companies vary too much –* the possibilities for successful companies and others:

- The boxed area represents the typical successful company as it ages. Read it from bottom left to upper right – speculative to aggressive growth to growth; then across to growth, dividend growth; and so on.

- The cells above the boxed area that do *not* say "value" represent companies that are slightly less successful than their boxed (successful) counterparts.

- The cells above the boxed area that say "value" correspond to companies that are unsuccessful, temporarily or otherwise.

- The cells below the boxed area correspond to companies that are temporarily *too* successful. Typically, few companies can sustain growth rates as high as these for long periods, (say) ten years or more.

In the table, the various combinations also correspond to various *investing styles*: speculative, aggressive growth, growth, dividend growth, conservative, and value. Our characterization of "value" differs from commonly accepted definitions. We simply suggest that *something* has gone wrong, that the stock has taken a detour, that it has deviated from the climbing, snaky path of the successful company depicted in Figure 6.2.[3] Of the twenty-one combinations, only three are suited to dividend growth:

- Midsize companies with expected five-year earnings per share growth rates of 8-12 percent a year;

- Midsize companies with expected five-year earnings per share growth rates of 12-16 percent a year; and

---

[3] Conventionally, a value stock is characterized as a stock with, for instance, a low P/E ratio, a high dividend yield, a low price to book ratio, or a low price to cash flow ratio. Typically, no comparison is made to the stock's underlying growth rate. Thus, many financials fall into the value category because their P/E ratios are generally low. Likewise, a cyclical stock at the top of the economic cycle falls into the value category because, at the top, earnings are high and the P/E ratio is low. Many investors implicitly believe that a value stock signals a bargain. In both these examples, however, the implicit sense that the stock is a bargain, that somehow valuation is favorable and risk is low, is incorrect. With our definition, we do not automatically take a value stock to be a bargain. We merely acknowledge that something has gone wrong.

Expected five-year earnings per share growth rate	Company size		
	Small	Midsize	Large
Below 0%	-	-	-
0-4%	Very slow	Very slow	Very slow
4-8%	Very slow	Slow	Slow
8-12%	Slow	Moderate	Moderate
12-16%	Moderate	Moderate	High
16-20%	High	High	Very high
Above 20%	Very high	Very high	Unsustainable

Table 6.2. Qualitative assessment of expected five-year earnings per share growth rate by company size. Because small companies are expected to grow faster than midsize companies, a moderate growth rate for a midsize company is typically a slow growth rate for a small company. Likewise, a moderate growth rate for a large company is typically a slow growth rate for a midsize company. As with the previous table, for any company that sits on an overlapping expected five-year earnings per share growth rate boundary, place the company in the slot you deem fit.

- Large companies with expected five-year earnings per share growth rates of 8-12 percent a year.

As a simple way of managing risk, mix and match stocks from the three combinations to suit your tolerance of risk. For instance, if you plan to buy twelve dividend growth stocks, but are very cautious, choose (say) zero stocks of the first kind, zero of the second, and twelve of the third. If you are slightly more adventurous, choose (say) two of the first kind, zero of the second, and ten of the third. If you are still more adventurous, choose (say) four of the first kind, two of the second, and six of the third. Or, three, three, and six. And so on.

In Chapter 8, we will see that a company's earnings per share growth rate ultimately caps its dividend growth rate. *Thus, the above ranges for the earnings per share growth rate – 8-16 percent for a midsize com-*

*pany and 8-12 percent for a large company – ultimately cap the divi-
dend growth rate for dividend growth stocks.*

Table 6.2 replaces the investing styles from Table 6.1 with *qualitative
assessments* of the expected five-year earnings per share growth rate. *For
the **long-term** investor, the boxed area – moderate growth – brackets the
ideal range. Companies do not run overheated, or anemically.* Dividend
growth from the earlier table is now a subset of the boxed area: the two
slots in the middle and the one slot to the right.

Management

"Experience is the name everyone gives to their mistakes." Oscar Wilde

Warren Buffett will not invest in a company if he does not believe in
the quality of its management. Management pulls most of the strings.
Management must be honest and capable with a track record that proves
it. Without superior management, companies cannot succeed.

But how do we judge the quality of management? It isn't easy. Glow-
ing financial results point the way – but sordid cases of fraud show that
we cannot depend on financial results alone. We also have to rely on
other incomplete – and imperfect – ways:

- Check that management has kept its word. Have managers done
  what they said they would do?

- Does management keep the right perspective? Do they balance
  near-term profits with long-term investment?

- Research management's track record. Did prior companies or
  divisions thrive under their stewardship? How fast did these prior
  companies or divisions grow?

- To get a feel for the company, its culture, and its management,
  read the CEO's letter to shareholders. Better yet, read several past
  letters as well.

- Management sets the standard for integrity. If management is dishonest, employees will follow. Gauge management's honesty during conference calls and presentations. Past behavior offers clues.

- Look for red flags such as insider sales and insider dealings. Both must be disclosed in filings with the SEC. Pay particular attention when many insiders sell suddenly and heavily. Among the insider dealings that take place but should not:

  - Nepotism.
  - The company makes loans to insiders.
  - Entities that insiders own are involved in business transactions with the company.

Excess pay and benefits add up. *When management (and employees) receive more than they are worth, shareholders receive less than they deserve.*

Shareholder Commitment: Paying Shareholders Their Fair Share

"Well done is better than well said." Benjamin Franklin

In its company credo, Johnson & Johnson has this to say about its obligation to shareholders (stockholders):

> Our final responsibility is to our stockholders. Business must make a sound profit. We must experiment with new ideas. Research must be carried on, innovative programs developed and mistakes paid for. New equipment must be purchased, new facilities provided and new products launched. Reserves must be created to provide for adverse times. When we operate according to these principles, the stockholders should realize a fair return.

Shareholders own the business. They provide companies with funds. They do so directly when companies start up. They do so indirectly when they buy shares in the stock market. Shareholders expect a return on their funds.

Companies pay shareholders in three ways:

- They pay (cash) dividends, a direct way.

- They buy back shares, another direct way. When companies buy back shares, earnings per share typically rises. Share prices are more stubborn.

- They operate better, an indirect way. In theory, the stock market rewards better-run companies (that were not initially overvalued) with higher stock prices. Better operations underpin the first two ways. Better operations lead to higher profits. Higher profits lead to higher dividends and bigger share buybacks.

Companies differ in how much they allocate between dividends and share buybacks. Some prefer the lower taxes and flexibility of share buybacks. Others value the explicit income that dividends provide.

Over the long term, with dividend growth stocks, share counts should remain flattish or fall. *As a rough guide – based entirely on the better stocks I have studied, so this is far from being a scientific sample – even with a reasonable dividend, share counts should fall 1-2 percent a year.* Companies should not pay everything possible as dividends. Instead, they should compromise with a reasonable dividend plus a reasonable share buyback. Typically, share counts that fall three percent or more a year are ambitious. These require that companies (not paying minuscule dividends) earn rich internal returns. More often than not, when companies buy back shares this aggressively, dividends are low.

Some companies use debt to buy back shares. As debt changes a company's risk profile, debt must be manageable. For instance, debt must not be too high in relation to equity, a plan must be in place to pay debt back at the right pace, interest rates must be fair, and debt maturities must not be concentrated.

Always study a company's long-term history to determine if it has paid back shareholders fairly. Some companies have shareholder-friendly cultures. Others do not. Value Line provides a history of dividends and share counts.

Business Risks

Companies face a multitude of business risks. Most of these risks relate to competition. Others relate to management. We covered competition and management earlier.

Another category of risks can plunge a company into bankruptcy. You have to be vigilant here. Never invest in a company with business risks so large that they can destroy it. For instance, a company may have a verdict go against it or it may not be able to refinance its debt or it may have had years of losses and does not have the financial strength to endure one more.

Companies list their business risks in the *Risk Factors* section of their annual reports – completed on so-called Form 10-Ks – that they file with the SEC. Here are some of the more common – and important – business risks that companies face:

- State of the economy.

- Litigation.

- Size.

- Cyclicality – of the whole business or one or more of its parts.

- Lumpy sales. Steady sales are better than lumpy sales.

- Labor costs.

- Commodity costs.

- Lack of diversification, commonly in customers or suppliers.

- Damage to the company's brand. A respected brand allows a company to charge a premium.

- Pension and other benefit plans. These have costs, sometimes unexpected costs.

- Acquisitions. Acquisitions boost growth – but they do not always work.

- Currency fluctuations.

- Maturity of the business or industry.

- New competition.

- Is the company's business in long-term decline? In the U.S., traditional cigarette use is in long-term decline.

- Does the company sell to the U.S. government or other governments? Government budgets can be fickle.

- Is the company's business intrinsically volatile? For instance, a company that sells stock funds is vulnerable to movements in the stock market.

- Key individuals. Does the success of the business depend on a handful of key individuals?

- Excess insider ownership. Although some insider ownership is better than none, too much insider ownership spoils the broth. The insiders do as they please, often with little regard for other shareholders.

If you are uncomfortable with a company's business risks, punt. There are always other choices, choices that are often separated by clean hard numbers.

In the next chapter, we turn to the numbers. ♣

CHAPTER 7

The Numbers

"If you have tears prepare to shed them now." Shakespeare

MANAGEMENT is too often overly optimistic. Perhaps it is a matter of survival or an excess of little chocolate donuts, or perhaps it is a matter of believing in the future despite the evidence, but history has not always backed management's starry-eyed optimism up.

Never use management's optimism as the sole basis for investing in a company, especially over the long term. What you have to unearth as well are the numerical signposts, the hard numbers that back management's optimism up. It is not that qualitative checks are unimportant. They are. But after you have done your qualitative checks – after you have determined that the company's business is stable and strong, that its future holds ample room for growth, that its management is capable, that the company understands it must pay shareholders their fair share, and that business risks are not excessive – roll up your sleeves, put on your thinking cap, and take a good hard look at the numbers, the fundamentals.

McDonald's 2012 Income Statement, simplified (in millions)	
Sales	**27,567**
Operating costs and expenses	18,962
Interest expense	517
Other expenses	9
Taxes	2,614
Earnings	**5,465**

Table 7.1. McDonald's 2012 income statement, simplified. Sales minus the sum of the next four items – operating costs and expenses, interest expense, other expenses, and taxes – equals earnings.

Profitability

"Nothing contributes so much to the prosperity and happiness of a country as high profits." David Ricardo

Profitability is the essence of a business. We measure a company's profitability by its *net profit margin* (more simply, profit margin):

$$Net\ Profit\ Margin = \frac{Earnings}{Sales}$$

Yahoo! Finance and Value Line publish this ratio. You can also calculate it quite readily. To do so, you need to understand the essentials, and no more, of a company's *income statement* – one of three key financial statements that a company produces at the end of a reporting period. *The purpose of an income statement is to record a company's sales during a period and show how, after deductions, these sales are transformed into earnings, also known as profits.* An income statement shows (1) sales; (2)

operating costs and expenses[1] incurred to make those sales; (3) interest expense; (4) other expenses; (5) taxes; and (6) earnings. Sales minus the sum of items (2) to (5) equals earnings. Earnings are what shareholders are – theoretically – left with after everyone (and everything) gets their share. These include suppliers, employees, and the accounting costs of things such as land and equipment (combined, these are operating costs and expenses); debt holders (interest expense); and the government (taxes). In addition to earnings, the income statement includes earnings per share.

As an example, Table 7.1 presents a simplified version of McDonald's 2012 income statement. All numbers are in millions. From the table, McDonald's sales are 27,567. The sum of the next four items – operating costs and expenses, interest expense, other expenses, and taxes – is 22,102. McDonald's 2012 earnings are therefore 27567 - 22102 or 5,465.

For 2012, McDonald's net profit margin, that is earnings divided by sales, is 5465 / 27567 or 20 percent. Incidentally, currently, mid-2015, net profit margins for the typical company range from five to eight percent. McDonald's net profit margins are so much higher because of the company's dominant market share and lucrative franchising model.

A company's net profit margin depends on many factors. For example:

- State of the economy. During expansions, profits rise. During recessions, profits fall. As a telling example, cyclical businesses go from boom to bust as the economy moves from expansion to recession. Alcoa, the aluminum giant, and canonical cyclical, earned $2.8 billion in the boom year of 2007; then *lost* $1.0 billion in the recessionary year of 2009. The company's net profit margin was ten percent in 2007; and *negative* five percent in 2009.

- General nature of the business or industry. Some businesses are naturally more profitable than others. For instance, manufacturing is naturally more profitable than services. Moreover, some

---

[1] In accounting jargon, operating costs and expenses include: cost of goods sold; selling, general, and administrative expenses; and research and development expenses. For our purposes, this breakdown is unimportant.

industries have naturally low net profit margins – though this does not mean we cannot find good dividend growth stocks in industries such as these.

- Industry age. First-movers enjoy good net profit margins. As imitators encroach, however, profits start to fall. Nevertheless, at least for a while, profitability remains fair. Companies survive. As competition intensifies, however, profitability starts to collapse. Companies fail. Only a few remain. Growth slows. As profitability remains under pressure, survivors merge. This cuts costs and improves profitability. Because the days of good industry growth are over, new competition fails to emerge. The remaining companies grow slowly. Profits are fair.

- Scale. Large companies are typically more profitable than small companies.

- Dominant market share. Partly because it dominates Internet search, Google (now part of Alphabet) has net profit margins of twenty-two percent.

- Value added. Typically, companies that add greater value to whatever they sell have higher net profit margins than companies that do not add as much value. For instance, companies that manufacture products have higher net profit margins than companies that distribute those products. And companies that sell innovative products have higher net profit margins than companies that sell standard products.

- Sacrificing profitability for growth. Companies sometimes sacrifice profitability for growth.

- Temporarily foregoing profitability to hurt the competition. Companies sometimes temporarily forgo profitability to hurt the competition. They lower their prices hoping that this hurts the competition more than it hurts them. When these price wars continue for too long, the weakest competitors fail.

- Lower costs. Some companies enjoy lower costs. For instance, they operate in low-cost regions.

- Debt and interest rates. The lower the interest expense, the higher the net profit margin. This has everything to do with how the business is financed and little to do with the business itself.

- Taxes. Some companies pay lower taxes because of where they are domiciled. Others, rightly or wrongly, use accounting chicanery to lower their taxes. This has everything to do with how the business is taxed and little to do with the business itself.

- Royalties and franchising. In some sense, these are almost pure profit.

Always prefer companies with good to strong net profit margins. Currently, mid-2015, a net profit margin of ten to fifteen percent is good. More than fifteen percent is strong.

Asset Turnover

Companies generate sales when they put their assets to productive use. One way to assess how *effective* they are at doing this is to calculate how much sales they generate per dollar of assets, their so-called *asset turnover*:

$$Asset\ Turnover = \frac{Sales}{Assets}$$

Asset turnover is not as broadly published as net profit margin. Nevertheless, it too is easy to calculate. Sales are part of the income statement. We looked at the income statement in the previous section. Assets are part of another financial statement, the *balance sheet*. *The balance sheet is a snapshot of a company's assets, debt, and equity at the end of a reporting period.* Equity is the portion of assets that shareholders own. Debt is the portion of assets that others own. Table 7.2 presents a simplified version of McDonald's 2012 balance sheet. For McDonald's 2012 asset turnover, the line that matters is (total) assets, 35,386 (all numbers are in millions). With sales of 27,567, as before, McDonald's 2012 asset turnover is 27567 / 35386 or 0.78.

McDonald's 2012 Balance Sheet, simplified (in millions)	
Current assets	4,922
Other assets	5,787
Net property and equipment	24,677
Assets	**35,386**
Current liabilities	3,403
Long-term debt	13,632
Other	3,057
Debt	**20,092**
Equity	**15,294**

Table 7.2. McDonald's 2012 balance sheet, simplified.

Financial Leverage

A company's assets are backed by debt and equity. Debt is money lent to the company. Equity is money given to the company in exchange for ownership (shares). Lenders provide debt. Shareholders provide equity. Assets equal debt plus equity:

$$Assets = Debt + Equity$$

One way to understand how debt impacts a company's business is to calculate its *financial leverage* (more simply, leverage):

$$Financial\ Leverage = \frac{Assets}{Equity}$$

As of mid-2015, Yahoo! Finance and Value Line do not publish this ratio. Nevertheless, it is easy to calculate. Assets and equity are on a company's balance sheet. Looking at McDonald's again, from Table 7.2, McDonald's

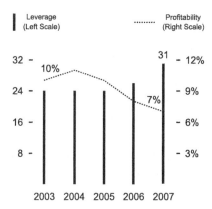

Figure 7.1. Lehman's numbers, trending in the wrong direction and cutting a line too fine.

assets (all numbers are in millions, no surprises here) are 35,386 with equity of 15,294. McDonald's 2012 financial leverage is 35386 / 15294 or 2.31.

If a company earns more on the assets financed by its debt than it pays as interest on that debt, shareholders benefit. In addition, because interest expense is tax deductible, debt is cheaper than it looks. At a tax rate of 40 percent, 6 percent debt costs 3.6 percent. Most companies prefer debt to equity.

The return-enhancing value of debt comes at a cost, however. *Debt is risky. If companies cannot pay the interest on their debt when due, or settle, or refinance, they fail.* The broader the sources of debt and the wider the range of maturities, the better. In the second half of 2008, as the capital markets froze, the stock market punished heavily indebted companies that had to refinance. Casino operator Las Vegas Sands fell 94 percent in 2008. As of mid-2015, it has recovered – though it has a long way to go before it reaches its 2007 peak. Mall owner General Growth Properties fell 97 percent in 2008. It filed for bankruptcy in 2009. (It has since emerged from bankruptcy.)

Investors sometimes consider long-term debt instead of all debt. For our purposes, all debt matters more – though long-term debt remains a useful adjunct.

Excess leverage exacts a heavy toll. Often, at precisely the wrong time, it shows its dangerous other side. Consider Lehman (Figure 7.1). In 2007, Lehman's already high leverage hit thirty-one. With profit margins falling – from ten percent in 2003 to seven percent in 2007 – Lehman was cutting a line too fine. Without an adequate cushion, it was asking for trouble if something went wrong. And, in 2008, something did go wrong. As asset prices fell, Lehman faced liquidity concerns and a run on the bank. At the same time, its colossal size made it a difficult target for buyers to consider or, perhaps, want to consider. On 15 September 2008, Lehman filed for bankruptcy, in turn, helping precipitate the Crash of 2008.

Prefer companies that use no more than moderate financial leverage. Because companies differ in so many ways, no guideline on financial leverage can universally apply. That said, as a *rough* guideline, *financial leverage less than 2.0 is reasonable*.[2] At 2.0, a dollar of debt is balanced by a dollar of equity. Exceptions abound – though they generally fall into two categories:

- Stable businesses. Companies such as Coca-Cola and IBM carry higher levels of debt because their business stability virtually guarantees that they can pay off their debts when due. How much debt can a stable business handle? It depends on the characteristics of the business. In general, however, if financial leverage of 2.0 is acceptable for most businesses, financial leverage of (say) 3.0 is acceptable for stable businesses.

- Financial intermediaries. These companies can handle higher levels of debt because all they do is *funnel* money from one part of the economy to another and their businesses are – usually – quite liquid. How much debt can a financial intermediary handle, however, is an open question. For instance, currently, mid-2015, financial leverage of fifteen or more is not uncommon. These companies

---

[2] Some tie the amount of debt a company can handle to how much it "earns" before adjustments (they use something called EBITDA, that is, earnings before interest, taxes, depreciation, and amortization). I do not take this route.

are different. But as the collapses of Bear Stearns, Washington Mutual, Indy Mac, and Lehman have shown, excess leverage is not without risk.

Financial leverage multiplies a company's return to shareholders – but it cuts both ways. During good times, shareholders benefit. During bad times, they potentially face ruin. Warren Buffett has said: "We will reject interesting opportunities rather than over-leverage our balance sheet." Likewise, be wary of companies that use excess financial leverage. In general, avoid them.

One Number

"One figure can sometimes add up to a lot." Mae West

Company ABC has high profit margins, moderate asset turnover, and high financial leverage. Company XYZ has moderate profit margins, high asset turnover, and low financial leverage. How do we compare the two when all three numbers matter?

One way is based on the product of the three numbers. Instead of comparing three things – and not knowing how to weigh the importance of each – we compare one thing. And the comparison is simple: Higher is better. We call this product *return on equity*:

$Return\ on\ Equity =$
$Net\ Profit\ Margin\ *\ Asset\ Turnover\ *\ Financial\ Leverage$

Using definitions from the last three sections:

$$Return\ on\ Equity = \frac{Earnings}{Sales}\ *\ \frac{Sales}{Assets}\ *\ \frac{Assets}{Equity}$$

Striking out the duplicate sales and assets terms:

$$Return\ on\ Equity = \frac{Earnings}{Equity}$$

McDonald's 2012 Return on Equity (in millions, except for calculated values)	
Net profit margin:	
Earnings	5,465
Sales	27,567
Net profit margin [Earnings / Sales]	**20%**
Asset turnover:	
Sales	27,567
Assets	35,386
Asset turnover [Sales / Assets]	**0.78**
Financial leverage:	
Assets	35,386
Equity	15,294
Financial leverage [Assets / Equity]	**2.31**
Return on equity (direct calculation):	
Earnings	5,465
Equity	15,294
Return on equity [Earnings / Equity]	**36%**
Return on equity (indirect calculation):	
Net profit margin (from above)	20%
Asset turnover (from above)	0.78
Financial leverage (from above)	2.31
Return on equity [Net profit margin * Asset turnover * Financial leverage]	**36%**

Table 7.3. McDonald's 2012 return on equity.

McDonald's 2012 Return on Beginning Equity (in millions, except for the calculated value)	
Return on beginning equity:	
Earnings in 2012	5,465
Equity at the end of the previous year, 2011	14,390
Return on beginning equity [Earnings / Beginning Equity]	**38%**

Table 7.4. McDonald's 2012 return on beginning equity. We consider equity at the beginning of a year the same as equity at the end of the previous year. Thus, McDonald's equity at the beginning of 2012 is the same as McDonald's equity at the end of 2011.

As an example, Table 7.3 calculates McDonald's 2012 return on equity, both directly, using this formula, and indirectly, using the first formula.

Earnings are what a company makes (earns) for its shareholders. Equity is what its shareholders invest. Thus, *provided we use equity at the beginning of a year*, return on equity – as a measure of what a company makes for its shareholders divided by what its shareholders invest – is a rough measure of investment return. It is rough because equity changes during the year but the formula does not reflect these changes. To differentiate between this version of the formula and the above one, let us call this version, *return on beginning equity.* For an example, again with McDonald's, see Table 7.4.

Return on beginning equity is an investment return within the company, an internal return. Return on beginning equity is not an investment return that you can get as a shareholder. Nevertheless, and this is key, **the returns are related because internal returns form the basis of shareholder returns.** *Thus, especially for long-term investors, knowing a company's internal return becomes an important part of investing in a company.* **Companies with poor long-term internal returns will never generate good long-term shareholder returns.**

Because we can think of return on beginning equity as a return, we can compare it to other returns. For instance, over a short period, we can compare it to the return on one-year Treasuries. During most years, a company's return on beginning equity should handily beat the return on one-year Treasuries. If not, the company should sell its assets and invest in one-year Treasuries instead. Likewise, shareholders should sell their shares and invest in something else instead – they are not getting paid for the risk that they are taking.

Always check long-run averages, (say) five- or ten-year averages, of a company's return on equity or return on beginning equity. Long-run averages smooth out a company's performance. They balance the good years with the bad. Rising internal returns (with no more than comfortable levels of debt) are good. High and stable internal returns are also good. In general, **avoid making long-term investments in companies with low or unstable or declining internal returns**.

As a guide, **a long-run return on beginning equity average of twenty percent or more is a good internal return**. *We will expect this of our dividend growth stocks.* Not only is this much higher than typical other returns, but, as we will see in the next chapter, *a twenty percent return on beginning equity allows a company to grow at a sensible and sustainable pace yet pay a reasonable share of its earnings as dividends.* It signals both maturity and high quality.

You may wonder how companies generate such high internal returns. One reason, not surprisingly, is superior business quality. Another reason, perhaps surprisingly, is financial leverage. Financial leverage magnifies internal returns. For many companies, financial leverage holds the key to these high internal returns.

With dividend growth stocks, it gets better. Dividend growth stocks can comfortably take on more financial leverage than an equivalent company without as stable a business. Thus, for dividend growth stocks, internal returns ratchet higher – which eventually translates into higher dividends and higher returns. Nevertheless, as always, even for dividend growth stocks, financial leverage should not be taken too far.[3]

---

[3] With all the favorable things that I have said about return on equity and return on beginning equity, I should point out that some investors look at other variables. For instance, some consider *company-wide* returns – for instance, *return on invested capital.* I prefer looking at returns to equity holders because these lead *directly* to investor returns. Nevertheless, I am mindful of debt. Debt cannot be too large, except in those

Fraud

"It is true that you may fool all the people some of the time; you can even fool some of the people all the time; but you can't fool all of the people all the time." Attributed to Abraham Lincoln

We have no choice but to rely on a company's financial statements. The numbers validate the story. If the numbers lie, the story lies. In the early 2000s, Enron and WorldCom were cataclysmic lies. In the late 2000s, Satyam was another. In all three cases, the auditors were rightly put to the task. Arthur Andersen ceased U.S. audit operations after Enron.

Even when auditors are honest and playing by (not with) the book(s), they cannot always unearth instances of fraud. Auditors do not examine every account and every transaction. Instead, they sample. Johnson & Johnson's auditor, PricewaterhouseCoopers, had this to say about its audit of Johnson & Johnson's financial statements in Johnson & Johnson's 2014 annual report:

> [W]e plan and perform the audits to obtain reasonable assurance about whether the financial statements are free of material misstatement ... Our audits of the financial statements included examining, on a *test* [emphasis added] basis, evidence supporting the amounts and disclosures in the financial statements ...

It is not too difficult for managers to commit fraud and escape detection – at least for a while. Many have done so in the past; many will do so in the future.

---

rare instances when businesses are extraordinarily stable. Others argue that return on equity is not a true return because it is based on accounting values. They use other variations, such as *economic* returns. Although this point is valid, our requirement of twenty percent should be large enough to account for most such distortions. In other words, twenty percent – as a relatively high requirement – affords us a margin of safety. In this book, I focus on long-term returns to shareholders. As long as these returns are reasonable, and sustainable, that's good enough for me.

Accounting Conservatism

History is littered with the remains of companies that made aggressive accounting their norm, companies that marked up their books to beat quarterly earnings targets and keep their stock prices high.

Warning signs of aggressive accounting include aggressive revenue recognition and an aggressive use of onetime charges. Stay away from companies with even the slightest whiff of aggressive accounting. The tiniest fudge today, the cloud no larger than a man's hand, warns of serious trouble later.

Conversely, one of the hallmarks of a properly managed company is conservative accounting. Sound companies do not use aggressive accounting to get noticed. They let their numbers speak for themselves.

In the next chapter, we return to dividends. We tie dividends to earnings. We establish several important ideas and relationships. ♣

Chapter 8

Dividend Payouts

"There's always money in the banana stand." George Bluth (Arrested Development)

How much *should* a company pay in dividends? It depends. It depends on how successful the company is and where it is in its life cycle:

- A struggling company should pay nothing. It needs all its cash to survive – or try something else.

- A young or vigorously growing company cannot pay anything either; other than, perhaps, a token amount. To support its growth it needs cash.

- A mature or slow-growing company can return as much as it wants. It does not need most of its cash because it has little, or nothing, to invest in. (But because it has little, or nothing, to invest in, its growth if not low already will eventually slow. Dividend growth will do the same.)

- Dividend growth companies sit somewhere in the happy middle between young and mature. They do not grow so quickly that they

131

consume large amounts of cash; they do not grow so slowly that they can return most of their cash to shareholders. What they can do is pay a reasonable and growing dividend.

The Dividend Payout Ratio

"Money makes money. And the money that money makes makes more money." Benjamin Franklin

Dividend payout ratio is dividends per share divided by earnings per share:

$$Dividend\ Payout\ Ratio\ =\ \frac{Dividends\ Per\ Share}{Earnings\ Per\ Share}$$

I am being slightly cavalier here. A better definition uses *(total) dividends divided by (total) earnings* – but this is more troublesome to calculate because while dividends per share and earnings per share are widely distributed, total dividends and total earnings are not.

As an example, in the first quarter of 2015, IBM paid $1.10 in dividends per share on $2.35 of earnings per share. IBM's dividend payout ratio was thus 1.10 / 2.35 or 47 percent.

In this definition, dividends per share and earnings per share must be consistent. Peanut butter must be paired with jelly; quarterly dividends per share must be paired with quarterly earnings per share; annual dividends per share with annual earnings per share; and so on.

To decide how much to pay as dividends, companies use dividend payout ratio *targets*. Typically, the more mature the company, the higher the target. *Larger companies typically use dividend payout ratio targets of 40 percent to 60 percent.*

The simplicity of this definition masks three subtleties:

- Timing. Dividends are typically paid out of the prior period's earnings.[1] Thus, the definition improves if it pairs dividends in one period with earnings from the period before.

- Earnings per share basis. Companies report earnings per share (eps) on both a basic and diluted basis. Basic eps uses shares outstanding. Diluted eps uses these plus the potential dilutive effect of things such as stock options. By contrast, dividends per share are always based on one number, shares outstanding. Thus, to remain consistent, the definition is better served if earnings per share is set to basic eps; instead, diluted eps is what is usually implied – and used.

- Share count. To calculate eps, accounting rules mandate that companies use time-weighted average share counts. Dividends, however, are not based on average share counts. Instead, they are based on shares outstanding on one date. Thus, "per share" has two connotations.

The first point is more of a nuisance than anything else. We ignore it. One way to address the second and third points is to change the definition of dividend payout ratio to the better definition noted above, *(total) dividends divided by (total) earnings.*

Figure 8.1 compares dividend payout ratios for the TJX Companies calculated three ways:

- Dividends per share / Diluted eps – our primary definition (implied)

- Dividends per share / Basic eps

- (Total) Dividends / (Total) Earnings – our better definition.

---

[1] Actually, dividends are paid out of cash not earnings. We delve into this little detail in the next section.

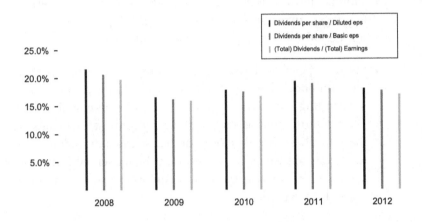

Figure 8.1. Comparing 2008-2012 dividend payout ratio calculations for the TJX Companies.

As the figure shows, the ratios do not match. But they are close, where close means they differ by a few percentage points. We keep our primary definition, *dividends per share divided by diluted eps* – only, for convenience, sometimes using the better definition, *(total) dividends divided by (total) earnings*.

 Dividend cover is the reciprocal of dividend payout ratio. I mention it for completeness. I do not use it.

Cash Flow

"Basically my wife was immature. I'd be at home in the bath and she'd come in and sink my boats." Woody Allen

Although we often use loose language to imply otherwise, dividends are not paid out of earnings. Dividends are paid out of cash. In theory, therefore, and contrary to what the dividend payout ratio implies, we must exercise care comparing dividends and earnings. Instead, we must compare like with like. We must compare dividends with cash-based metrics. As a side benefit, when we use cash-based metrics, we quickly discover whether a company can *afford* to pay its dividends.

But which cash-based metrics should we use? To find out, we need to understand the last of a company's three key financial statements, the *cash flow statement*, also known as the *statement of cash flows*. *The cash flow statement summarizes a company's cash transactions,* categorizing them as follows:

- *Operating Cash Flow* – cash generated by a company's business activities. Operating cash flow is more volatile than earnings.

- *Investing Cash Flow* – changes in cash related to investments that a company makes. The best example is capital expenditures, the cash that a company uses to buy land, buildings, and equipment. Investing cash flow includes acquisitions.

- *Financing Cash Flow* – changes in cash related to financing the business. *Financing cash flow includes dividends, share buybacks, and proceeds from shares issued.*

Total cash flow is the sum of the three types above. The *change in cash* is this plus a usually tiny contribution from the *effect of exchange rates*. Table 8.1 summarizes McDonald's 2012 cash flow statement.

So which cash-based metrics should we use? Because the ultimate source of a company's dividends is its operating cash flow – this, after all, is the cash that a company generates by its *business* activities – *the most appropriate cash-based metric for dividend comparisons is operating cash flow.*

A slight variation of operating cash flow is also sometimes used:

- Free Cash Flow – a hybrid, generally taken to mean operating cash flow minus capital expenditures.

As an example, let us calculate these ratios for McDonald's. From Table 8.1, McDonald's operating cash flow is the total from the first section,

McDonald's 2012 Cash Flow Statement, simplified (in millions)	
Operating:	
Net income	**5,465**
Depreciation and amortization	1,489
Other	12
Cash provided by operations	**6,966**
Investing:	
Capital expenditures	**(3,049)**
Other investing activities	(118)
Cash used for investing activities	(3,167)
Financing:	
Stock purchases	**(2,615)**
Dividends	**(2,897)**
Proceeds from stock option exercises	**329**
Other financing activities	1,333
Cash used for financing activities	(3,850)
Effect of exchange rates	51
Change in cash	0

Table 8.1. McDonald's 2012 cash flow statement, simplified.

6,966 (all numbers in millions); capital expenditures are in the second section, (3,049); and dividends are in the third section, (2,897). We have everything we need:

- Dividends compared to Operating Cash Flow: 2897 / 6966 or 42 percent.

- Dividends compared to Free Cash Flow: Free cash flow is 6966 - 3049, or 3,917. Our ratio is therefore 2897 / 3917 or 74 percent.

How do these ratios compare to McDonald's 2012 dividend payout ratio? As before, McDonald's earnings are in its income statement – though they are also the first item in its cash flow statement, 5,465, from Table 8.1. McDonald's 2012 dividend payout ratio, calculated for convenience here as (total) dividends divided by (total) earnings, is thus 2897 / 5465 or 53 percent, falling in between the dividend to cash flow ratios of 42 percent and 74 percent.

If cash flow matters so much why then do so many investors look at dividend payout ratio? Because cash flow is volatile. Earnings are much less so – as a side benefit of accounting rules. Consequently, dividend to cash flow ratios behave like a bouncing ball – whereas dividend payout ratio is comparatively stable. Moreover, over a company's lifetime, total earnings equal total operating cash flow. In a cumulative sense, therefore, we are looking at the same thing. Investors typically look at dividend to cash flow ratios for companies in distress. In such cases, understanding whether a company can continue to pay its dividend becomes paramount.

During recessions, as earnings fall and dividend payout ratios rise, investors worry about dividend cuts. Instead, consider the company's operating cash flow. Even with anticipated decreases in earnings, there may still be enough room in operating cash flow for the company to pay its dividend. The dividend might be safer than it looks.

The Link Between P/E Ratio and Dividend Yield

A company's P/E ratio is price per share (P) divided by earnings per share (E). Here, E is an annual value based typically on earnings for the trailing four quarters, the next four quarters, or two quarters in the past plus two quarters in the future. On financial websites, P/E ratios based on earnings for the trailing four quarters are most common.

With D as dividends per share, the following equation holds as the P's cancel:

$$\frac{P}{E} * \frac{D}{P} = \frac{D}{E}$$

Dividing both sides by $\frac{D}{P}$:

$$\frac{P}{E} = \frac{\left(\frac{D}{E}\right)}{\left(\frac{D}{P}\right)}$$

In English:

$$P/E \ Ratio = \frac{Dividend \ Payout \ Ratio}{Dividend \ Yield}$$

In other words, *dividend payout ratio provides the link between P/E ratio and dividend yield*. This result has an important corollary: **Whenever dividend payout ratio is constant (or reasonably so), P/E ratio and dividend yield are opposing faces of the same coin. When one is high, the other must be low.** Thus, for example, when we talk of buying a stock with a high dividend yield we are almost always saying, equivalently, that we are buying a stock with a low P/E ratio. And, assuming the stock pays a dividend, vice versa.

In expensive markets, those characterized by high P/E ratios, and thus low dividend yields, investors expect future earnings to drive most of their gains. *Implicitly*, they assume a rosy future. During the late 1990s NASDAQ Bubble, when people took their parrots to work and the giddy

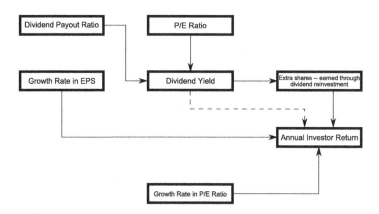

Figure 8.2. Adding dividend payout ratio and P/E ratio to our figure of annual (investor) return.

exuberance about the Internet translated into heady expectations about the future, the market's P/E soared – and its dividend yield collapsed.

Conversely, in inexpensive markets, those characterized by low P/E ratios, and thus high dividend yields, investors prefer the certainty of dividends today to the promise of gains in the future. *Explicitly*, they assume a gloomy future. During the immediate aftermath of the Crash of 2008, dividend yields soared as investors, fearing a deep and developing catastrophe, lost all faith and confidence in the future.

Figure 8.2 adds dividend payout ratio and P/E ratio to our figure of annual (investor) return.

Sustainable Growth Rate

"The future is much like the present, only longer." Dan Quisenberry

If a portfolio experiences no deposits and no withdrawals in a given year, the portfolio's growth rate, its change in equity divided by its equity at the beginning of the year, must match its rate of return.[2] It has to. The money could not have come from anywhere else.

For companies, the logic is identical, except that dividends weave in a little wrinkle. Dividends are akin to withdrawals. Without dividends, a company's growth equals its earnings. Dividends reduce a company's growth by exactly the amount of the dividends. Thus, *growth = earnings – dividends*. Importantly, *this relationship assumes no net "deposits," that is, no net additions to a company's equity*. We call this amount of growth, *sustainable growth*. Thus, more accurately, *sustainable growth = earnings – dividends*. Using the definition of dividend payout ratio as dividends divided by earnings, with a bit of algebra:

$$Sustainable\ Growth = (1 - Dividend\ Payout\ Ratio) * Earnings$$

Dividing both sides by *beginning equity*:

$$Sustainable\ Growth\ Rate$$
$$= (1 - Dividend\ Payout\ Ratio) * Return\ on\ Beginning\ Equity$$

Thus, a company's sustainable growth rate is tied to how much it pays in dividends and the quality of its business. Pay too much, or run a poor business, and the company's sustainable growth rate suffers.

Knowing a company's long-term sustainable growth rate is crucial to long-term investors because it is the most a company can grow without raising net new equity. Companies cannot grow slower or faster than this without doing *something* different. If they were growing slower, we would want to know why. If they were growing faster, we would want to know how. In turn, **long-term sustainable growth rate is linked to growth rate of the company's underlying markets and the company's**

---

[2] Though we generally think of portfolios as not including debt, they can. Much like assets in a company, in general, assets in a portfolio are made up of debt and equity. Debt is what an investor borrows – it is what others own. Equity is what the investor owns.

competitive position within those markets. Theoretically, companies first judge the growth rates of their markets, then return what they do not need to investors, perhaps keeping a bit for adverse times.

Suppose a company (1) wants to pay half of its earnings as dividends; yet (2) still grow ten percent a year. What should its return on beginning equity be? In the equation above, on substituting a dividend payout ratio of fifty percent and a sustainable growth rate of ten percent, we get the following:

$$0.10 = (1 - 0.50) * Return\ on\ Beginning\ Equity$$

Or:

$$Return\ on\ Beginning\ Equity = \frac{0.10}{(1 - 0.50)} = 0.20 = 20\%$$

This result confirms an observation made in the previous chapter: *A twenty percent return on beginning equity allows a company to grow at a sensible and sustainable pace yet pay a reasonable share of its earnings as dividends*. It signals both maturity and high quality. This is an important result for long-term investing and, in particular, for investing in dividend growth stocks.

From Return on Beginning Equity to Investor Return

"Where the telescope ends the microscope begins, and who can say which has the wider vision?" Victor Hugo

Figure 8.3, a culmination of similar such figures throughout the book – and an important one – includes return on beginning equity.

The figure shows the interplay between company, stock market, and investor. Think of company as primarily the boxes in the left column; stock market, as primarily the boxes in the middle column; and investor, as primarily the boxes in the right column.

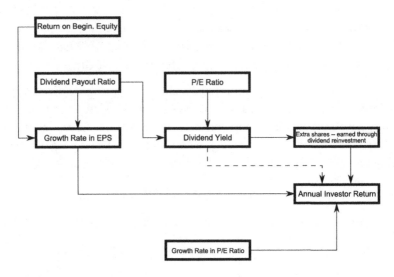

Figure 8.3. Adding return on beginning equity to our figure of annual (investor) return. For dividend growth stocks, this completes the picture.

In the left column, return on beginning equity is a fundamental company number, establishing how much the company earns on its shareholders' investment. Dividend payout ratio is a company decision, primarily guided by underlying growth rates in the company's business. It equals the portion of earnings that the company can pay as dividends, yet maintain its growth. What remains of return on beginning equity after paying dividends translates into growth rate in earnings per share.

In the middle column, P/E ratio is the multiple that the stock market accords the company's earnings per share. Dividend yield is equivalent annual dividend divided by current stock price. Growth rate in P/E ratio contributes to returns but is difficult to forecast.

In the right column, the investor has two choices with the dividends that he receives: (1) He may choose to not reinvest his dividends, in which case, dividend yield adds directly to his annual investor return. (Moreover, he may earn an additional return on these dividends by investing them in something else.) (2) He may choose to reinvest his dividends, in which case, dividend yield adds indirectly to his annual investor return through the extra shares that he earns through dividend reinvestment. Growth rate in earnings per share and growth rate in P/E ratio also contribute to annual investor return.

For dividend growth stocks, this completes the picture. With other stocks, another box leads to return on beginning equity, representing money that the company raises in the stock market. This causes share dilution and must be incorporated into the calculation of return, normally as a change in growth rate in earnings per share. Dividend growth stocks are self-funding. They do not need to raise money in the stock market.

Investors often make arbitrary estimates of a stock's return, generating estimates out of thin air, not realizing the connections among the various pieces leading up to it. As the figure shows, the various pieces are connected. They lead in a definite path to investor return.

Other Payout Ratios

Dividend payout ratio does not account for share buybacks and shares issued. To fix this, we modify it. Our first fix, *gross payout ratio*, includes cash spent on share buybacks:

Gross Payout Ratio

$$= \frac{Dividends \ + \ Cash \ Spent \ on \ Share \ Buybacks}{Earnings}$$

Continuing our month-long Happy Meal, from Table 8.1 on page 136, McDonald's earnings are 5,465 (all numbers are still in millions, no goblins here), dividends are 2,897, and share buybacks (stock purchases) are 2,615. Gross payout ratio is thus (2897 + 2615) / 5465 or 101 percent. In other words, McDonald's returned slightly more than all its 2012 earnings to shareholders.

To include cash received when a company issues shares, our second fix, an improvement over gross payout ratio, results in a more useful ratio, *net payout ratio:*[3]

---

[3] As in Chapter 3, on page 54, in calculating cash received from shares issued, there

Net Payout Ratio

$$= \frac{Dividends\ +\ Cash\ Spent\ on\ Share\ Buybacks}{Earnings}$$

$$-\ \frac{Cash\ Received\ From\ Shares\ Issued}{Earnings}$$

Net payout ratio is gross payout ratio minus a natural adjustment when a company issues shares. It is equivalent to dividends plus cash spent on share buybacks minus cash received from shares issued, all divided by earnings. For McDonald's, from Table 8.1 on page 136, the company did not issue shares directly, as in a public offering, but instead received cash through the exercise of stock options by its employees and management, "Proceeds from stock option exercises," 329. If a company issues shares, you will see an item such as "Proceeds from the issuance of common stock." (Because dividend growth companies are self-funding, you will usually not see such items for dividend growth companies.) McDonald's net payout ratio is thus (2897 + 2615 - 329) / 5465 or 95 percent. Contrast this, and the company's gross payout ratio, with its dividend payout ratio, 2897 / 5465, or 53 percent. The dividend payout ratio completely misses the mark.

Some companies behave too conservatively, keeping more cash than they should. In the next chapter, when we learn how to value dividend growth stocks, *we will update the net payout ratio to include additional cash that a company can return to shareholders but for whatever reason does not – we call this new ratio the payout ratio.*[4] *The numerator of the payout ratio is the maximum that a company can return to shareholders.* Any company can return more than it should, but its growth will then suffer – or it will have to raise money in the markets to compensate. The payout ratio is subjective because we have to estimate the extra part.

---

are complicating factors, for instance, potential tax effects related to stock options. These are potentially complex and perhaps not always clear. For many years, companies did not even disclose them. In general, for simplicity and comparability, I ignore these complications. However, the impact can sometimes be significant. You may choose to include them. The idea is to account for *all* cash that the company receives as a result of issuing shares.

[4] Do not confuse this terminology with the dividend payout ratio. In this book, I will be careful to mention dividend payout ratio if I am only interested in dividends. The payout ratio is much more important to us.

All else equal, the payout ratio for our dividend growth stocks must average at least fifty percent. This guarantees that companies are paying a reasonable share of their earnings to shareholders and that the companies are suitable candidates – in terms of maturity and quality – for dividend growth investment.

In general, because of the discretionary nature of share buybacks, gross and net payout ratios fluctuate much more than dividend payout ratio. Ratios that fluctuate too much are the bane of financial analysis. By contrast, because payout ratio is the maximum that a company can pay, it removes the discretion of share buybacks. It fluctuates less. Moreover, because of the steady nature of the typical dividend growth company's business, fluctuations are even more muted. Thus, payout ratio becomes a "good" ratio – well-behaved instead of haphazard – for the financial analysis of dividend growth stocks. For us, it plays a prominent role in valuation.

Similar to the cash flow changes to the dividend payout ratio that we considered earlier, we can change the ratios here to use either operating cash flow or free cash flow in the denominator, instead of earnings. But we do not need to make such changes. For high-quality dividend growth stocks, they do not tell us much.

How Companies Grow Their Dividends (per share)[5]

Companies grow their dividends per share through:

- Growth in dividend payout ratio; and

- Growth in earnings per share, which in turn arises from:

    - Growth in earnings; and

    - Reduction in shares outstanding.

---

[5] In this section, I emphasize dividends *per share* to more carefully differentiate this from (total) dividends. Thus, while in the rest of the book I say dividend growth, in this section, I say dividends per share growth.

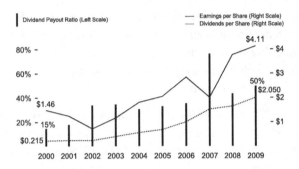

Figure 8.4. McDonald's dividends per share rose smartly from $0.215 per share in 2000 to $2.050 per share in 2009 not only because its earnings per share rose a robust 12 percent a year – from $1.46 per share in 2000 to $4.11 per share in 2009 – but also because its dividend payout ratio rose steadily from 15 percent in 2000 to 50 percent in 2009.

The primary factor driving long-term growth in dividends per share is growth in earnings per share. Unlike earnings per share, dividend payout ratio cannot keep rising – this limits its long-term influence.

But in the short- and intermediate-term, growth in dividend payout ratio can have a dramatic impact on growth in dividends per share. For instance, McDonald's dividends per share rose smartly from $0.215 per share in 2000 to $2.050 per share in 2009 not only because its earnings per share rose a robust 12 percent a year – from $1.46 per share in 2000 to $4.11 per share in 2009 – but also because its dividend payout ratio rose steadily from 15 percent in 2000 to 50 percent in 2009 (Figure 8.4). Investors in McDonald's got a double shot of dividend growth espresso.

This magic cannot continue forever, however – because the dividend payout ratio cannot rise forever. For instance, given its current size, McDonald's dividends per share will never again compound, over a reasonably long period, (say) three to five years, at the rate that it did between 2000 and 2009. That 28.5 percent compound annual growth rate is history.

Suppose we know next year's earnings per share growth rate and the change in dividend payout ratio from this year to the next. Can we calculate the *dividends per share growth rate*? Yes. The exact answer is:

$$\left(1 + \frac{DPR_{next\,year} - DPR_{this\,year}}{DPR_{this\,year}} \right) * (1 + EPSGR) - 1$$

Here, DPR is the dividend payout ratio and EPSGR is the earnings per share growth rate. An approximation usually suffices:

$$\left(\frac{DPR_{next\,year} - DPR_{this\,year}}{DPR_{this\,year}} \right) + EPSGR$$

Think of the piece in parentheses as the *dividend payout ratio growth rate*. As an example, suppose this year's dividend payout ratio is 15 percent, next year's expected dividend payout ratio is 20 percent, and expected earnings per share growth rate is 10 percent. What is the expected one-year dividends per share growth rate? The exact answer is (1 + (20 - 15) / 15) * (1 + 0.10) - 1 or 46.7 percent. The rough answer is (20 - 15) / 15 + 0.10 or 43.3 percent.

Therefore, *a stock's expected one-year dividends per share growth rate equals, roughly, its dividend payout ratio growth rate plus its earnings per share growth rate. Thus, once dividend payout ratio does not change, which we typically assume for well-established companies, dividends per share growth rate equals earnings per share growth rate.* In other words, as noted, *earnings per share growth rate is the primary factor driving long-term growth rate in dividends per share.*

Table 8.2 shows McDonald's dividends per share, total dividends, and basic shares outstanding from 2010 to 2012. During this period, McDonald's dividends per share growth rate exceeded its total dividends growth rate because *dividends per share growth rate was boosted by continually declining share counts.* For instance, in 2012, dividends per share grew 13.4 percent and total dividends grew 11.0 percent – the reduced share count of 2.1 percent explains the difference. This spread total dividends across fewer shares – thus boosting the dividends per share growth rate. The same is true of the other years.

In Table 8.2, dividends per share growth rate equals, roughly, total dividends growth rate minus growth rate in (basic) shares outstanding.

	2010	2011	2012
Dividends per share	2.26	2.53	2.87
Growth rate (in percent)	10.2	11.9	**13.4**
Total dividends (in millions)	2,408.1	2,609.7	2,896.6
Growth rate (in percent)	7.7	8.4	**11.0**
Basic shares outstanding (weighted) (in millions)	1,066.0	1,032.1	1,010.1
Growth rate (in percent)	(2.4)	(3.2)	**(2.1)**

Table 8.2. From 2010 to 2012, McDonald's dividends per share growth rate exceeded its total dividends growth rate.

Though these calculations are made even less accurate because of how basic shares outstanding are calculated in the table, *in general*, the following relationship between dividends per share growth rate, total dividends growth rate, and growth rate in shares is roughly true:

Dividends Per Share Growth Rate

> = *Total Dividends Growth Rate − Growth Rate in Shares*

Thus, when growth rate in shares is negative, as in a share buyback, for instance, dividends per share growth rate exceeds total dividends growth rate. In other words, **companies can boost their dividends per share growth rate when they undertake share buybacks to reduce shares outstanding**.

Moreover, *companies can show dividends per share growth with no growth in total dividends.* All they have to do is to buy back enough shares to show whatever dividends per share growth they want.

Some consider this an artificial boost, a heel lift. In another sense, however, this criticism is unfair. After all, an investor looking at his or her income is most interested in dividends *per share*. How it gets there almost does not matter.

Nevertheless, this additional boost is worth watching. If a company reduces the pace of its share buybacks or the share buybacks have less of an impact in reducing share count (for instance, because of a higher share price), dividends per share growth suffers.

History

Long-term dividend increases must average far more than inflation; otherwise, you are losing out. You are not getting paid for the risk that you are taking. Be wary of companies that raise their dividends by the tiniest of amounts.

Use the following resources to research a company's dividend history:

- **Company investor relations websites.**

- **Value Line *Investment Survey*,** available at most libraries, if not as a printed copy, then at least online.

- As of mid-2015, **Yahoo! Finance** includes a dividend history on each stock's *Historical Prices* page.

Do not feel compelled to research a company's entire dividend history. Ten to fifteen years is ample – clearly, dividends paid during Nixon's presidency do not tell us much. Ultimately, we want to know what the future will bring – we are far less interested in the distant past. Check that the company's dividend growth rate has exceeded long-term inflation, three percent. Always watch for problems such as decreases. Check the trend.

In addition to dividend history, research the history of the dividend payout ratio. The standard edition of the Value Line *Investment Survey* has an eleven-year history of the dividend payout ratio. As before, study the trend. Is it stable, increasing, or decreasing? Stability does not mean dividend payout ratio is constant. It just means it is reasonably bounded, for instance, between 45 percent and 50 percent, with no obvious trend. Earnings sometimes dip for onetime reasons. This disrupts the trend.

Do not discard a stock simply because of a limited or damaged dividend history. With a limited history, you can view the start of a dividend as a sign of confidence, or maturity, or both. Likewise, a damaged dividend history is not necessarily the end of the world. Even big companies make mistakes serious enough that they have to lower their dividends. If they resume their dividends, however, take another look. For instance, in the early 2000s, Lockheed Martin slashed its dividend to pay down debt. Since then, it has emerged stronger. It has bought back shares; it has raised its dividend.

Conversely, a strong dividend history does not always suggest a strong dividend growth stock – the past does not extrapolate without error. Pay attention to dividend history but do not be fooled by it. *The eight-hundred-pound gorilla in the room is how the business performs in the future*. Consider Lehman. Between 2002 and 2006, the company grew its dividend at a more than 25 percent a year clip. Lehman outperformed the market and many of its peers. Yet, in 2008, in the blink of an investment eye, the company declared bankruptcy. The dividend was gone. Lehman's dividend history proved meaningless.

Successful long-term investors value their stocks properly – if not, they risk paying too much. Next, we turn to valuation. ♣

CHAPTER 9

Forecasts and Valuation

"Weather forecast for tonight: dark." George Carlin

SHORT-TERM forecasting is difficult – history has this uneasy habit of not always repeating in the way that it once did. What was important in the past, gradually, imperceptibly, becomes unimportant. Conversely, what was unimportant becomes important. Even if someone gets it right once, the market often proves them wrong later. Most people guess. And history has often proved such guesses wrong.

Over a short period – a few weeks, a few months, or even a year – prices parade in a game of chance, the roll of the market-pricing die not counting for much. Short-term returns are random.

Over a longer period – five years, ten years, or even more – returns reflect the underlying business. The market noise averages out. What remains is the signal, the characteristics of the underlying business.

Though supporters of Modern Portfolio Theory may disagree, I believe returns over a longer period are not random. A distinction between short- and long-term returns is important. Short-term, returns are random. Long-term, I believe, not so much.

Relative Valuation Models

"In the business world, the rearview mirror is always clearer than the windshield." Warren Buffett

To value stocks, we use valuation models. Valuation models are of two primary types:

- *relative valuation models* – where we compare our stock to something else; and

- *absolute valuation models* – where we value our stock directly.

With relative valuation models, we consider our stock undervalued – *relative to that something else* – if it comes out ahead in the comparison. With absolute valuation models, we calculate – either directly or indirectly – the stock's expected return; and invest if the risk-return profile is favorable.

The most well-known category of relative valuation models uses P/E ratios. With these models, we compare our stock's P/E ratio to that of the market, its peers, or even itself in the past. We consider our stock undervalued relative to the comparison if its P/E ratio is lower. For example, if our stock's P/E ratio is twelve and the market's P/E ratio is fifteen, we consider our stock undervalued relative to the market.

P/E models may work when comparing a stable company to itself in the past. They may also work when comparing the market to itself in the past, assuming the market is stable. On the other hand, P/E models fail with cyclical companies and often fail with rapidly growing companies. In general, P/E models fail when earnings per share is meager – so that P/E ratio makes little sense; and when earnings per share is zero or negative – so that P/E ratio is undefined.

Like a puzzle with missing pieces, P/E models are incomplete. They have at least two common shortcomings: (1) They do not account for growth; and (2) they do not account for dividends.

Peter Lynch addressed these omissions in his book, *One Up on Wall Street*. For non-dividend-paying companies, he advocated the use of models that use the PEG ratio. The PEG ratio is P/E ratio divided by earnings per share growth rate, G, in percentage points. For example, a stock with a P/E ratio of twelve and a G of ten percent has a PEG ratio of 12 / 10 or 1.2. Implicitly, most investors use a one-year earnings per share growth rate in this comparison. For longer-term investors, a longer-term earnings per share growth rate, (say) a five-year value, may be more appropriate. Lynch considered PEGs of 0.5 or less, very positive; and PEGs of 2.0 or more, very negative.

Many investors believe that a PEG of 1.0 indicates a fairly valued stock. This has little justification. For this to be valid, P/E ratios have to, at a minimum, (ideally) be proportional to growth and must not depend on anything else other than growth. But the relationship of P/E ratios to growth is nonlinear; and P/E ratios depend on factors such as risk.

Instead, think of PEG models, in general, and the PEG rule of 1.0, in particular, as *heuristics*. A PEG of 1.0 is a demarcating line – but only if a stock's PEG is far below 1.0 or far above 1.0. Even then it is not always right – but at least it has a *chance* of being in the right ballpark. (To be fair, the broad range of Lynch's criteria does seem to reflect this.)

For dividend-paying companies, Lynch tweaked the PEG ratio. Dividends reduce growth. Additionally, because dividend yield is part of an investor's return, it cannot be excluded when considering returns, even indirectly. It seems natural therefore to compare P/E ratio to the sum of dividend yield (Y) and earnings per share growth rate (again, G), both in percentage points. Both Y and G are components of return and the ratio now treats them equally. Moreover, the ratio now snuggles up to all three terms of the return equation of Chapter 1. Let us call this ratio the PEYG ratio. Lynch considered PEYGs of 0.5 or below attractive and PEYGs of 1.0 or above unattractive. For the unattractive criterion, he used 1.0, not the 2.0 he used for PEGs.

As with PEG models, think of PEYG models, in general, as heuristics. Both sets of models fail when P/E ratio and G are meager, zero, or negative.

When applying these models, estimates of earnings and growth rates are credible only with many independent estimates, (say) a minimum of 10-15. This is usually not a problem with large companies; this is often a problem with small and midsize companies.

Likewise, be wary when estimates are too broad. An average earnings per share estimate of 10¢ is meaningless when the range of estimates is broad, (say) 2¢ to 15¢. It becomes more meaningful when the range narrows, (say) 9¢ to 11¢. A narrow range indicates certainty. A broad range indicates uncertainty. Uncertainty is a shaky path. The same criticism applies to growth rates – though this is hard to catch because the range of growth rates is typically not published.

Another category of relative valuation models uses P/S ratios. P/S ratio is price per share divided by sales per share. With these models, we compare our stock's P/S ratio to that of other stocks, including its peers, or even itself in the past. We consider our stock undervalued relative to the comparison if its P/S ratio is lower. Thus, for example, if our stock's P/S ratio is 1.25, and that of a peer is 1.50, we consider our stock undervalued relative to the peer.

P/S models do not account for profitability. A company can generate enormous sales by acting like Santa Claus – giving away its products, with or without ribbons and wrapping paper. Based on its P/S ratio, it will look cheap. But without profits, unless the company regularly comes to the market for money, it will not survive for long. *Because of an emphasis on the top line, sales, and no accounting for the bottom line, profits; or in general, returns to shareholders, be wary of P/S models.* Although they may help spot very overvalued companies (P/S ratios more than (say) 10, for instance) and very cheap companies (P/S ratios less than (say) 0.2, for instance), you will find exceptions even here. In general, do not use P/S models.

Of the four models mentioned here, the P/E and PEYG models may apply to our dividend growth stocks, when comparing these companies to themselves in the past.

Still, relative valuation has many problems:

- The stock must resemble its comparison in all important details.

- None of the models (directly) account for risk. Ignoring risk is risky.

- *Relative valuation never tells you whether your stock is overvalued or undervalued.* It only tells you that your stock is *relatively* overvalued or *relatively* undervalued. During the late 1990s NASDAQ Bubble, one Internet stock may have looked undervalued relative to another. In fact, all were overvalued.

- Relative valuation makes more sense when you *hedge*, where, for instance, you buy the cheaper stock and short the more expensive comparison. It is an open question whether it makes sense when you do not hedge, which will often be the case for most individual investors, who typically do not go short.

T. S. Eliot once quipped, "it's not wise to violate rules until you know how to observe them." Likewise, **because of the many subtleties involved, use relative valuation only as a quick and dirty approach to valuation – and only as a start**. Appreciate the pitfalls of its simplicity – simplicity that is almost impossible to defend. Do not apply relative valuation blindly.

Absolute Valuation Models

"Do not worry about your difficulties in Mathematics. I can assure you mine are still greater." Albert Einstein

In 1962, M. J. Gordon, working off earlier work by John Burr Williams in 1938, derived the granddaddy of the absolute valuation models, today called the Gordon Model or Gordon Growth Model. It features dividends prominently:

$$V = \frac{D_1}{(r - g)}$$

Here, V is the value of one share of stock; D_1 is the annual dividend per share one year from today; r is the expected return, that is, the

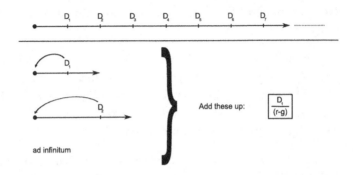

Figure 9.1. The Gordon Model, in conceptual terms, and without the mathematics: (1) Project the dividends (indefinitely), assuming they grow at a constant rate. (2) Discount each dividend to the present. (3) Add these up.

annual return you expect to earn from investing in the stock; and g is the dividend (per share) growth rate, which the model assumes is constant.

To produce this formula requires a three-step recipe (Figure 9.1): First, project the dividends (indefinitely), assuming they grow at a constant rate. Second, discount each dividend to the present. Third, add these up. The constant dividend growth rate is a key feature of this model. It simplifies the mathematics.

By rearranging terms in the formula, we have the following expression for the expected return, r:

$$r = \frac{D_1}{V} + g$$

In English:

Expected Return = Dividend Yield + Dividend Growth Rate

How does this compare to what we have seen already? In Chapter 1, we saw that return is the sum of dividend yield (where, strictly speaking, the dividend is paid at the end of the year), growth rate in earnings per share, growth rate in P/E ratio, and the product of these growth rates. Here, the last two terms drop out because P/E ratio does not change. In Chapter 8, we saw that once dividend payout ratio does not change – which is the case here – growth rate in earnings per share equals dividend (per share) growth rate. Thus, return is the sum of dividend yield and dividend growth rate – just as the Gordon Model advocates. In some sense, therefore, the model tells us nothing new – it's a review of a movie we have already seen, just couched in different language.

Although the Gordon Model formula provided investors with deep insight at the time, and its underlying principle still applies, the direct use of this formula, strictly as is, has problems that nullify its use for most companies today:[1]

- Inflexible dividend growth rates

  - The dividend growth rate has to be constant. But no company grows at one rate forever. Growth rates change. Typically, a company's growth rate slows as it ages.
  - Even with a constant dividend growth rate, it cannot be too large. For instance, it cannot exceed the growth rate of the economy. If it did, the company would one day become the economy.
  - The formula cannot be used – it does not apply – when dividend growth rate equals or exceeds expected return.

- Inflexible amounts

  - Not all companies pay dividends.
  - The formula implicitly requires that companies pay the maximum possible as dividends. Few companies do.

For companies that pay dividends and buy shares back, some argue that the Gordon Model has a crucial flaw because it does not account for

---

[1]To be fair, its purpose may have always been to illustrate more than anything else.

share buybacks. This rationale is incorrect. Share buybacks reduce the number of shares. They show up implicitly as a higher dividend (per share) growth rate.

Because dividend growth rate has to be constant and not too large, and the company has to pay the maximum possible as dividends, about the only stocks for which the Gordon Model *directly* applies, at least roughly, are slow-growing utilities and other similarly slow-growing companies that pay most of their free cash flow as dividends. We cannot apply the Gordon Model, *strictly as is*, to value our dividend growth stocks.

A Reasonable Model to Value Dividend Growth Stocks

"Looks like there's gonna be a cleanup on aisle five." Michael Scott (The Office)

In the Gordon Model, we project, discount, add. This principle of projecting, discounting, and adding underpins all absolute valuation models. In fact, it is broader. On 27 August 1999, in a speech at Jackson Hole, Wyoming, none other than Alan Greenspan asserted that this principle underlies the valuation of all assets:

> The value ascribed to any asset is a discounted value of future expected returns, even if no market participant consciously makes that calculation. In principle, forward discounting lies behind the valuation of all assets, from an apple that is about to be consumed to a hydroelectric plant with a hundred-year life expectancy.

It is undoubtedly correct. Yet, if the general concept works, but we cannot apply the Gordon Model to value our dividend growth stocks, what do we do? We create a model.

Our model uses a spreadsheet.[2] Using it is easy. Typically, you enter the stock ticker and eight numbers – the stock price and seven estimates, four of which are (related) growth rates – and out jumps the answer. You can download a copy immediately by typing this link into your web browser: *http://goo.gl/*qSTFJR. I created the spreadsheet in Windows 7 using Excel 2007. Thus, in an ideal world, you have the same or compatible operating system and spreadsheet application – and the link, which depends on Google Drive (and Google URL Shortener), continues to work. As an alternative, the following link will let you at least view the spreadsheet (in Google Sheets): *http://goo.gl/*etw143. If you do this, you will notice that I do not make the file editable – thus, one errant entry by one person does not spoil it for everyone else. Once you have the spreadsheet open, you may be able to download it as an Excel or other spreadsheet. Google Sheets ruins the original formatting – if this happens to you, you will need to tidy things up. I do not believe Google Sheets ruins the calculations but you will want to, ideally, check your downloaded spreadsheet's formulas against the formulas below and, as well, check your downloaded spreadsheet's results against the results of the examples in this chapter and Chapter 11. In case you run into problems, the instructions below on how to create the spreadsheet should help. It should take no more than an hour or two to create the spreadsheet.

As other ways of using our model, refer to the next two sections. In the first, you look up the model's result from tables. In the second, you calculate the model's result using a formula. I used the spreadsheet to derive the tables; and the tables to create the formula. The tables do not cover every possibility (that would be impossible) but they cover enough to be useful. The formula also does not cover every possibility – but it applies more broadly than the tables.

The spreadsheet addresses the two problems with the Gordon Model. To address inflexible dividend growth rates, it allows a range of growth

---

[2] Do not fear the Muffin Man. Even if you are uncomfortable with spreadsheets, what we do here is not difficult. Give the spreadsheet a try. You will find that using it is straightforward. If you do not have a spreadsheet application, Google offers one for free, Google Sheets, part of Google's productivity suite. Another free offering is by the Apache Software Foundation, Apache OpenOffice Calc, part of the Apache OpenOffice productivity suite.

rates. To address inflexible amounts, it requires that we use *payouts per share*, not dividends (per share).[3] Our estimates are not arbitrary. We (and the spreadsheet) create them in four steps:

- First, we calculate a long-term *payout ratio*. This is not the company's current dividend payout ratio. Instead, it reflects what the company can return to shareholders, in any form, over the long term. It recognizes that the company needs to keep some of the cash it generates to invest in the business, and perhaps a bit more for adverse times. Payouts include dividends, net share buybacks, and anything else the company can return to shareholders but for whatever reason does not. (We want to avoid situations where the company keeps accumulating cash it does not need.) For instance, if a company returns forty percent of earnings as dividends and buys back, net of shares issued, another ten percent as shares, and these numbers look sustainable, we tentatively assume a payout ratio of fifty percent. Then, if in our opinion the company can comfortably return another ten percent, we assume a payout ratio of sixty percent.

- Second, we calculate the starting assumed payout per share as the payout ratio from the first step times earnings per share.

- Third, we calculate the next assumed payout per share as the starting assumed payout per share accumulated at the earnings growth rate for the first year.

- Fourth, we calculate the next assumed payout per share as the payout per share from the third step accumulated at the earnings growth rate for the second year. We calculate the others in sequence, similarly.

Now for the spreadsheet. I first explain how to create it; I then explain how to use it. I conclude with examples of Johnson & Johnson at the

---

[3] Valuing stocks is difficult because of the many moving parts. Here, I try to get one thing right – or as right as I possibly can, the cash payouts. I believe getting the cash payouts wrong – and hoping to paper this over with other details – gets you into a heap of trouble.

beginning of 2000 and the beginning of 2013. If you do not want to know how to create the spreadsheet and just want to know how to use it, skip to page 165.

The instructions that follow apply to Excel 2007. I do not use anything too difficult. Other spreadsheets should be similar.

In the Excel 2007 descriptions that follow, when I say enter =...., enter everything from the equal sign up to and including the character just before the closing period of the sentence. Do not enter the closing period. Here we go:

- Create a new blank spreadsheet. To simplify things, give cells H4, C17, C18, C19, C20, and C21 the names return, gr_1, gr_2, gr_3, gr_4, and gr_5 respectively. (Gr stands for growth rate.) To do this in Excel 2007, click the relevant cell, (say) H4, move the cursor to the Name Box (the input box to the left of the Formula Bar in Excel 2007), click, then enter the name, (say) return.

- The spreadsheet has four required sections: Projections, Input, Result, and Miscellaneous. Start with the Projections section (Figure 9.2). Enter the titles as shown in the figure. Next, do the following:

  - In cell J5, enter =NOW(). This gets today's date (and time, though we are not interested in time). I was able to format it as a short date to hide the time.

  - In cell J6, enter =J5+365. This gets the date one 365-day year from today. Copy this to cells J7, J8, ..., and J205. This gets the dates further out. As a check, J205 should read =J204+365.

  - Next, enter the growth rates:
    * In cell K6, enter =gr_1. Copy this to cells K7, K8, K9, and K10. Each cell should read =gr_1.
    * In cell K11, enter =gr_2. Copy this to cells K12, K13, K14, and K15. Each cell should read =gr_2.
    * In cell K16, enter =gr_3. Copy this to cells K17, K18, ..., and K25. Each cell should read =gr_3.

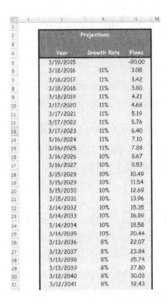

Year	Growth Rate	Flows
3/19/2015		-90.00
3/18/2016	11%	3.08
3/18/2017	11%	3.42
3/18/2018	11%	3.80
3/18/2019	11%	4.21
3/17/2020	11%	4.68
3/17/2021	11%	5.19
3/17/2022	11%	5.76
3/17/2023	11%	6.40
3/16/2024	11%	7.10
3/16/2025	11%	7.88
3/16/2026	10%	8.67
3/16/2027	10%	9.53
3/15/2028	10%	10.49
3/15/2029	10%	11.54
3/15/2030	10%	12.69
3/15/2031	10%	13.96
3/14/2032	10%	15.35
3/14/2033	10%	16.89
3/14/2034	10%	18.58
3/14/2035	10%	20.44
3/13/2036	8%	22.07
3/13/2037	8%	23.84
3/13/2038	8%	25.74
3/13/2039	8%	27.80
3/12/2040	8%	30.03
3/12/2041	8%	32.43

Figure 9.2. Spreadsheet to value dividend growth stocks – Projections.

- * In cell K26, enter =gr_4. Copy this to cells K27, K28, ...,
  and K35. Each cell should read =gr_4.
- * In cell K36, enter =gr_5. Copy this to cells K37, K38, ...,
  and K205. Each cell should read =gr_5.
  - In cell L5, enter =-C5. This is the negative of the current
    stock price, which we will enter later in the Input section.
  - In cell L6, enter =H17*(1+K6). This is the payout per share
    one 365-day year from today. It uses the starting assumed
    payout per share, which is calculated later in the Miscella-
    neous section, and the first-year growth rate, which we will
    enter later in the Input section.
  - In cell L7, enter =L6*(1+K7). Copy this to cells L8, L9, ...,
    and L205. These are the later payouts per share. As a check,
    L205 should read =L204*(1+K205).
  - Format the cells as in the figure or any way you wish.
- • Moving to the Input section, refer to Figure 9.3. Enter the title
  and text as shown. This is a data entry section. It has no formulas.

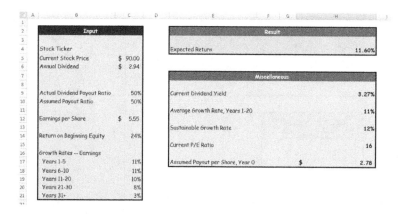

Figure 9.3. Spreadsheet to value dividend growth stocks – Input, Result, and Miscellaneous.

Format as appropriate. Enter the data in the figure. This will allow you to check your spreadsheet against mine.

- Next for the Result and Miscellaneous sections. Refer to Figure 9.3 again. Complete the titles and text as shown. Then, do the following:

  – In cell H4, enter =XIRR(L5:L205,J5:J205,0.1). This calculates the expected return. Ignore the Excel #NUM! error. It arises because the Miscellaneous section is incomplete. The 0.1 in this function is a guess to help Excel along.

  – In cell H9, enter =C6/C5.

  – In cell H11, enter =Average(K6:K25).

  – In cell H13, enter =C14*(1-C10).

  – In cell H15, enter =Round(C5/C12,0).

  – In cell H17, enter =C10*C12. The #NUM! error from earlier should vanish.

  – Format as appropriate.

That's it. Check that the numbers in your spreadsheet's Result and Miscellaneous sections match those of Figure 9.3. The most important number

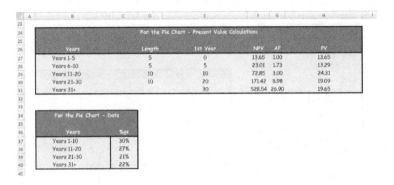

Figure 9.4. Spreadsheet to value dividend growth stocks – sections for the pie chart.

is the expected return, here, 11.60 percent. If you wish, tidy up superficial details – for instance, increase row heights, remove guidelines, and change names of tabs. Save your spreadsheet.

(The following portion is for the pie chart in the spreadsheet. It is optional, it is ugly; but it is useful. Refer to Figure 9.4. Enter the titles and text as shown. The formulas are involved. Here we go:

- The values in cells D27, D28, D29, and D30 are fixed. Enter 5, 5, 10, and 10 respectively.

- In cell E27, enter 0. In cell E28, enter =E27+D27. Copy this to cells E29, E30, and E31. As a check, E31 should read =E30+D30. Cells E27 to E31 should read 0, 5, 10, 20, and 30 respectively.

- Cells F27 to F31 contain values of segments of the payout per share stream at points in the future.[4] The segments correspond to the text in cells B27 to B31, namely, Years 1-5, Years 6-10, Years 11-20, Years 21-30, and Years 31+. Enter the formulas as follows:

  - In cell F27, enter =NPV(return,L6:L10).

  - In cell F28, enter =NPV(return,L11:L15).

---

[4]In the spreadsheet, I refer to these as net present values, NPV, based on the Excel function that I use. Except for the first entry, these are not net present values in a strict financial sense.

- In cell F29, enter =NPV(return,L16:L25).

- In cell F30, enter =NPV(return,L26:L35).

- In cell F31, enter =NPV(return,L36:L205).

- In cell G27, enter =(1+return)^E27. Copy this to cells G28, G29, G30, and G31. As a check, G31 should read =(1+return)^E31. In financial jargon, these are accumulation factors, AF.

- In cell H27, enter =F27/G27. Copy this to cells H28, H29, H30, and H31. As a check, H31 should read =F31/G31. These are values of segments of the payout per share stream discounted to the present. In financial jargon, these are present values, PV, that is, values discounted to the present. Check that the sum of cells H27 to H31 equals the current stock price.

- Cells C37 to C40 contain the numerical values for the pie chart. In cell C37, enter =(H27+H28)/\$C\$5. In cell C38, enter = H29/\$C\$5. Copy this to cells C39 and C40. As a check, C40 should read =H31/\$C\$5. The first two segments are combined into one ten years long. This makes it comparable to the next two segments. If you entered the input data from Figure 9.3, check that the results in cells C37 through C40 match those of Figure 9.4. As the figure shows, starting from C37 and moving down, the results are 30 percent, 27 percent, 21 percent, and 22 percent respectively.

- Format as appropriate.

- Select cells B37 to C40. Press the F11 key to generate the default chart. Change the chart type to exploded pie (Figure 9.5). Format as appropriate. Save your spreadsheet.)

Here's **how to use** the spreadsheet:

- Enter the data in the Input section. There are twelve entries, namely, the stock ticker and eleven numerical entries. Of the eleven, two are optional; seven are required; one is recommended, though not required; and one you generally should not change.

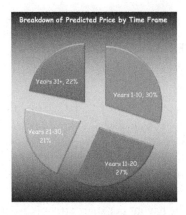

Figure 9.5. Spreadsheet to value dividend growth stocks – pie chart.

The two optional entries are *annual dividend* and *actual dividend payout ratio*. The seven required entries are *current stock price, assumed payout ratio, earnings per share,* and four *earnings growth rates*. The one recommended, though not required, entry is *return on beginning equity*. The one entry you generally should not change is a fifth *earnings growth rate*. For details, see below.

- Read the *expected return* from the Result section. If the expected return is high relative to the risk of investing in the stock or relative to the risk-adjusted returns of other investments such as long-term bonds the stock is a buy. Otherwise, the stock is a hold or a sell. This assessment is subjective.

Risk is a vast subject that needs a separate chapter, or two, or three, to do it justice. Instead, I will sketch it in a few sentences. *For stocks, risk comes in two primary flavors: business risk and valuation risk* – as distinct from each other as bacon is from eggs. *For dividend growth stocks, business risk is relatively low*. This is risk *within* the company. A good understanding of the company's business and a check of its earnings history will give you a good assessment of business risk. The business should be simple and stable with a high return on equity and no more than a comfortable level of debt. In addition, earnings history should show steady growth with few, if any, negative surprises. *As with all stocks,*

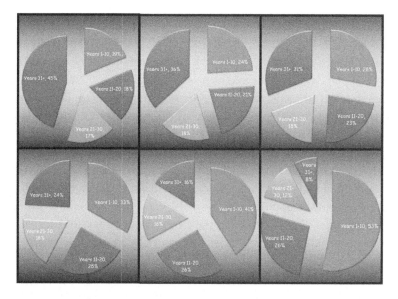

Figure 9.6. Pie charts under various scenarios, from most risky in the upper left to least risky in the lower right.

valuation risk is low, reasonable, or high. This is stock price risk, risk *external* to the company. Essentially, P/E ratio is the ultimate arbiter of valuation risk. All else equal, high P/E ratios imply high valuation risk; low P/E ratios, low valuation risk. Yet, how high is high and how low is low remains the Riddler's question. A general way to assess valuation risk is to compare the stock's expected return to that of safer investments, for example, ten-year Treasuries. (This assumes ten-year Treasuries are safe. As of mid-2015, with yields so low, ten-year Treasuries are not safe, at least from a return point of view. In this one instance, you may want to use high-quality intermediate-term corporate bonds as the comparison – though, unlike Treasuries, they are not free of default risk.) *For us, another way to gauge valuation risk is with the spreadsheet's pie chart: If too much of a stock's value arises from distant years, the stock is risky; if a big enough proportion arises from near years, the stock is not as risky. This, admittedly, hand-wavy guideline is based on the premise that depending on the hereafter is risky and the lower that dependence the less risky the stock.* This approach is imperfect –

and thus not foolproof – but I believe it is fair. For stocks that are *very overvalued* to *overvalued*, the Years 1-10 slice is relatively small. For instance, very overvalued stocks may have a Years 1-10 slice equal to less than 20 percent of the pie and overvalued stocks may have a Years 1-10 slice equal to 20-25 percent of the pie. For stocks that are *fairly valued* to *undervalued* to *very undervalued*, the Years 1-10 slice is quite large. For instance, fairly valued stocks may have a Years 1-10 slice equal to 25-30 percent of the pie; undervalued stocks, 30-40 percent of the pie; and very undervalued stocks, more than 40 percent. For percents on a boundary, classify the stock as you deem fit. In all cases, the Years 31+ slice works in the opposite way, roughly. *View these guidelines as rough, not sacrosanct.* Figure 9.6 shows the pie charts under various scenarios, from most risky in the upper left to least risky in the lower right. To create these charts, I ratcheted down price – thus lowering P/E ratio – keeping everything else the same.[5] As risk lessens, the slices change, in particular, the first and last slices – *the first slice progressively expands and the last slice progressively shrinks.* Not surprisingly, expected return runs opposite to risk. The upper left has the lowest expected return of 6.76 percent (because it has the highest risk, that is, the highest P/E ratio); the lower right, the highest expected return of 14.25 percent (because it has the lowest risk, that is, the lowest P/E ratio). Because of the many variables involved, it is difficult to make this argument unassailable. For instance, stocks with high payout ratios tend to have large Years 1-10 slices – and thus appear less risky. That is probably how it should be, and might partly explain, for instance, why the market considers stocks with big and sustainable dividends less risky; still, this nicety, if we're in a good mood, or "bias," if the bacon's out, is worth keeping in mind. We will see real-world examples of the pie chart to assess valuation risk when we value Johnson & Johnson.

Details about entries in the Input section follow:

- **Stock Ticker**. (Self-explanatory.)

---

[5] I used these assumptions: assumed payout ratio (75 percent); earnings per share (1.00); years 1-5 (7 percent); years 6-10 (7 percent); years 11-20 (6 percent); years 21-30 (6 percent); years 31+ (3 percent). To create the six pie charts, I varied current stock price from 40 (most risky) to 30 to 25 to 20 to 15 to 10 (least risky).

- **Current Stock Price**. (Self-explanatory.)

- **Annual Dividend**. Annual Dividend is not used in the valuation. You may leave it blank. It is used to calculate current dividend yield in the Miscellaneous section – but that is for reference only. If you enter it, use dividends (per share) six months in the past plus estimated dividends (per share) six months in the future.

- **Actual Dividend Payout Ratio**. Actual Dividend Payout Ratio is not used in the valuation. You may leave it blank. It is for reference only. If you enter it, use the current actual dividend payout ratio; or a value that takes into account a historical longer-term trend, (say) a five- or ten-year trend; or an estimated long-run average for the next several years, where "several" is something in the range of ten. If you enter it this last way, use it to check that the next entry, assumed payout ratio – an important number – looks reasonable. When looking at history, remove or adjust any strange years, for instance, when the dividend payout ratio looks unreasonably high because earnings are temporarily depressed. For historical data, use Value Line.

- **Assumed Payout Ratio**. The spreadsheet uses Assumed Payout Ratio and the next number, earnings per share, to establish the starting assumed payout per share. The simplest way to develop this ratio is to work backward. Assuming you have a good feel for the earnings growth rates, which in many cases you will because dividend growth stocks tend to be stable growers – and history and analyst estimates can at least help point the way – the spreadsheet calculates in the Miscellaneous section the average growth rate for Years 1-20 and the sustainable growth rate. Adjust the assumed payout ratio for these two values to come close or match. (For details, see the second bullet point in the discussion of the Miscellaneous section below.) This exercise is imperfect but gives you a reasonable way out. Do not enter an assumed payout ratio that is negative, zero, or one-hundred percent or more.[6]

---

[6] You can also calculate this ratio from first principles – though this requires more effort – by studying the cash flow statement and a fourth financial statement I do not cover here, the statement of shareowners' equity. Study a long sequence, (say) ten years,

- **Earnings per Share**. Earnings per Share equals earnings per share six months in the past plus estimated earnings per share six months in the future.[7] These are diluted earnings per share not basic earnings per share or any other earnings per share. Use a value that reflects the company's ongoing business. Consider removing onetime effects – especially if they are distorting and large. Do not enter a value that is zero or negative.

- **Return on Beginning Equity**. Although you can leave Return on Beginning Equity blank because it is not used in the projection, I recommend entering it. The spreadsheet uses return on beginning equity to calculate an important sanity check in the Miscellaneous section. This is a long-run average for the next several years, (say) ten. Look at ten years of history to gauge fluctuations and trends.

- **Growth Rates – Earnings**. *These are growth rates in earnings, not growth rates in earnings per share*. We do not use earnings per share because we would then be including share buybacks twice – indirectly in earnings per share and directly in assumed payout ratio. When we use growth rates in earnings, our criteria for the expected five-year earnings per share growth rate – 8-12 percent for a large-cap and 8-16 percent for a midcap – shift downward, the degree of shift depending on size and effectiveness of the share buyback. Thus, do not be alarmed by growth rates in earnings of less than 8 percent in the examples in this chapter and Chapter 11. In general, use growth rates that decrease over time, as companies age. (Moreover, using lower growth rates results in a more conservative valuation.) Check your assumed earnings growth rates against the company's earnings growth rates over the last five or ten years. Generally, leave the growth rate for Years 31+ at three percent. Three percent approximates inflation – companies do not grow forever. If you feel long-term inflation

---

of these statements to understand what the company can pay to shareholders – and to remove the effects of fluctuations and uncover any trends.

[7] This is not the mathematically precise answer – but it should be close. To do this precisely, we need to add earnings over the last six months to estimated earnings over the next six months and divide the resulting sum by the weighted average share count (somehow magically obtained) over the twelve months.

will be lower, consider using two percent. If you feel long-term inflation will be higher, consider using four percent. If I had to choose between the two, for the U.S. economy, I think two percent is more likely than four percent. The lower the Years 31+ growth rate, the lower the expected return. A change from three percent to two percent results in a drop in expected return of about a tenth or two of a percentage point – within our tolerance of error, thus not worth our bother. Do not worry about the huge flows in outer years. Much like watching pedestrians from higher and higher floors of a skyscraper, they become tiny when discounted to the present. (Other programs use a P/E multiple, (say) after five or ten years, but this introduces a potential error.) Account for excess earnings volatility with lower growth rates. With most stocks, we have to study the business in depth to determine growth rates. Because of their stability, this type of study is often unnecessary with dividend growth stocks. I generally do not bother – as I'd rather be eating homemade waffles instead – whereas with many other types of stocks I am much more careful.

The Miscellaneous section has five variables. Four are for sanity checks and one is used in the Projections section:

- **Current Dividend Yield** and **Current P/E Ratio** are for market comparisons. To maintain consistency, the spreadsheet requires dividends and earnings per share six months in the past plus six months in the future. Thus, current dividend yield and current P/E ratio reflect this span.

- **Average Growth Rate, Years 1-20** and **Sustainable Growth Rate**. Sustainable Growth Rate here is similar to sustainable growth rate from Chapter 8 – except that here it includes everything offsetting earnings not just dividends. Do not assume growth rates that result in an average growth rate, years 1-20, higher than the sustainable growth rate. I believe, in general, that this is an aggressive assumption – and dangerous. An average growth rate, years 1-20, lower than the sustainable growth rate by one or two percentages points is fair – and perhaps conservative – and typically can be ignored. If the difference is three or more percentage points, consider raising the growth rates.

- The spreadsheet uses **Assumed Payout per Share, Year 0** to start the payouts per share stream in the Projections section.

The **pie chart on the second tab** provides a check on valuation risk, as explained in detail earlier.

As examples, consider Johnson & Johnson at the beginning of 2000 and the beginning of 2013. Table 9.1 shows the spreadsheet data and results. At the beginning of 2000 – despite aggressive long-term growth rates – the expected return is 9.94 percent; at the beginning of 2013, it is 11.97 percent. Figures 9.7 and 9.8 show the pie charts. For 2000, as a sign of overvaluation, the last slice, Years 31+, is large (32 percent) relative to the other slices, and the first slice, Years 1-10, is quite small (22 percent). By contrast, for 2013, as a sign of undervaluation, the first slice, Years 1-10, is huge (44 percent), bloated, relative to the other slices. The pie charts (and the sharp difference in results) highlight the difference in valuation risk. Not surprisingly, the difference is evident in the stock's P/E ratio: It was 30 at the beginning of 2000 and 13 at the beginning of 2013. The stock looked overvalued at the beginning of 2000; it looked undervalued at the beginning of 2013.

A few concluding points:

- We use a spreadsheet because the calculation of expected return requires solving a complex equation iteratively.

- For more examples, see Chapter 11.

- A constant return on beginning equity is not ideal – it will change over time. Still, the more stable this number historically the better.

- To keep things simple, I do not include error checks.

- Err toward conservative valuations. They give us a margin of safety.

Johnson & Johnson: Spreadsheet Data and Results		
	Beginning of 2000	Beginning of 2013
Stock Ticker	JNJ	JNJ
Current Stock Price	93.25	70.10
Annual Dividend	1.16	2.49
Actual Dividend Payout Ratio	35%	45%
Assumed Payout Ratio	60%	75%
Earnings per Share	3.15	5.25
Return on Beginning Equity	30%	28%
Growth Rates – Earnings		
Years 1-5	12%	7%
Years 6-10	11%	7%
Years 11-20	10%	6%
Years 21-30	9%	6%
Years 31+	3%	3%
Expected Return	9.94%	11.97%

Table 9.1. Valuing Johnson & Johnson at the beginning of 2000 and the beginning of 2013, spreadsheet data and results. The current stock price, annual dividend, and earnings per share in 2000 do not reflect a subsequent 2-1 stock split in 2001. Nostradamus was not in the house.

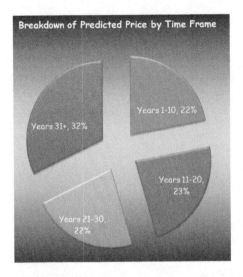

Figure 9.7. Pie chart, Johnson & Johnson, beginning of 2000. As a sign of overvaluation, the last slice, Years 31+, is large (32 percent) relative to the other slices, and the first
slice, Years 1-10, is quite small (22 percent).

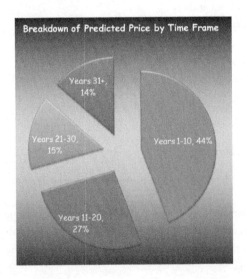

Figure 9.8. Pie chart, Johnson & Johnson, beginning of 2013. As a sign of undervaluation, the first slice, Years 1-10, is huge (44 percent), bloated, relative to the other
slices.

- Investors often make arbitrary guesses about growth rates. Few realize that too high a growth rate means the company has to take on more debt than otherwise expected – thus becoming riskier – or the company has to take on new equity – thus diluting existing shareholders. Valuations become corrupt. By calculating a sustainable growth rate, the spreadsheet forces us to think about reasonable growth rates. The sustainable growth rate is relevant to high-quality dividend growth companies because these companies rarely, if ever, need to raise net new equity. They are profitable enough to fund both growth and payouts to shareholders.

- In general, averages of input values are unsuitable in projections. Ideally, we need exact future flows. That's impossible. Alternatively, we run scenarios. That still requires judgment.

- Try various stock prices to see how expected return changes.

- More generally, try other assumptions and what-ifs. For instance, what if return on beginning equity is lower by three percentage points? How does this impact growth rates of earnings, and thus valuation?

- Our model implies dividends are reinvested.

- Do not ignore small differences in expected return. Even a small difference results in a big difference in long-term wealth. A difference of one percentage point is huge.

- *Keep it simple. The biggest unknowns are the values of the parameters.* The future will never turn out the way we expect.

- You may argue that incorporating numbers so far out into the future is silly. That may be, but any other system, even implicitly, does the same.

- Our model calculates the return *built into* the stock price. In other words, it looks at what the market gives us.

- As always, you will need to update expected return if a company's earnings or outlook are well above or well below what you expect.

- Our model does not produce a stock price target. In general, as a long-term investor, avoid short-term stock price targets. They force you to think short term. What matters is your long-term return. Nevertheless, if you feel you must have a one-year stock price target, multiply the stock price by (1 + Expected Return). Because we use normalized growth rates over long periods, this target is useless.

- Our model does not use dividend yield. This is different from what many investors do when they buy stocks based solely on dividend yield. Do not buy most stocks based solely on dividend yield.

- Our model does not include tax calculations.

- Expected return does not change if we divide current stock price and earnings per share by the same non-zero number. Thus, we divide both by earnings per share – current stock price becomes current P/E ratio and earnings per share becomes 1.0. In effect, our model depends on current P/E ratio and we dispense with current stock price and earnings per share. Thus, overall, *our model depends on just three factors: assumed payout ratio, growth rates (of earnings), and current P/E ratio*.

A Tabular Shortcut[8]

Use the tables in this section to look up expected return. These tables do not cover every possibility (that would be impossible) but they cover enough to be useful. I used the spreadsheet to calculate the entries in these tables.

To use these tables do the following:

---

[8] If you understand how to use the spreadsheet, you may skip this section. That said, you can use the tables in this section to quickly read your stock's expected return. Moreover, you can study the tables to understand how expected return varies with changes in P/E ratio and changes in growth rates.

1. Estimate your stock's assumed payout ratio. This will identify which table to use. Tables 9.2, ..., 9.10 cover assumed payout ratios of 50 percent to 90 percent in percentage point increments of five.

2. Determine your stock's current P/E ratio. This will identify the column in your table. Each table covers P/E ratios from 10.0 to 27.5, in increments of 2.5. The P/E ratio uses earnings per share six months in the past plus estimated earnings per share six months in the future. These are diluted earnings per share not basic earnings per share or any other form of earnings per share.

3. Estimate your stock's growth rates for Years 1-5, Years 6-10, Years 11-20, and Years 21-30. This will identify the row in your table. These are earnings growth rates, not earnings per share growth rates or any other growth rates. The tables list twenty-six possibilities.

4. With the table, column, and row identified, read the expected return from the relevant cell.

Our range of assumed payout ratios should cover most scenarios. As a rule, it makes little sense to stipulate an assumed payout ratio of (say) 51.3. In this case, 50 is fine. Likewise, 55 makes more sense than (say) 53.7.

Current P/E ratio is another matter. More often than not, because our stock's current P/E ratio will not match one of the current P/E ratios in the columns, we have to hazard a guess.[9] For example, suppose our stock's assumed payout ratio is 75 percent. We have to use Table 9.7. Suppose growth rates are 11, 11, 10, and 8. Let current P/E ratio be 18. From the table, expected return for a current P/E ratio of 17.5 is 13.6 percent and expected return for a current P/E ratio of 20.0 is 12.7 percent. Thus, with a current P/E ratio of 18, one-fifth of the way from 17.5 to 20.0, we take one-fifth of 13.6 percent minus 12.7 percent, namely 0.2 percent rounded, and subtract this from 13.6. Thus, our guess is 13.6 percent - 0.2 percent, or 13.4 percent.

---

[9] More precisely, we use linear interpolation.

Expected return (**assumed payout ratio of 50 percent**)							
Growth rates	Current P/E ratio						
– earnings	10.0	12.5	15.0	17.5	20.0	22.5	25.0	27.5
12, 12, 10, 8	15.2%	13.6%	12.5%	11.6%	10.9%	10.3%	9.9%	9.5%
12, 11, 9, 8	14.7%	13.1%	12.0%	11.1%	10.5%	9.9%	9.4%	9.0%
12, 10, 9, 7	14.3%	12.7%	11.6%	10.8%	10.1%	9.6%	9.1%	8.7%
12, 10, 8, 6	13.9%	12.3%	11.2%	10.3%	9.7%	9.1%	8.7%	8.3%
12, 9, 7, 6	13.4%	11.8%	10.7%	9.9%	9.2%	8.7%	8.3%	7.9%
11, 11, 10, 8	14.7%	13.1%	12.0%	11.2%	10.5%	10.0%	9.5%	9.1%
11, 11, 9, 7	14.2%	12.7%	11.6%	10.7%	10.1%	9.5%	9.1%	8.7%
11, 11, 8, 6	13.8%	12.2%	11.1%	10.3%	9.6%	9.1%	8.7%	8.3%
11, 9, 8, 7	13.5%	12.0%	10.9%	10.1%	9.5%	8.9%	8.5%	8.1%
10, 10, 9, 8	13.8%	12.4%	11.3%	10.5%	9.9%	9.4%	8.9%	8.6%
10, 10, 8, 7	13.4%	11.9%	10.9%	10.1%	9.4%	8.9%	8.5%	8.1%
10, 9, 8, 6	13.0%	11.6%	10.5%	9.7%	9.1%	8.6%	8.2%	7.8%
10, 9, 7, 7	12.9%	11.4%	10.4%	9.6%	9.0%	8.5%	8.1%	7.8%
10, 8, 7, 6	12.5%	11.1%	10.1%	9.3%	8.7%	8.2%	7.8%	7.4%
9, 9, 9, 8	13.3%	11.9%	10.9%	10.1%	9.5%	9.0%	8.6%	8.2%
9, 9, 8, 7	12.9%	11.5%	10.5%	9.7%	9.1%	8.6%	8.2%	7.8%
9, 8, 8, 6	12.5%	11.1%	10.1%	9.3%	8.7%	8.3%	7.9%	7.5%
9, 8, 7, 5	12.1%	10.7%	9.7%	8.9%	8.3%	7.9%	7.5%	7.1%
9, 7, 7, 6	12.0%	10.6%	9.6%	8.9%	8.3%	7.9%	7.5%	7.2%
9, 7, 6, 5	11.6%	10.2%	9.2%	8.5%	7.9%	7.5%	7.1%	6.8%
8, 8, 8, 7	12.4%	11.0%	10.0%	9.3%	8.7%	8.3%	7.9%	7.5%
8, 8, 7, 6	12.0%	10.6%	9.6%	8.9%	8.3%	7.9%	7.5%	7.1%
8, 7, 7, 5	11.6%	10.2%	9.3%	8.6%	8.0%	7.5%	7.2%	6.9%
7, 7, 7, 6	11.5%	10.2%	9.2%	8.5%	8.0%	7.5%	7.2%	6.9%
7, 7, 6, 5	11.0%	9.7%	8.8%	8.1%	7.6%	7.2%	6.8%	6.5%
7, 6, 5, 5	10.6%	9.3%	8.4%	7.7%	7.2%	6.8%	6.5%	6.2%

Table 9.2. Expected return – using our spreadsheet – given growth rates (of earnings) and current P/E ratio. The assumed payout ratio is **50 percent**. The current P/E ratio is based on earnings in the last six months plus estimated earnings in the next six months. The four growth rates in each line are for Years 1-5, Years 6-10, Years 11-20, and Years 21-30 respectively. In the spreadsheet, the growth rate for Years 31+ is kept at 3 percent.

Growth rates	Expected return (**assumed payout ratio of 55 percent**)							
	Current P/E ratio							
– earnings	10.0	12.5	15.0	17.5	20.0	22.5	25.0	27.5
12, 12, 10, 8	15.9%	14.3%	13.1%	12.1%	11.4%	10.8%	10.3%	9.9%
12, 11, 9, 8	15.4%	13.7%	12.6%	11.7%	10.9%	10.3%	9.9%	9.4%
12, 10, 9, 7	15.0%	13.4%	12.2%	11.3%	10.6%	10.0%	9.5%	9.1%
12, 10, 8, 6	14.6%	12.9%	11.8%	10.8%	10.1%	9.6%	9.1%	8.7%
12, 9, 7, 6	14.1%	12.4%	11.3%	10.4%	9.7%	9.1%	8.7%	8.3%
11, 11, 10, 8	15.4%	13.8%	12.6%	11.7%	11.0%	10.4%	9.9%	9.5%
11, 11, 9, 7	15.0%	13.3%	12.1%	11.3%	10.5%	10.0%	9.5%	9.1%
11, 11, 8, 6	14.5%	12.9%	11.7%	10.8%	10.1%	9.5%	9.1%	8.7%
11, 9, 8, 7	14.2%	12.6%	11.5%	10.6%	9.9%	9.4%	8.9%	8.5%
10, 10, 9, 8	14.5%	13.0%	11.9%	11.0%	10.3%	9.8%	9.3%	8.9%
10, 10, 8, 7	14.1%	12.5%	11.4%	10.6%	9.9%	9.3%	8.9%	8.5%
10, 9, 8, 6	13.8%	12.2%	11.0%	10.2%	9.5%	9.0%	8.6%	8.2%
10, 9, 7, 7	13.6%	12.0%	10.9%	10.1%	9.4%	8.9%	8.5%	8.1%
10, 8, 7, 6	13.2%	11.7%	10.6%	9.7%	9.1%	8.6%	8.2%	7.8%
9, 9, 9, 8	14.0%	12.5%	11.4%	10.6%	9.9%	9.4%	9.0%	8.6%
9, 9, 8, 7	13.6%	12.1%	11.0%	10.2%	9.5%	9.0%	8.5%	8.2%
9, 8, 8, 6	13.2%	11.7%	10.6%	9.8%	9.2%	8.7%	8.2%	7.9%
9, 8, 7, 5	12.8%	11.3%	10.2%	9.4%	8.7%	8.2%	7.8%	7.5%
9, 7, 7, 6	12.7%	11.2%	10.1%	9.4%	8.7%	8.2%	7.8%	7.5%
9, 7, 6, 5	12.3%	10.8%	9.7%	8.9%	8.3%	7.8%	7.4%	7.1%
8, 8, 8, 7	13.1%	11.6%	10.5%	9.8%	9.1%	8.6%	8.2%	7.9%
8, 8, 7, 6	12.6%	11.1%	10.1%	9.3%	8.7%	8.2%	7.8%	7.5%
8, 7, 7, 5	12.3%	10.8%	9.8%	9.0%	8.4%	7.9%	7.5%	7.2%
7, 7, 7, 6	12.1%	10.7%	9.7%	8.9%	8.4%	7.9%	7.5%	7.2%
7, 7, 6, 5	11.7%	10.3%	9.3%	8.5%	8.0%	7.5%	7.1%	6.8%
7, 6, 5, 5	11.2%	9.8%	8.8%	8.1%	7.6%	7.1%	6.8%	6.5%

Table 9.3. Expected return – using our spreadsheet – given growth rates (of earnings) and current P/E ratio. The assumed payout ratio is **55 percent**. The current P/E ratio is based on earnings in the last six months plus estimated earnings in the next six months. The four growth rates in each line are for Years 1-5, Years 6-10, Years 11-20, and Years 21-30 respectively. In the spreadsheet, the growth rate for Years 31+ is kept at 3 percent.

Expected return (**assumed payout ratio of 60 percent**)							
Growth rates	Current P/E ratio						
– earnings	10.0	12.5	15.0	17.5	20.0	22.5	25.0	27.5
12, 12, 10, 8	16.7%	14.9%	13.6%	12.6%	11.9%	11.2%	10.7%	10.3%
12, 11, 9, 8	16.1%	14.4%	13.1%	12.2%	11.4%	10.8%	10.3%	9.8%
12, 10, 9, 7	15.8%	14.0%	12.7%	11.8%	11.0%	10.4%	9.9%	9.5%
12, 10, 8, 6	15.4%	13.6%	12.3%	11.3%	10.6%	10.0%	9.5%	9.0%
12, 9, 7, 6	14.8%	13.1%	11.8%	10.9%	10.1%	9.5%	9.0%	8.6%
11, 11, 10, 8	16.1%	14.4%	13.1%	12.2%	11.5%	10.8%	10.3%	9.9%
11, 11, 9, 7	15.7%	13.9%	12.7%	11.7%	11.0%	10.4%	9.9%	9.5%
11, 11, 8, 6	15.3%	13.5%	12.2%	11.3%	10.6%	10.0%	9.5%	9.0%
11, 9, 8, 7	14.9%	13.2%	12.0%	11.1%	10.3%	9.8%	9.3%	8.9%
10, 10, 9, 8	15.2%	13.6%	12.4%	11.5%	10.8%	10.2%	9.7%	9.3%
10, 10, 8, 7	14.8%	13.1%	11.9%	11.0%	10.3%	9.7%	9.3%	8.8%
10, 9, 8, 6	14.4%	12.8%	11.6%	10.7%	10.0%	9.4%	8.9%	8.5%
10, 9, 7, 7	14.3%	12.6%	11.4%	10.6%	9.9%	9.3%	8.8%	8.4%
10, 8, 7, 6	13.9%	12.2%	11.1%	10.2%	9.5%	9.0%	8.5%	8.1%
9, 9, 9, 8	14.7%	13.1%	11.9%	11.0%	10.4%	9.8%	9.3%	8.9%
9, 9, 8, 7	14.2%	12.6%	11.5%	10.6%	9.9%	9.4%	8.9%	8.5%
9, 8, 8, 6	13.9%	12.3%	11.1%	10.2%	9.6%	9.0%	8.6%	8.2%
9, 8, 7, 5	13.5%	11.8%	10.7%	9.8%	9.1%	8.6%	8.2%	7.8%
9, 7, 7, 6	13.4%	11.8%	10.6%	9.8%	9.1%	8.6%	8.2%	7.8%
9, 7, 6, 5	12.9%	11.3%	10.2%	9.4%	8.7%	8.2%	7.8%	7.4%
8, 8, 8, 7	13.7%	12.1%	11.0%	10.2%	9.5%	9.0%	8.6%	8.2%
8, 8, 7, 6	13.3%	11.7%	10.6%	9.8%	9.1%	8.6%	8.2%	7.8%
8, 7, 7, 5	12.9%	11.3%	10.2%	9.4%	8.8%	8.3%	7.8%	7.5%
7, 7, 7, 6	12.7%	11.2%	10.2%	9.4%	8.7%	8.2%	7.8%	7.5%
7, 7, 6, 5	12.3%	10.8%	9.7%	8.9%	8.3%	7.8%	7.4%	7.1%
7, 6, 5, 5	11.8%	10.3%	9.3%	8.5%	7.9%	7.4%	7.1%	6.7%

Table 9.4. Expected return – using our spreadsheet – given growth rates (of earnings) and current P/E ratio. The assumed payout ratio is **60 percent**. The current P/E ratio is based on earnings in the last six months plus estimated earnings in the next six months. The four growth rates in each line are for Years 1-5, Years 6-10, Years 11-20, and Years 21-30 respectively. In the spreadsheet, the growth rate for Years 31+ is kept at 3 percent.

Expected return (**assumed payout ratio of 65 percent**)							
Growth rates	Current P/E ratio						
– earnings	10.0	12.5	15.0	17.5	20.0	22.5	25.0	27.5
12, 12, 10, 8	17.4%	15.5%	14.2%	13.1%	12.3%	11.7%	11.1%	10.6%
12, 11, 9, 8	16.8%	15.0%	13.6%	12.6%	11.8%	11.2%	10.6%	10.2%
12, 10, 9, 7	16.5%	14.6%	13.3%	12.3%	11.5%	10.8%	10.3%	9.8%
12, 10, 8, 6	16.1%	14.2%	12.8%	11.8%	11.0%	10.4%	9.9%	9.4%
12, 9, 7, 6	15.5%	13.7%	12.3%	11.3%	10.6%	9.9%	9.4%	9.0%
11, 11, 10, 8	16.8%	15.0%	13.7%	12.7%	11.9%	11.3%	10.7%	10.3%
11, 11, 9, 7	16.4%	14.5%	13.2%	12.2%	11.4%	10.8%	10.3%	9.8%
11, 11, 8, 6	16.0%	14.1%	12.8%	11.8%	11.0%	10.4%	9.8%	9.4%
11, 9, 8, 7	15.6%	13.8%	12.5%	11.5%	10.8%	10.2%	9.6%	9.2%
10, 10, 9, 8	15.9%	14.1%	12.9%	11.9%	11.2%	10.6%	10.1%	9.6%
10, 10, 8, 7	15.5%	13.7%	12.4%	11.5%	10.7%	10.1%	9.6%	9.2%
10, 9, 8, 6	15.1%	13.3%	12.1%	11.1%	10.4%	9.8%	9.3%	8.9%
10, 9, 7, 7	15.0%	13.2%	11.9%	11.0%	10.3%	9.7%	9.2%	8.8%
10, 8, 7, 6	14.6%	12.8%	11.6%	10.6%	9.9%	9.3%	8.9%	8.4%
9, 9, 9, 8	15.3%	13.6%	12.4%	11.5%	10.8%	10.2%	9.7%	9.3%
9, 9, 8, 7	14.9%	13.2%	12.0%	11.0%	10.3%	9.7%	9.3%	8.8%
9, 8, 8, 6	14.5%	12.8%	11.6%	10.7%	10.0%	9.4%	8.9%	8.5%
9, 8, 7, 5	14.1%	12.4%	11.2%	10.2%	9.5%	9.0%	8.5%	8.1%
9, 7, 7, 6	14.0%	12.3%	11.1%	10.2%	9.5%	9.0%	8.5%	8.1%
9, 7, 6, 5	13.6%	11.9%	10.7%	9.8%	9.1%	8.5%	8.1%	7.7%
8, 8, 8, 7	14.3%	12.7%	11.5%	10.6%	9.9%	9.4%	8.9%	8.5%
8, 8, 7, 6	13.9%	12.2%	11.1%	10.2%	9.5%	8.9%	8.5%	8.1%
8, 7, 7, 5	13.5%	11.9%	10.7%	9.8%	9.1%	8.6%	8.2%	7.8%
7, 7, 7, 6	13.3%	11.7%	10.6%	9.8%	9.1%	8.6%	8.1%	7.8%
7, 7, 6, 5	12.9%	11.3%	10.2%	9.3%	8.7%	8.2%	7.7%	7.4%
7, 6, 5, 5	12.4%	10.8%	9.7%	8.9%	8.3%	7.8%	7.4%	7.0%

Table 9.5. Expected return – using our spreadsheet – given growth rates (of earnings) and current P/E ratio. The assumed payout ratio is **65 percent**. The current P/E ratio is based on earnings in the last six months plus estimated earnings in the next six months. The four growth rates in each line are for Years 1-5, Years 6-10, Years 11-20, and Years 21-30 respectively. In the spreadsheet, the growth rate for Years 31+ is kept at 3 percent.

Expected return (**assumed payout ratio of 70 percent**)							
Growth rates	Current P/E ratio						
– earnings	10.0	12.5	15.0	17.5	20.0	22.5	25.0	27.5
12, 12, 10, 8	18.1%	16.1%	14.7%	13.6%	12.8%	12.1%	11.5%	11.0%
12, 11, 9, 8	17.5%	15.6%	14.2%	13.1%	12.3%	11.6%	11.0%	10.5%
12, 10, 9, 7	17.2%	15.2%	13.8%	12.7%	11.9%	11.2%	10.7%	10.2%
12, 10, 8, 6	16.8%	14.8%	13.4%	12.3%	11.5%	10.8%	10.2%	9.8%
12, 9, 7, 6	16.2%	14.2%	12.8%	11.8%	11.0%	10.3%	9.8%	9.3%
11, 11, 10, 8	17.5%	15.5%	14.2%	13.1%	12.3%	11.6%	11.1%	10.6%
11, 11, 9, 7	17.1%	15.1%	13.7%	12.7%	11.9%	11.2%	10.6%	10.2%
11, 11, 8, 6	16.7%	14.7%	13.3%	12.2%	11.4%	10.8%	10.2%	9.7%
11, 9, 8, 7	16.3%	14.3%	13.0%	12.0%	11.2%	10.5%	10.0%	9.5%
10, 10, 9, 8	16.5%	14.7%	**13.4%**	12.4%	11.6%	10.9%	10.4%	10.0%
10, 10, 8, 7	16.1%	14.3%	**12.9%**	11.9%	11.1%	10.5%	10.0%	9.5%
10, 9, 8, 6	15.8%	13.9%	12.6%	11.6%	10.8%	10.2%	9.6%	9.2%
10, 9, 7, 7	15.6%	13.7%	12.4%	11.4%	10.7%	10.0%	9.5%	9.1%
10, 8, 7, 6	15.2%	13.4%	12.1%	11.1%	10.3%	9.7%	9.2%	8.8%
9, 9, 9, 8	15.9%	14.1%	12.9%	11.9%	11.2%	10.5%	10.0%	9.6%
9, 9, 8, 7	15.5%	13.7%	12.4%	11.5%	10.7%	10.1%	9.6%	9.2%
9, 8, 8, 6	15.2%	13.3%	12.1%	11.1%	10.4%	9.8%	9.3%	8.8%
9, 8, 7, 5	14.8%	12.9%	11.6%	10.7%	9.9%	9.3%	8.8%	8.4%
9, 7, 7, 6	14.6%	12.8%	11.6%	10.6%	9.9%	9.3%	8.8%	8.4%
9, 7, 6, 5	14.2%	12.4%	11.1%	10.2%	9.5%	8.9%	8.4%	8.0%
8, 8, 8, 7	14.9%	13.2%	11.9%	11.0%	10.3%	9.7%	9.2%	8.8%
8, 8, 7, 6	14.5%	12.8%	11.5%	10.6%	9.9%	9.3%	8.8%	8.4%
8, 7, 7, 5	14.2%	12.4%	11.2%	10.2%	9.5%	8.9%	8.5%	8.1%
7, 7, 7, 6	13.9%	12.2%	11.0%	10.2%	9.5%	8.9%	8.4%	8.1%
7, 7, 6, 5	13.5%	11.8%	10.6%	9.7%	9.0%	8.5%	8.0%	7.7%
7, 6, 5, 5	13.0%	11.3%	10.1%	9.3%	8.6%	8.1%	7.6%	7.3%

Table 9.6. Expected return – using our spreadsheet – given growth rates (of earnings) and current P/E ratio. The assumed payout ratio is **70 percent**. The current P/E ratio is based on earnings in the last six months plus estimated earnings in the next six months. The four growth rates in each line are for Years 1-5, Years 6-10, Years 11-20, and Years 21-30 respectively. In the spreadsheet, the growth rate for Years 31+ is kept at 3 percent.

Growth rates – earnings	Expected return (**assumed payout ratio of 75 percent**) Current P/E ratio							
	10.0	12.5	15.0	17.5	20.0	22.5	25.0	27.5
12, 12, 10, 8	18.8%	16.7%	15.2%	14.1%	13.2%	12.5%	11.9%	11.4%
12, 11, 9, 8	18.2%	16.1%	14.7%	13.6%	12.7%	12.0%	11.4%	10.9%
12, 10, 9, 7	17.9%	15.8%	14.3%	13.2%	12.3%	11.6%	11.0%	10.5%
12, 10, 8, 6	17.5%	15.4%	13.9%	12.8%	11.9%	11.2%	10.6%	10.1%
12, 9, 7, 6	16.9%	14.8%	13.4%	12.3%	11.4%	10.7%	10.1%	9.6%
11, 11, 10, 8	18.1%	16.1%	14.7%	**13.6%**	**12.7%**	12.0%	11.5%	11.0%
11, 11, 9, 7	17.7%	15.7%	14.2%	13.1%	12.3%	11.6%	11.0%	10.5%
11, 11, 8, 6	17.3%	15.3%	13.8%	12.7%	11.8%	11.1%	10.6%	10.1%
11, 9, 8, 7	16.9%	14.9%	13.5%	12.4%	11.6%	10.9%	10.3%	9.9%
10, 10, 9, 8	17.2%	15.2%	13.8%	12.8%	12.0%	11.3%	10.8%	10.3%
10, 10, 8, 7	16.8%	14.8%	13.4%	12.4%	11.5%	10.9%	10.3%	9.8%
10, 9, 8, 6	16.4%	14.4%	13.0%	12.0%	11.2%	10.5%	10.0%	9.5%
10, 9, 7, 7	16.3%	14.3%	12.9%	11.9%	11.1%	10.4%	9.9%	9.4%
10, 8, 7, 6	15.9%	13.9%	12.5%	11.5%	10.7%	10.1%	9.5%	9.1%
9, 9, 9, 8	16.6%	14.7%	13.3%	12.3%	11.5%	10.9%	10.4%	9.9%
9, 9, 8, 7	16.2%	14.2%	12.9%	11.9%	11.1%	10.5%	9.9%	9.5%
9, 8, 8, 6	15.8%	13.9%	12.5%	11.5%	10.7%	10.1%	9.6%	9.1%
9, 8, 7, 5	15.4%	13.5%	12.1%	11.1%	10.3%	9.7%	9.1%	8.7%
9, 7, 7, 6	15.3%	13.4%	12.0%	11.0%	10.3%	9.6%	9.1%	8.7%
9, 7, 6, 5	14.9%	12.9%	11.6%	10.6%	9.8%	9.2%	8.7%	8.3%
8, 8, 8, 7	15.5%	13.7%	12.4%	11.4%	10.7%	10.0%	9.5%	9.1%
8, 8, 7, 6	15.1%	13.3%	12.0%	11.0%	10.2%	9.6%	9.1%	8.7%
8, 7, 7, 5	14.8%	12.9%	11.6%	10.6%	9.9%	9.3%	8.8%	8.4%
7, 7, 7, 6	14.5%	12.7%	11.5%	10.5%	9.8%	9.2%	8.7%	8.3%
7, 7, 6, 5	14.1%	12.3%	11.0%	10.1%	9.4%	8.8%	8.3%	7.9%
7, 6, 5, 5	13.6%	11.8%	10.6%	9.6%	8.9%	8.4%	7.9%	7.5%

Table 9.7. Expected return – using our spreadsheet – given growth rates (of earnings) and current P/E ratio. The assumed payout ratio is **75 percent**. The current P/E ratio is based on earnings in the last six months plus estimated earnings in the next six months. The four growth rates in each line are for Years 1-5, Years 6-10, Years 11-20, and Years 21-30 respectively. In the spreadsheet, the growth rate for Years 31+ is kept at 3 percent.

Expected return (**assumed payout ratio of 80 percent**)							
Growth rates	Current P/E ratio						
– earnings	10.0	12.5	15.0	17.5	20.0	22.5	25.0	27.5
12, 12, 10, 8	19.4%	17.2%	15.7%	14.5%	13.6%	12.9%	12.2%	11.7%
12, 11, 9, 8	18.9%	16.7%	15.2%	14.0%	13.1%	12.4%	11.8%	11.2%
12, 10, 9, 7	18.5%	16.3%	14.8%	13.6%	12.7%	12.0%	11.4%	10.9%
12, 10, 8, 6	18.2%	15.9%	14.4%	13.2%	12.3%	11.6%	10.9%	10.4%
12, 9, 7, 6	17.6%	15.4%	13.9%	12.7%	11.8%	11.1%	10.5%	10.0%
11, 11, 10, 8	18.8%	16.6%	15.1%	14.0%	13.1%	12.4%	11.8%	11.3%
11, 11, 9, 7	18.4%	16.2%	14.7%	13.6%	12.7%	12.0%	11.4%	10.8%
11, 11, 8, 6	18.0%	15.8%	14.3%	13.2%	12.2%	11.5%	10.9%	10.4%
11, 9, 8, 7	17.6%	15.4%	14.0%	12.8%	12.0%	11.3%	10.7%	10.2%
10, 10, 9, 8	17.8%	15.8%	14.3%	13.2%	12.4%	11.7%	11.1%	10.6%
10, 10, 8, 7	17.4%	15.4%	13.9%	12.8%	11.9%	11.2%	10.7%	10.2%
10, 9, 8, 6	17.1%	15.0%	13.5%	12.4%	11.6%	10.9%	10.3%	9.8%
10, 9, 7, 7	16.9%	14.8%	13.4%	12.3%	11.4%	10.8%	10.2%	9.7%
10, 8, 7, 6	16.5%	14.5%	13.0%	11.9%	11.1%	10.4%	9.8%	9.4%
9, 9, 9, 8	17.2%	15.2%	13.8%	12.7%	11.9%	11.2%	10.7%	10.2%
9, 9, 8, 7	16.8%	14.8%	13.4%	12.3%	11.5%	10.8%	10.2%	9.8%
9, 8, 8, 6	16.4%	14.4%	13.0%	11.9%	11.1%	10.4%	9.9%	9.4%
9, 8, 7, 5	16.0%	14.0%	12.6%	11.5%	10.7%	10.0%	9.5%	9.0%
9, 7, 7, 6	15.9%	13.9%	12.5%	11.4%	10.6%	10.0%	9.4%	9.0%
9, 7, 6, 5	15.5%	13.5%	12.1%	11.0%	10.2%	9.5%	9.0%	8.6%
8, 8, 8, 7	16.1%	14.2%	12.8%	11.8%	11.0%	10.4%	9.8%	9.4%
8, 8, 7, 6	15.8%	13.8%	12.4%	11.4%	10.6%	9.9%	9.4%	9.0%
8, 7, 7, 5	15.4%	13.4%	12.0%	11.0%	10.2%	9.6%	9.1%	8.6%
7, 7, 7, 6	15.1%	13.2%	11.9%	10.9%	10.2%	9.5%	9.0%	8.6%
7, 7, 6, 5	14.7%	12.8%	11.5%	10.5%	9.7%	9.1%	8.6%	8.2%
7, 6, 5, 5	14.2%	12.3%	11.0%	10.0%	9.3%	8.7%	8.2%	7.8%

Table 9.8. Expected return – using our spreadsheet – given growth rates (of earnings) and current P/E ratio. The assumed payout ratio is **80 percent**. The current P/E ratio is based on earnings in the last six months plus estimated earnings in the next six months. The four growth rates in each line are for Years 1-5, Years 6-10, Years 11-20, and Years 21-30 respectively. In the spreadsheet, the growth rate for Years 31+ is kept at 3 percent.

Expected return (**assumed payout ratio of 85 percent**)							
Growth rates	Current P/E ratio						
– earnings	10.0	12.5	15.0	17.5	20.0	22.5	25.0	27.5
12, 12, 10, 8	20.1%	17.8%	16.2%	15.0%	14.0%	13.2%	12.6%	12.0%
12, 11, 9, 8	19.5%	17.3%	15.7%	14.5%	13.5%	12.7%	12.1%	11.6%
12, 10, 9, 7	19.2%	16.9%	15.3%	14.1%	13.1%	12.4%	11.7%	11.2%
12, 10, 8, 6	18.8%	16.5%	14.9%	13.7%	12.7%	11.9%	11.3%	10.8%
12, 9, 7, 6	18.3%	16.0%	14.3%	13.1%	12.2%	11.4%	10.8%	10.3%
11, 11, 10, 8	19.4%	17.2%	15.6%	14.4%	13.5%	12.8%	12.1%	11.6%
11, 11, 9, 7	19.0%	16.8%	15.2%	14.0%	13.1%	12.3%	11.7%	11.2%
11, 11, 8, 6	18.7%	16.4%	14.8%	13.6%	12.6%	11.9%	11.3%	10.7%
11, 9, 8, 7	18.2%	16.0%	14.4%	13.3%	12.4%	11.6%	11.0%	10.5%
10, 10, 9, 8	18.4%	16.3%	14.8%	13.6%	12.7%	12.0%	11.4%	10.9%
10, 10, 8, 7	18.1%	15.9%	14.4%	13.2%	12.3%	11.6%	11.0%	10.5%
10, 9, 8, 6	17.7%	15.5%	14.0%	12.8%	11.9%	11.2%	10.6%	10.1%
10, 9, 7, 7	17.5%	15.4%	13.8%	12.7%	11.8%	11.1%	10.5%	10.0%
10, 8, 7, 6	17.2%	15.0%	13.5%	12.3%	11.5%	10.7%	10.2%	9.7%
9, 9, 9, 8	17.8%	15.7%	14.2%	13.1%	12.3%	11.6%	11.0%	10.5%
9, 9, 8, 7	17.4%	15.3%	13.8%	12.7%	11.8%	11.1%	10.6%	10.1%
9, 8, 8, 6	17.0%	14.9%	13.4%	12.3%	11.5%	10.8%	10.2%	9.7%
9, 8, 7, 5	16.7%	14.5%	13.0%	11.9%	11.0%	10.3%	9.8%	9.3%
9, 7, 7, 6	16.5%	14.4%	12.9%	11.8%	11.0%	10.3%	9.7%	9.3%
9, 7, 6, 5	16.1%	14.0%	12.5%	11.4%	10.6%	9.9%	9.3%	8.9%
8, 8, 8, 7	16.7%	14.7%	13.3%	12.2%	11.4%	10.7%	10.1%	9.7%
8, 8, 7, 6	16.4%	14.3%	12.8%	11.8%	10.9%	10.3%	9.7%	9.2%
8, 7, 7, 5	16.0%	13.9%	12.5%	11.4%	10.6%	9.9%	9.4%	8.9%
7, 7, 7, 6	15.7%	13.7%	12.3%	11.3%	10.5%	9.8%	9.3%	8.9%
7, 7, 6, 5	15.3%	13.3%	11.9%	10.9%	10.1%	9.4%	8.9%	8.5%
7, 6, 5, 5	14.8%	12.8%	11.4%	10.4%	9.6%	9.0%	8.5%	8.0%

Table 9.9. Expected return – using our spreadsheet – given growth rates (of earnings) and current P/E ratio. The assumed payout ratio is **85 percent**. The current P/E ratio is based on earnings in the last six months plus estimated earnings in the next six months. The four growth rates in each line are for Years 1-5, Years 6-10, Years 11-20, and Years 21-30 respectively. In the spreadsheet, the growth rate for Years 31+ is kept at 3 percent.

	Expected return (**assumed payout ratio of 90 percent**)							
Growth rates	Current P/E ratio							
– earnings	10.0	12.5	15.0	17.5	20.0	22.5	25.0	27.5
12, 12, 10, 8	20.7%	18.4%	16.7%	15.4%	14.4%	13.6%	12.9%	12.4%
12, 11, 9, 8	20.2%	17.8%	16.1%	14.9%	13.9%	13.1%	12.4%	11.9%
12, 10, 9, 7	19.8%	17.4%	15.8%	14.5%	13.5%	12.7%	12.1%	11.5%
12, 10, 8, 6	19.5%	17.1%	15.4%	14.1%	13.1%	12.3%	11.6%	11.1%
12, 9, 7, 6	19.0%	16.5%	14.8%	13.6%	12.6%	11.8%	11.1%	10.6%
11, 11, 10, 8	20.0%	17.7%	16.1%	14.9%	13.9%	13.1%	12.5%	11.9%
11, 11, 9, 7	19.7%	17.3%	15.7%	14.4%	13.5%	12.7%	12.0%	11.5%
11, 11, 8, 6	19.3%	16.9%	15.3%	14.0%	13.0%	12.2%	11.6%	11.0%
11, 9, 8, 7	18.9%	16.5%	14.9%	13.7%	12.7%	12.0%	11.3%	10.8%
10, 10, 9, 8	19.1%	16.8%	15.2%	14.0%	13.1%	12.4%	11.7%	11.2%
10, 10, 8, 7	18.7%	16.4%	14.8%	13.6%	12.7%	11.9%	11.3%	10.8%
10, 9, 8, 6	18.3%	16.0%	14.4%	13.2%	12.3%	11.6%	10.9%	10.4%
10, 9, 7, 7	18.2%	15.9%	14.3%	13.1%	12.2%	11.4%	10.8%	10.3%
10, 8, 7, 6	17.8%	15.5%	13.9%	12.7%	11.8%	11.1%	10.5%	10.0%
9, 9, 9, 8	18.4%	16.2%	14.7%	13.5%	12.6%	11.9%	11.3%	10.8%
9, 9, 8, 7	18.0%	15.8%	14.2%	13.1%	12.2%	11.5%	10.9%	10.4%
9, 8, 8, 6	17.6%	15.4%	13.9%	12.7%	11.8%	11.1%	10.5%	10.0%
9, 8, 7, 5	17.3%	15.0%	13.5%	12.3%	11.4%	10.7%	10.1%	9.6%
9, 7, 7, 6	17.1%	14.9%	13.4%	12.2%	11.3%	10.6%	10.0%	9.6%
9, 7, 6, 5	16.8%	14.5%	12.9%	11.8%	10.9%	10.2%	9.6%	9.1%
8, 8, 8, 7	17.3%	15.2%	13.7%	12.6%	11.7%	11.0%	10.4%	10.0%
8, 8, 7, 6	17.0%	14.8%	13.3%	12.2%	11.3%	10.6%	10.0%	9.5%
8, 7, 7, 5	16.6%	14.4%	12.9%	11.8%	10.9%	10.2%	9.7%	9.2%
7, 7, 7, 6	16.3%	14.2%	12.7%	11.7%	10.8%	10.2%	9.6%	9.1%
7, 7, 6, 5	15.9%	13.8%	12.3%	11.2%	10.4%	9.7%	9.2%	8.7%
7, 6, 5, 5	15.4%	13.3%	11.8%	10.7%	9.9%	9.3%	8.7%	8.3%

Table 9.10. Expected return – using our spreadsheet – given growth rates (of earnings) and current P/E ratio. The assumed payout ratio is **90 percent**. The current P/E ratio is based on earnings in the last six months plus estimated earnings in the next six months. The four growth rates in each line are for Years 1-5, Years 6-10, Years 11-20, and Years 21-30 respectively. In the spreadsheet, the growth rate for Years 31+ is kept at 3 percent.

For growth rates, we are most constrained. If our stock's growth rates do not match one of the possibilities in the tables, we have to find the row that most resembles ours, compare expected returns, and make a reasonable adjustment. This is naturally imprecise. For instance, suppose our stock's assumed payout ratio is 70 percent. We have to use Table 9.6. Suppose current P/E ratio is 15.0; and growth rates are 10, 10, 9, and 7. This row is not present in the table. The most appropriate comparison is the row with growth rates of 10, 10, 9, and 8 – this combination matches in the first three growth rates (the more important ones) and differs by just one percentage point in the fourth (the less important one). Expected return for this row is 13.4 percent. As our stock's last growth rate, 7 percent, is lower than this row's 8 percent, we expect a lower expected return. Looking at how expected returns change in the surrounding rows, we expect expected return to be lower by a tenth or two of a percentage point, so 13.3 percent or 13.2 percent. The exact expected return from the spreadsheet is 13.22 percent.

A Formulaic Shortcut[10]

"Another such victory over the Romans, and we are undone." Pyrrhus

Using the tables in the previous section, Figure 9.9 plots expected return versus current P/E ratio for a variety of assumed payout ratios and a sample earnings growth rate combination. The playground-slide curves show every sign that they are well-behaved (in a mathematical sense). Moreover, they show a smooth transition as the assumed payout ratio changes. Because of these characteristics, we use a bit of mathematical magic – more precisely two rounds of function-fitting algorithms – on the tables in the previous section to derive the following ***generic formula for the expected return***:

$$(ar + b) * p^3 + (cr + d) * p^2 + (er + f) * p + (gr + h)$$

Here a, …, h are parameters from Tables 9.11 and 9.12. In these tables, the rows correspond to the twenty-six growth rate combinations from the

---

[10] This section is excessively mathematical. If you understand how to use the spreadsheet, you may skip this section.

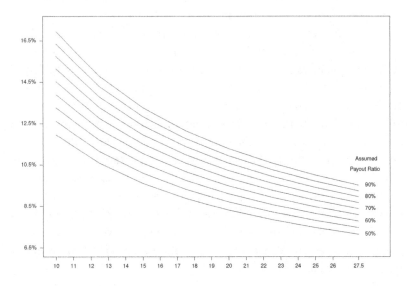

Figure 9.9. Expected return versus current P/E ratio for a variety of assumed payout ratios and a sample earnings growth rate combination, here, 8 percent for Years 1-5, 8 percent for Years 6-10, 7 percent for Years 11-20, and 6 percent for Years 21-30. Years 31+ remains at 3 percent. The curves are similar and, not unexpectedly, show every sign that they are well-behaved (in a mathematical sense). Moreover, they show a smooth transition as the assumed payout ratio changes.

tables in the previous section. Once you have a growth rate combination, look up the parameters in the tables and substitute these into the formula. You will then have an expression in *r*, the assumed payout ratio, and, *p*, the current P/E ratio. Given an *r* and a *p*, the formula calculates the expected return as a percent. Thus, a result of 11 from the formula means the expected return is 11 percent.

Importantly, this formula applies not just to the specific values of assumed payout ratio and current P/E ratio from the tables in the previous section, but to a much broader range, *namely, assumed payout ratios between 50 percent and 90 percent and current P/E ratios between 10.0 and 27.5.* This should cover the vast majority of dividend

Growth rates	Parameters - I			
– earnings	a	b	c	d
12, 12, 10, 8	-0.001089	-0.0001708	0.08030	0.01438
12, 11, 9, 8	-0.001120	-0.0001567	0.08253	0.01325
12, 10, 9, 7	-0.001125	-0.0001583	0.08299	0.01330
12, 10, 8, 6	-0.001142	-0.0001678	0.08447	0.01382
12, 9, 7, 6	-0.001176	-0.0001528	0.08705	0.01256
11, 11, 10, 8	-0.001069	-0.0001583	0.07870	0.01343
11, 11, 9, 7	-0.001088	-0.0001646	0.08032	0.01375
11, 11, 8, 6	-0.001105	-0.0001734	0.08180	0.01423
11, 9, 8, 7	-0.001129	-0.0001393	0.08327	0.01175
10, 10, 9, 8	-0.001070	-0.0001406	0.07875	0.01202
10, 10, 8, 7	-0.001092	-0.0001455	0.08059	0.01221
10, 9, 8, 6	**-0.001098**	**-0.0001473**	**0.08110**	**0.01225**
10, 9, 7, 7	-0.001126	-0.0001293	0.08303	0.01089
10, 8, 7, 6	-0.001132	-0.0001307	0.08366	0.01087
9, 9, 9, 8	-0.001047	-0.0001291	0.07698	0.01113
9, 9, 8, 7	**-0.001071**	**-0.0001323**	**0.07896**	**0.01119**
9, 8, 8, 6	-0.001078	-0.0001331	0.07959	0.01115
9, 8, 7, 5	-0.001100	-0.0001394	0.08150	0.01138
9, 7, 7, 6	-0.001113	-0.0001154	0.08214	0.00970
9, 7, 6, 5	-0.001137	-0.0001215	0.08426	0.00986
8, 8, 8, 7	-0.001050	-0.0001193	0.07728	0.01021
8, 8, 7, 6	-0.001075	-0.0001222	0.07942	0.01020
8, 7, 7, 5	-0.001083	-0.0001234	0.08010	0.01014
7, 7, 7, 6	-0.001054	-0.0001081	0.07780	0.009113
7, 7, 6, 5	-0.001082	-0.0001107	0.08017	0.009011
7, 6, 5, 5	-0.001122	-0.00008898	0.08311	0.007212

Table 9.11. The first four parameters – a, b, c, d – of our generic formula for the expected return.

Growth rates	Parameters - II			
– earnings	e	f	g	h
12, 12, 10, 8	-2.154	-0.4868	28.39	11.95
12, 11, 9, 8	-2.211	-0.4498	28.74	11.17
12, 10, 9, 7	-2.229	-0.4450	28.89	10.73
12, 10, 8, 6	-2.280	-0.4462	29.49	10.17
12, 9, 7, 6	-2.348	-0.4035	29.91	9.347
11, 11, 10, 8	-2.108	-0.4588	27.64	11.43
11, 11, 9, 7	-2.161	-0.4567	28.22	10.85
11, 11, 8, 6	-2.212	-0.4571	28.81	10.29
11, 9, 8, 7	-2.233	-0.3943	28.53	9.726
10, 10, 9, 8	-2.106	-0.4126	27.24	10.46
10, 10, 8, 7	-2.165	-0.4063	27.86	9.851
10, 9, 8, 6	**-2.184**	**-0.3997**	**28.02**	**9.406**
10, 9, 7, 7	-2.227	-0.3631	28.21	9.046
10, 8, 7, 6	-2.250	-0.3543	28.39	8.586
9, 9, 9, 8	-2.056	-0.3860	26.45	9.973
9, 9, 8, 7	**-2.117**	**-0.3760**	**27.07**	**9.344**
9, 8, 8, 6	-2.140	-0.3670	27.25	8.886
9, 8, 7, 5	-2.203	-0.3583	27.89	8.260
9, 7, 7, 6	-2.205	-0.3199	27.60	8.070
9, 7, 6, 5	-2.274	-0.3080	28.28	7.420
8, 8, 8, 7	-2.068	-0.3467	26.27	8.858
8, 8, 7, 6	-2.135	-0.3330	26.92	8.205
8, 7, 7, 5	-2.161	-0.3217	27.11	7.733
7, 7, 7, 6	-2.088	-0.3008	26.12	7.718
7, 7, 6, 5	-2.161	-0.2824	26.80	7.036
7, 6, 5, 5	-2.235	-0.2258	27.17	6.190

Table 9.12. The next four parameters – e, f, g, h – of our generic formula for the expected return.

growth stocks, at least under normal times. You can likely use this formula *slightly* beyond these ranges but, since I used data *within* the tables to derive the formula, just to be careful, I would not go too far.

The formula produces results close to the exact answers from the spreadsheet – but they do not always match. Partly this is in the nature of the algorithms and partly this is because of the rounding of entries in Tables 9.11 and 9.12. Of the hundred or so cases that I checked, the biggest difference was one-tenth of a percentage point, thus, for instance, 10.4 percent versus an exact answer of 10.5 percent. This is well within our range of tolerance. Figure 9.10 compares expected returns from the formula to expected returns from the spreadsheet for a sample assumed payout ratio and earnings growth rate combination. The expected returns match almost perfectly. The maximum difference is one-tenth of a percentage point.

Here are more details on how to use the formula:

1. As in the previous section, estimate your stock's assumed payout ratio, determine its current P/E ratio, and estimate its earnings growth rates for Years 1-5, Years 6-10, Years 11-20, and Years 21-30.

2. Ideally, the earnings growth rates match one of our twenty-six combinations. If not, see if you can ratchet the earnings growth rates up or down to match one of the twenty-six. If you are unwilling to, or cannot, then you cannot continue.[11]

3. Your stock's assumed payout ratio must be between 50 percent and 90 percent.

4. Your stock's current P/E ratio must be between 10.0 and 27.5.

5. Look up parameters a, …, h in Tables 9.11 and 9.12 and substitute for them in the formula above.

6. Using your stock's assumed payout ratio and current P/E ratio, substitute for r and p, respectively, in the formula above to get

---

[11] That said, you may be able to take an approach similar to that in the previous section of finding the growth rates that most resemble yours, calculating the expected return with the formula, then making a reasonable adjustment.

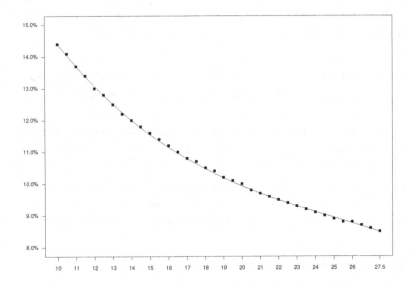

Figure 9.10. Expected return versus current P/E ratio from the formula (the line) and the spreadsheet (the markers) for a sample assumed payout ratio and earnings growth rate combination. The expected returns match almost perfectly. The maximum difference is one-tenth of a percentage point. Here, assumed payout ratio is 60 percent and earnings growth rates are 10 percent for Years 1-5, 9 percent for Years 6-10, 8 percent for Years 11-20, and 6 percent for Years 21-30. Years 31+ remains at 3 percent.

your stock's expected return. Better yet, just substitute for *r*, leave *p* as a variable, and see how your stock's expected return varies by current P/E ratio. For instance, the huge variation in expected returns is clear from Figure 9.10.

Let us now turn to our very own high-quality dividend growth Picasso (Figure 9.11). Consider a *canonical* high-quality dividend growth stock with a return on beginning equity of 25 percent, higher than our required minimum of 20 percent. If we assume a payout ratio of 65 percent, the company can grow at a sustainable rate of about 9 percent a year – we assume the company's markets and competition are such that the

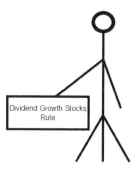

Figure 9.11. Our very own high-quality dividend growth Picasso.

company can actually grow at this rate. To be careful, let us reduce this growth rate for later years. Thus, we assume earnings growth rates of 9 percent for Years 1-5, 9 percent for Years 6-10, 8 percent for Years 11-20, and 7 percent for Years 21-30. We assume the business is stable and we do not reduce these rates further to account for earnings volatility. Years 31+ remains at 3 percent. From the generic formula, and Tables 9.11 and 9.12, with a payout ratio of 65 percent, we get the following formula for our canonical dividend growth stock's expected return in terms of its current P/E ratio, p:[12]

$$-0.000828 * p^3 + 0.0625 * p^2 - 1.75 * p + 26.9$$

For instance, at a current P/E ratio of 17, expected return is 11.1 percent. Figure 9.12 graphs this formula over our range of current P/E ratios, 10.0 to 27.5. In this case, any current P/E ratio of 21 or less leads to an expected return of 10 percent or more. You can work out similar formulas and acceptability of returns for your dividend growth stocks. These expressions are not quite magic formulas but they are useful. Assuming you have growth rates and payout ratio reasonably right, they calculate expected long-term return based on the one factor the market controls, P/E ratio.[13]

---

[12] Be careful when rounding the coefficients of the cubed and squared terms.

[13] The derivative of the last expression tells you how much expected return changes for a small change in P/E ratio. This allows you to understand how *sensitive* expected

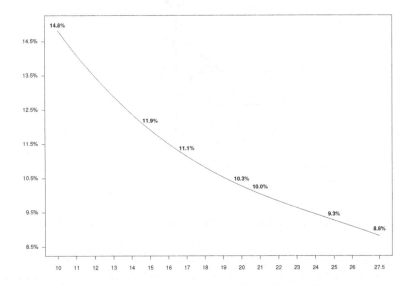

Figure 9.12. Using the formula, expected return versus current P/E ratio for our canonical high-quality dividend growth stock. Return on beginning equity is 25 percent. Assumed payout ratio is 65 percent. Earnings growth rates are 9 percent for Years 1-5, 9 percent for Years 6-10, 8 percent for Years 11-20, and 7 percent for Years 21-30. Years 31+ remains at 3 percent.

Data

"The charm of history and its enigmatic lesson consist in the fact that, from age to age, nothing changes and yet everything is completely different."
Aldous Huxley

Use the following sources for data. The first three are broadly applicable:

Nasdaq, *http://www.nasdaq.com/*, for instance, among various other general-purpose finance websites

---

return is to small changes in P/E ratio. Moreover, for a given payout ratio, this logic applies identically to the generic formula at the start of this section.

SEC EDGAR, *http://goo.gl/1iUiL*

Value Line, *http://www.valueline.com/*

The fourth is company-specific:

Company investor relations websites, *(for example, as of mid-2015, for Johnson & Johnson, http://goo.gl/zY2TK)*

As a dividend growth investor, you will find the following stock-specific pages on Nasdaq useful, as of mid-2015:

- Summary Quote, for stock price, market capitalization, P/E ratios, earnings per share, annualized dividend, dividend yield, headlines, and company description;

- Company Headlines and Press Releases, for company-released news;

- Analyst Research, for forecasted earnings per share and estimated earnings per share growth rates, among many other useful earnings-related data;

- Stock Report, for many key financials;

- "Income Statement," for Income Statement, Balance Sheet, and Cash Flow (Statement) figures for the four most recent years and four most recent quarters;

- "Income Statement," Financial Ratios, for return on equity;

- Dividend History, for dividend history.

Use the SEC's EDGAR database to search for company filings. Read the filings to understand what a company does, learn about its business risks, and access its financial statements. Like shoulder checks, it is always good practice to read a company's SEC EDGAR filings before you invest.

Value Line's *Investment Survey* is indispensable for historical financial data on large companies. As of mid-2015, you will find the following items on each stock's *Investment Survey* page useful for dividend growth investing:

- Header, for stock price, P/E ratio, and dividend yield;

- Business, for a description of the company;

- Earnings per share;

- Dividends declared per share;

- Common shares outstanding;

- Net profit margin;

- Long-term debt;

- Capital structure;

- Return on shareholders' equity;

- All dividends to net profit;

- (Estimated) annual rates of change of earnings per share and dividends (per share).

Investor relations websites are useful for events, presentations, dividend histories, annual reports, and links to SEC EDGAR filings. Some investor relations websites have documents that explain how the business works. ♣ ♣

A Summary: Part II

"Welcome back, Lord Nibbler, Ambassador to Earth, home world of the pizza bagel." (Futurama)

Here are the more important points from this part of the book. First, we list our criteria for picking dividend growth stocks. Next, we list other important points.

Primarily, our criteria revolve around the traits of good long-term businesses with dividends falling out almost naturally from companies of the right maturity and quality and valuation putting the defining mark to the whole story. Here are our criteria for picking dividend growth stocks, categorized by quality, return, risk, and shareholder commitment:

- *Quality*

    - A strong business is the logical starting point.
    - What is the competition? Ask that first of all your long-term investments. You will do your portfolio an immense amount of good when you invest in companies that face stable or falling competition. Avoid investing in companies that face rising competition.
    - Stable modestly growing profits form the basis of dividend growth. Profits should not vary wildly, like a yo-yo, from year to year.

- Stability helps companies survive. Stable companies persist. Large companies generally have an intrinsic advantage here. Diversification aids stability.

- Management must be honest and capable with a track record that proves it. That said, never use management's optimism as the sole basis for investing in a company, especially over the long term.

- Always prefer companies with good to strong net profit margins. Currently, mid-2015, a net profit margin of ten to fifteen percent is good. More than fifteen percent is strong.

- ***The company's long-run return on beginning equity must average twenty percent or more.*** This allows a company to grow at a sensible and sustainable pace yet pay a reasonable share of its earnings as dividends. It signals both maturity and high quality.

- *Return*

  - The company's expected five-year earnings per share growth rate must be 8-12 percent a year for large companies and 8-16 percent a year for midsize companies.

  - Over the long term, with dividend growth stocks, share counts should remain flattish or fall. Companies should not pay everything possible as dividends. Instead, they should compromise with a reasonable dividend plus a reasonable share buyback.

  - Consider a canonical high-quality dividend growth stock with a return on beginning equity of 25 percent, higher than our required minimum of 20 percent. Assume a payout ratio of 65 percent and earnings growth rates of 9 percent for Years 1-5, 9 percent for Years 6-10, 8 percent for Years 11-20, 7 percent for Years 21-30, and 3 percent for Years 31+. For current P/E ratios of 10.0 to 27.5, the formula for expected return in terms of current P/E ratio, p, is:

  $$-0.000828 * p^3 + 0.0625 * p^2 - 1.75 * p + 26.9$$

- *Risk*

    - Know the business risks that your company faces. Most relate to competition.

    - Never invest in a company with business risks so large that they can destroy it.

    - Read the *Risk Factors* section of your company's annual reports.

    - If you are uncomfortable with a company's business risks, punt. There are always other choices.

    - Excess financial leverage exacts a heavy toll. Often, at precisely the wrong time, it shows its dangerous other side.

    - Prefer companies with no more than moderate financial leverage. As a rough guideline, financial leverage less than 2.0 is reasonable. For stable companies, the limit can be higher, (say) 3.0. Financial intermediaries can get away with higher ratios, but not without risk.

- *Shareholder Commitment*

    - The company must pay shareholders their fair share. Shareholders own the business.

    - Payout ratio includes dividends, net share buybacks, and any additional cash that the company can return to shareholders but for whatever reason does not. All else equal, the payout ratio for our dividend growth stocks must average at least fifty percent.

- *Quality, Return, Risk, Shareholder Commitment*

    - ***Value your dividend growth stocks properly.*** Be wary of simple valuations. Simple valuations are often misleading. Do not buy most stocks based solely on dividend yield. Use relative valuation only as a quick and dirty approach to valuation – and only as a start. Use our spreadsheet as a reasonable model to value dividend growth stocks. As alternatives, for a range of special cases, use the tables or the formula. The formula is more broadly applicable than the tables. In general, err toward conservative valuations. They give us a margin of safety. Our model depends on just three factors: assumed payout ratio, growth rates (of earnings), and current P/E ratio.

This completes our criteria. As a side note, here are other important points from this part of the book:

- *Informational*

    - As companies age, they travel along a well-cobbled path. At the dividend growth stage, not only does the company fund itself, but it generates so much extra cash it can afford to pay dividends.
    - When management (and employees) receive more than they are worth, shareholders receive less than they deserve.
    - One of the hallmarks of a properly managed company is conservative accounting.
    - Dividend growth companies sit somewhere in the happy middle between young and mature. They do not grow so quickly that they consume large amounts of cash; they do not grow so slowly that they can return most of their cash to shareholders. What they can do is pay a reasonable and growing dividend.
    - Larger companies typically use dividend payout ratio targets of forty percent to sixty percent.
    - Dividends are not paid out of earnings. Dividends are paid out of cash.
    - Total cash flow is the sum of operating cash flow, investing cash flow, and financing cash flow. The change in cash is this plus a usually tiny contribution from the effect of exchange rates.

- During recessions, as earnings fall and dividend payout ratios rise, investors worry about dividend cuts. Instead, consider the company's operating cash flow.

- Dividend payout ratio provides the link between P/E ratio and dividend yield: P/E ratio equals dividend payout ratio divided by dividend yield. Whenever dividend payout ratio is constant (or reasonably so), P/E ratio and dividend yield are opposing faces of the same coin. When one is high, the other must be low.

- Knowing a company's long-term sustainable growth rate is crucial to long-term investors because it is the most a company can grow without raising net new equity.

- In turn, long-term sustainable growth rate is linked to growth rate of the company's underlying markets and the company's competitive position within those markets.

- Companies grow dividends per share through a combination of growth in dividend payout ratio and growth in earnings per share. A stock's expected one-year dividends per share growth rate equals, roughly, its dividend payout ratio growth rate plus its earnings per share growth rate. Dividend payout ratio cannot keep rising. This limits its long-term influence. The primary factor driving long-term growth in dividends per share is growth in earnings per share. For a dividend growth stock, the earnings per share growth rate range of 8-16 percent a year for a midsize company and 8-12 percent a year for a large company ultimately caps the dividend growth rate. Companies can boost their dividends per share growth rate when they undertake share buybacks to reduce shares outstanding.

- Long-term dividend increases must average far more than inflation.

- Do not discard a stock simply because of a limited or damaged dividend history.

- A strong dividend history does not always suggest a strong dividend growth stock. Pay attention to dividend history but do not be fooled by it. The eight-hundred-pound gorilla in the room is how the business performs in the future.

– Over a short period – a few weeks, a few months, or even a year – prices parade in a game of chance. Short-term returns are random.

– Over a longer period – five years, ten years, or even more – returns reflect the underlying business. The market noise averages out.

– Valuation models are of two primary types: (1) relative valuation models, where we compare our stock to something else; and (2) absolute valuation models, where we value our stock directly.

– P/E models do not account for growth and dividends.

– PEG models account for growth.

– PEYG models account for growth and dividends.

– In general, use PEG and PEYG models as heuristics only.

– Be wary of P/S models.

– Relative valuation only tells you that your stock is relatively overvalued or relatively undervalued.

***

This concludes the second part of the book. For long-term investors, the traits of the underlying business hold the key. We saw why a strong return on equity matters. We studied the link between return on beginning equity, (sustainable) growth rates, and dividends. We understood the importance of the payout ratio. We created a spreadsheet to value our dividend growth stocks. For a range of special cases, we created tables and a formula. Our model depends on three factors: assumed payout ratio, growth rates (of earnings), and current P/E ratio. We summarized our criteria for picking dividend growth stocks.

In the third and final part of the book, we learn how to search for dividend growth stocks; we study a sample of twenty dividend growth stocks, including valuing them based on what we have learned so far; we look at a few dividend growth mutual funds and ETFs; and we close with a discussion of portfolios and other odds and ends. ♣ ♣ ♣

Part III

Picks

"A good example is far better than a good precept."

Dwight Moody

CHAPTER 10

The Search is On

"Ponder and deliberate before you make a move." Sun-tzu

Today, the information spigot is always on. With such a deluge, you might expect the search for dividend growth stocks to be easy. It isn't. As with an excess of anything, much of the trumpeted value is noise. Besides, almost everyone focuses on the short term. The long-term investor finds little of value here.

The pundits muse: What will Intel's earnings per share be tomorrow? Why did analyst so-and-so cut Intel's earnings per share estimate one cent? Unless Intel is egregiously overvalued or the questions have longer-term implications, the value of questions such as these to long-term investors is nil. Business fluctuates. For a good company, most fluctuations are blips. More relevant: What can Intel do to offset the decline in its PC business? How will Intel address new markets? What is Intel's long-term growth rate? These questions have a bearing on Intel's long-term return. What Intel earns tomorrow rarely does.

So when you search for your long-term investment ideas, read, watch, and listen – but focus on those who ask the right questions. Prefer long-term insight and careful analysis. Tune out the noise.

Wal-Mart

Johnson & Johnson

Coca-Cola

PepsiCo

QUALCOMM

Exxon Mobil

CVS Health

IBM

3M

United Technologies

Table 10.1. Top ten stocks in VDAIX as of 31 December 2014.

Holdings of Mutual Funds, ETFs, and Indexes

"The majority of those who put together collections of verses or epigrams resemble those who eat cherries or oysters; they begin by choosing the best and end by eating everything." Chamfort

Holdings of mutual funds and ETFs (exchange-traded funds) afford us a wealth of investment ideas. The experts do the first phase of the hard work for us. We then winnow down their selections to a manageable few. (Of course, if we like enough of their selections, and do not mind the expenses, we simply buy the mutual fund or ETF.)

Two caveats:

- Only consider mutual funds and ETFs with good long-term records.

- Only consider mutual funds and ETFs with low turnover. Low turnover is twenty percent or less. With high turnover, what is a brilliant new idea one month somehow becomes a pariah the next.

Johnson & Johnson

Roper

United Technologies

Medtronic

Praxair

Air Products and Chemicals

Pentair

Bunge

Honeywell

Archer-Daniels-Midland

Table 10.2. Top ten stocks in FRDPX as of 31 December 2014.

Vanguard's Dividend Appreciation Index Fund Investor Shares, VDAIX, a mutual fund – or its ETF clone, Vanguard Dividend Appreciation ETF, VIG – is an excellent source of dividend growth investment ideas. In its May 2015 prospectus, Vanguard describes VDAIX's investment approach as follows:

> The Fund employs an indexing investment approach designed to track the performance of the NASDAQ US Dividend Achievers Select Index, which consists of common stocks of companies that have a record of increasing dividends over time. The Fund attempts to replicate the target index by investing all, or substantially all, of its assets in the stocks that make up the Index, holding each stock in approximately the same proportion as its weighting in the Index.

Table 10.1 lists the top ten stocks in VDAIX as of 31 December 2014.

Another good source of dividend growth investment ideas is Franklin Rising Dividends Fund (Class A Shares), FRDPX. Although this fund has a front-end load and a 12b-1 charge, turnover is extremely low and it has fared well over time. In its February 2015 prospectus, Franklin Templeton, the fund's parent, describes FRDPX's investment approach as follows:

> Under normal market conditions, the Fund invests at least 80% of its net assets in investments of companies that have paid consistently rising dividends. The Fund invests predominantly in equity securities, primarily common stock. Companies that have paid consistently rising dividends include those companies that currently pay dividends on their common stocks and have maintained or increased their dividend rate during the last four consecutive years.

Table 10.2 lists the top ten stocks in FRDPX as of 31 December 2014.

Moving to indexes, the S&P 500[®] Dividend Aristocrats[®] index and the NASDAQ US Dividend Achievers[TM] Select Index – mentioned by Vanguard above – offer a rich vein of dividend growth investment ideas.

Always take a look at stocks common to high-quality investment vehicles, say, for example, for us, a VDAIX and an FRDPX. Although this method naturally favors large-caps, the presence of a stock in more than one vehicle proves it has passed more than one battery of tests. Success likes company. Table 10.3 lists the stocks common to VDAIX and FRDPX as of 31 December 2014.

Screens

"I knew I should've checked your showboating Globetrotter algebra." Professor Farnsworth (Futurama)

Stock screeners provide another approach – but one that requires more effort – to find dividend growth stocks. Stock screeners are not foolproof. They are not comprehensive. The data have errors. You will often overlook good opportunities. Nevertheless, they help establish a starting point.

Abbott	John Wiley & Sons
ABM Industries	Johnson & Johnson
Aflac	Matthews
Air Products and Chemicals	McCormick
Albermale	Medtronic
Archer-Daniels-Midland	Nike
Becton Dickinson	Nucor
Bemis	Occidental Petroleum
Brady	Pentair
Bunge	PepsiCo
Carlisle	Praxair
Chubb	QUALCOMM
Cintas	RLI
Colgate-Palmolive	Roper
CVS Health	Ross Stores
Donaldson Company	Stryker
Dover	Target
Ecolab	Texas Instruments
EOG Resources	United Technologies
Exxon Mobil	Walgreens Boots Alliance
General Dynamics	Wal-Mart
Grainger (W. W.)	West Pharmaceutical Services
IBM	

Table 10.3. Stocks common to VDAIX and FRDPX as of 31 December 2014.

In a happy world for dividend growth stocks, stock screeners have the following screening variables:

- Quality

    - Return on Beginning Equity (most recent year, or, ideally, a longer-term average, such as a five- or ten-year average)

    - Return on Equity (most recent year, or, ideally, a longer-term average, such as a five- or ten-year average)

- Return

    - Expected EPS Growth Rate (current, or, ideally, a five-year average)

    - Historical EPS Growth Rate (a longer-term average, such as a five- or ten-year average)

- Risk

    - Market Capitalization

    - Financial Leverage

    - Beta

- Shareholder Commitment

    - Dividend Payout Ratio, or, even better, Net Payout Ratio.

Some investors include quasi-valuation variables such as P/E ratio and dividend yield as screening variables. I prefer to keep screening distinct from valuation. That way, if I like a business but the stock is expensive, I have at least found a good company and can keep an eye on it. You may disagree with this approach. If so, include P/E ratio and dividend yield in your screens. Note that because dividend payout ratio, P/E ratio, and dividend yield are linked, as we saw in Chapter 8, you do not need to include all three variables in your screen – knowing two tells you the other.

Variables	Categories - Preferences	Criteria
Quality: Return on Beginning Equity		
Most Recent Year	(1 - C)	>= 20%
Longer-Term Average	(1 - A)	>= 20%
Quality: Return on Equity		
Most Recent Year	(1 - D)	>= 20%
Longer-Term Average	(1 - B)	>= 20%
Return: EPS Growth Rate		
Expected, Current	(3 - C)	>= 8%
Expected, Five-Year Average	(3 - A)	>= 8%
Historical, Longer-Term Average	(3 - B)	>= 8%
Risk:		
Market Capitalization	(5)	>= 2.0 Billion
Financial Leverage	(4)	<= 3.0
Beta	(6)	<= 0.9, positive
Shareholder Commitment:		
Dividend Payout Ratio	(2 - B)	>= 20%
Net Payout Ratio	(2 - A)	>= 40%

Table 10.4. Dividend growth screening variables, categories - preferences, and criteria. In general, return on equity does not equal return on beginning equity. Thus, strictly speaking, criteria for return on equity should differ from criteria for return on beginning equity. But for a screen, this difference is not crucial.

We have covered these variables before, except for beta. Beta is a variable from Modern Portfolio Theory. It has multiple interpretations. One is that it gauges the risk of a stock relative to the market by how much the stock moves in relation to the market. A stock's beta can be negative, zero, or positive. Most stocks have positive betas. A beta of 0.6 means the stock has historically moved, and, by extension, is expected to move sixty percent of what the market moves. For instance, if the market moves ten percent, the stock has historically moved, and is expected to move, six percent – in this sense, beta is a measure of a stock's "springiness." The market has a beta of 1.0. Most large-cap dividend growth stocks probably have betas between 0.5 and 0.8, give or take 0.1 – and dependent on market conditions. This reflects their superior business stability – thus lower risk – relative to the market. Do not treat this range as sacrosanct – betas change over time. In recent years, beta has come under attack. Many believe it to be too simplistic.

I use market capitalization as an indicator of risk because, all else equal, the larger the stock the lower the risk. If your screener does not have dividend payout ratio, you need to include dividend yield as a screening variable, if for no other reason, than to get stocks that pay dividends.

Consider including additional *descriptive* variables in your screen. For instance, you may want to exclude non-U.S. stocks, REITs, and MLPs. Also, you may want to restrict your selections to stocks with share prices above a minimum price, say $25. Do not add variables that overlap existing variables. Likewise, do not add so many variables that the screen results in few or no stocks. A good guideline is to have at most ten variables. Start with ours, then add yours.

In our list, some variables are preferred. Others are alternatives. Use an alternative if the screener does not provide the preferred variable. See Table 10.4. From the table, enter one variable each from categories 1-6. Within each category, when multiple options are available, A is best, B is second, C is third, and D is fourth. If the screener has A, use it. If A is unavailable, use B, and so on. If using all categories results in too few stocks, remove the variables in reverse categorical order. That is, remove category 6 first and see if you get enough stocks. If not, remove category 5, and so on. Do not remove more than three categories. Instead, relax the criteria. For the longer-term averages, a ten-year average is ideal followed by a five-year average. In the table, I use 2.0 Billion to select midcaps and larger, appropriate as of mid-2015. In later years, you will need to adjust this value as ranges of market capitalization bubble up over time. The criteria are generous by design so that we do not overlook good opportunities. Tighten them if you get too many results. A well-designed screen in a normal market should result in (say) thirty to sixty stocks as initial dividend growth candidates – if so, the porridge is probably just right. If you get hundreds, the porridge is too hot. If you get ten, that too is (usually) a problem – the porridge is too cold.

Of the free stock screeners available on the web as of mid-2015, Finviz (a favorite) and Google Finance provide two of the more capable ones. They are easy to use and offer most of the variables we need (Table 10.5). Finviz is unusual in that it offers only predefined ranges. That is, you cannot enter the precise values of Table 10.4. Instead, you have to choose an appropriate range – though even this may not be sufficient for some variables, where the ranges we need are not available. Just choose a more generous range and sort your results to narrow your choices further. For instance, the Finviz variable "EPS growth next 5 years" includes ranges of "over 5 percent" and "over 10 percent." We cannot enter our criterion of at least 8 percent. To overcome this restriction, choose "over 5 percent" and sort your results by "EPS growth next 5 years." You will now readily see the subset of results with growth rates of at least 8 percent. Ignore the rest.

You can access the Finviz and Google Finance stock screeners at the following web addresses:

- Finviz: *http://goo.gl/c9UnZ*

- Google Finance: *http://goo.gl/30YZ2*

Value Line, which you should be able to access through your local library, also has a good stock screener. Use the following Value Line variables and criteria:

- Quality

| | Stock Screeners | |
Variables	Finviz	Google Finance
Quality: Return on Beginning Equity		
Most Recent Year	no	*
Longer-Term Average	no	*
Quality: Return on Equity:		
Most Recent Year	yes (trailing 12 months)	*
Longer-Term Average	no	*
Return: EPS Growth Rate		
Expected, Current	yes	no
Expected, Five-Year Average	yes	no
Historical, Longer-Term Average	yes (5-year)	yes (5- and 10-year)
Risk:		
Market Capitalization	yes	yes
Financial Leverage**	yes	yes
Beta	yes	yes
Shareholder Commitment:		
Dividend Payout Ratio	yes	no
Net Payout Ratio	no	no

Table 10.5. Availability of variables for the Finviz and Google Finance stock screeners, as of mid-2015. *No return on beginning equity or return on equity; instead, return on *average* equity, for the most recent year and a 5-year average, which you may use instead. In general, these returns do not match; for a screen, this difference is not crucial. **Not financial leverage as such, but a related variable, total debt divided by equity, instead. (Finviz calls this Debt/Equity and Google Finance calls it Total Debt/Equity.) Financial leverage = total debt divided by equity + 1. Thus, our financial leverage criterion of <= 3.0 becomes <= 2.0 when applied to total debt divided by equity. Because Google Finance does not have dividend payout ratio, you need to include dividend yield to get stocks that pay dividends. Just set dividend yield greater than 0 percent.

– Return on Shareholders' Equity. Set 20 percent as the minimum.

- Return

  – Proj EPS Growth Rate. Set 8 percent as the minimum.

- Risk

  – Market Capitalization: Use "Market Cap \$ (Mil)." Set 2000 as the minimum. This selects midcaps and larger, appropriate as of mid-2015. In later years, you will need to adjust this value as ranges of market capitalization bubble up over time.
  – Select Financial Strength of A++, A+, A.
  – Beta: Set 0 as the minimum and 0.9 as the maximum.

- Shareholder Commitment

  – Dividend Payout Ratio: Use "% All Divs/Net Inc Trail 12 Mo." Set 20 percent as the minimum.

Value Line also regularly screens for dividend growth stocks in its *Investment Survey*. Other publications may do the same. Understand the criteria that Value Line and these other publications use.

Once you have a list of candidate stocks from your stock screener, do the following:

1. Exclude those that make you uncomfortable for ethical or other reasons.

2. Exclude those that *clearly* do not meet the numerical criteria listed in the conclusion to Part II (if you do not already use those numerical criteria in your screener).

3. Order your favorite pizza. The next step requires work.

4. Study the remaining businesses, keeping those that meet the criteria listed in the conclusion to Part II, up to, but excluding, the last step, the valuation step.

5. Order another pizza.

6. Complete the valuation step: (1) Collect historical data. (2) Use the spreadsheet model from Chapter 9. (If applicable, instead, use the tables or the formulaic shortcut – though these tell you little about risk.)

7. Write each story up. Include notes about the business, risks, the financial numbers, dividends and share buybacks, and – if you used the spreadsheet – spreadsheet parameters and spreadsheet results. (Alternatively, if you used the tables or formulaic shortcut, include your assumptions and results.) Consider investing in those stocks that, in your opinion, offer a reasonable to good risk-adjusted return.

8. Take a nap. You've earned it.

Next, we pick twenty dividend growth stocks. ♣

CHAPTER 11

Twenty Dividend Growth Stocks to Consider

"Hitch your wagon to a star." Ralph Waldo Emerson

T HIS chapter profiles twenty dividend growth stocks. The entry for each stock consists of an introduction followed by a commentary. The introduction consists of ticker, sector, size, and website.

Ticker and website are what you expect – certainly, here, ticker has nothing to do with cardiology and website is not a club for spiders. Sector refers to one of the market's ten sectors (Table 11.1). Size refers to market capitalization, that is, third time's a charm, share price times number of shares outstanding, grouped as follows:

- Megacap: $200 billion or more in market capitalization.

- Large-cap: between $10 billion and $199.9 billion in market capitalization.

Consumer Discretionary

Consumer Staples

Energy

Financials

Healthcare

Industrials

Information Technology

Materials

Telecommunication Services

Utilities

Table 11.1. Market Sectors. This is one accepted categorization. There are others.

- Midcap: between $2 billion and $9.9 billion in market capitalization.

As our selections are dividend growth stocks by this book's guidelines, none of our selections is smaller than a midcap. The above ranges are not universally accepted. In any case, they will bubble up over time. The large-cap range is wide enough to drive a Hummer through – it is not useful. For dividend growth stocks, as of mid-2015, the sweet *growth* spot is likely between $5 billion and $15 billion.

Each commentary is subdivided into the following sections:

- **The Business** (based on Chapter 6)

- (Business) **Risks** (based on Chapter 6)

- **The Numbers** (based on Chapter 7)

- **Dividends and Share Buybacks** (an obvious general theme of this book, especially with dividends, here based primarily on Chapters 2, 3, and 8)

- **Spreadsheet Parameters** (based on Chapter 9)

- **Sample Spreadsheet Results** (based on Chapter 9)

I list (business) risks separately because they are an important part of the story. Understand the risks before you invest – you never want to be surprised by the unexpected, like running out of milk when you are ready to open a bag of Oreos. Update the spreadsheet parameters as you see fit. As a reminder, the actual dividend never matters in the valuation.

With the exception of current dividend data, which is more recent, the commentaries include data up to the most recently completed fiscal year, or the fiscal year before that, available as of mid-2015. In particular, this means current dividend data is typically out of sync with the rest of the data. It's just a flesh wound. I do not quote exact fiscal dates because they are not that relevant for the typical dividend growth stock, which is stable. I used company websites and SEC filings through EDGAR for data. You may, instead, find virtually all the data in Value Line. Value Line uses slightly different definitions of items such as earnings per share – so make sure to understand the differences, especially if they are large.

I do not adjust share buybacks for debt-related buybacks, if any. Doing so is not easy, especially if the buyback started a long time ago. Just study the data, and trends, of items such as return on equity and leverage to see if anything looks "off." In general, because our dividend growth stocks are stable, we are more interested in averages – and if the averages look reasonable and steady that's good enough.

Regarding averages, the averages here are simple averages, that is, sum divided by number. Moreover, because of how averages work, the product of averages generally does not equal the average of the product. Thus, for instance, multiplying average profit margin by average asset turnover by average financial leverage generally does not equal average return on equity.

Earnings growth rates are not arbitrary. They relate to return on beginning equity and payout ratio. We do consider history – but sustainable growth rate provides a useful gating factor.

Toward the end of each commentary, I include expected return from the spreadsheet and a comment on valuation. Expected return is a long-term compound return. Year-to-year returns will vary. *As always, update expected return if a company's earnings or outlook are well above or well below what you expect.* For the comment on valuation, I comment along a spectrum of *very undervalued to undervalued to fairly valued to overvalued to very overvalued.* These are *rough* indications of return relative to risk. I primarily use the pie chart to gauge risk. You can also gauge a stock's historical risk by checking the volatility of its stock price and the volatility of its earnings per share. For the majority of dividend growth stocks, risk should be below average.

You do not need to only buy undervalued or very undervalued stocks to earn a good long-term return. You can, and should, put at least some (or even most) of your money in stocks that you think are fairly valued. If you are right, over long enough periods (assuming, for example, that you buy regularly to even out the effect of growth rate in P/E ratio on annual return), you will earn an annual return equal to each year's dividend yield plus each year's growth rate in earnings per share. If the sum of these two terms is fair, and volatility is reasonable, so that compound return does not get steadily nibbled away, you will do just fine. Many financial headaches have been caused by chasing high returns.

Alternatively, some investors *only* buy stocks that they think are undervalued or very undervalued. They hope for a large return as the stock rises to fair value. Even if they are right, however, they need to continually replace stocks that return to fair value. This trading has tax implications. Moreover, this continual decision-making is difficult. *In the stock market, it is a truism that the fewer, presumably good, decisions you make the greater your chances of success.* Importantly, with too many decisions, your returns will almost certainly trend toward market returns, at best. At worst, portfolios badly underperform.

Our list consists of one megacap, fifteen large-caps, and four midcaps. **They reflect the compromise of real-world choice**. Not all are perfect – in general, perfect stocks, like four-leaf clovers, are rare. The real world differs from the stylized world of theory. *By design, I choose a range of businesses.*

Do not treat these as immediate buys. For one, you may disagree with my assumptions. For another, new company information may have arrived. In any case, stock prices will have changed by the time you read this. Ideally, think of these selections as examples. Contrast them with your selections. Pay attention to business risks.

I used the criteria at the end of Part II to pick these stocks. I assumed a ten-year investing time frame. I looked for the following key attributes:

- Quality

    - A strong business.

    - Low volatility of earnings per share.

    - A diversified business.

    - A long-run return on beginning equity average of at least twenty percent. If a company looked otherwise attractive, one or two percentage points less than twenty percent was not a dealbreaker. Here, long-run average is the average of the last ten years.

- Return

    - Historical earnings per share growth over the last ten years of at least eight percent a year and expected earnings per share growth over the next ten years of at least eight percent a year. Ideally, growth in earnings per share is steady.

- Risk

    - Reasonable.

    - Moderate leverage.

- Shareholder Commitment

    - A shareholder-friendly culture. A growing dividend and a falling share count. An emphasis on shareholder returns.

    - A payout ratio of at least fifty percent. More, of course, is better, but not at the expense of expected growth.

Though an ideal stock meets all these guidelines, often something will be amiss – like a picture that does not quite hang straight – in which case, you have to make a judgment call. There may be enough positives to offset the negatives.

You may be surprised by some of the stocks *not* on this list. For instance, I do not include Coca-Cola, bank stocks, drug stocks (I include Johnson & Johnson, but it is more than a drug stock), and energy stocks:

- Coca-Cola has been a fine long-term stock – with exceptional dividend growth – but demand for sugary drinks is slowing. In addition, potential regulations to restrict sales are another threat.

- Banks generally do not have returns on beginning equity of at least twenty percent. Moreover, I am uncomfortable with high leverage and many big banks are impossible to understand. For instance, Wells Fargo's 2014 annual report is about 240 pages long. Not to be outdone, Bank of America's is about 254 pages long. With Wells Fargo and Bank of America, we have to read not annual reports – but annual "books." By contrast, McDonald's, one of our picks, needed just 60 pages. As a rough – and only slightly facetious – rule, the longer the report, the more complex the business and the more likely it is that something will go wrong. In addition, banks must abide by stringent regulations, regulations that hinder their profitability and hamper their growth. Still, all this does not mean banks cannot be good investments. Many are, and many will be. Warren Buffett's Berkshire Hathaway owns banks. If you feel you must own a bank – but do not want the risk of owning one or two banks or trying to understand their often overly complex financials – consider a banking or financial ETF instead.

- Sales for drug companies are often dominated by a few multibillion-dollar drugs, which when they go off patent become a shareholder's multiyear nightmare. In addition, the government squeezes profits out of the system. I prefer companies with more diversified sales streams and I avoid businesses where one participant, here the government, wields too much power – the hammer can come down at any time.

- Energy companies such as Chevron and Exxon Mobil may experience slower growth as supplies increase, investments in green energy climb, and things such as automobiles and houses continue to become more efficient. In addition, energy prices are volatile.

Finally, **always** *be aware of overriding economic and related conditions.* For instance, interest rates are low, currently, mid-2015. Low interest rates boost profit margins, return on equity, and return on beginning equity – and encourage companies to take on debt to buy back shares. Likewise, changing demographics, labor relations, and new regulations always play a role.

Accenture

Ticker: ACN

Sector: Information Technology

Size: Large-cap

Website: http://www.accenture.com

The Business: Accenture provides management consulting, technology services, and outsourcing services to clients in more than one-hundred-and-twenty countries. The company's clients include eighty-nine of the Fortune Global 100 and more than three-quarters of the Fortune Global 500. Consulting-related services make up fifty-one percent of the company's sales; outsourcing, forty-nine percent. The company splits its business into five groups: products (25 percent of sales); financial services (21 percent); communications, media, and technology (20 percent); resources (16 percent); and health and public service (18 percent). Forty-six percent of sales are from North America; thirty-five percent from Europe; and nineteen percent from elsewhere. The company is based in Ireland. It is very shareholder-friendly.

Risks: Technology changes rapidly. The stock is more volatile than a typical dividend growth stock of the same size. The company faces competition from lower-cost providers in countries such as India, the Philippines, and China – though it does have a big presence, through its Global Delivery Network, in India and the Philippines. Currency fluctuations are another risk. The company has seen declines in earnings per share in two of the last ten years. In Fiscal Years 2009 and 2014, earnings per share fell eight percent.

The Numbers: Profit margins have averaged eight percent the last ten years. Asset turnover is 1.7. Financial leverage is 3.0. Long-term debt is relatively minuscule. Return on equity is an impressive fifty-one percent. It has averaged an even higher fifty-nine percent the last ten years. Accenture does not need much capital because it is a consulting company. This boosts internal returns.

Dividends and Share Buybacks: The company paid its first dividend during Fiscal Year 2006. The company's dividends are subject to an

Irish dividend withholding tax – though investors in certain countries, the U.S. included, may be exempt. Check how the withholding tax applies to you. The company pays semiannual dividends. In September 2015, the company announced an eight percent increase in its annual dividend to $2.20. Its dividend history is skewed because it switched from annual dividends to semiannual dividends in Fiscal Year 2010 and began paying its semiannual dividend midway through that fiscal year. The dividend payout ratio is forty-one percent. The company complements its dividend with a vigorous share buyback program.

Spreadsheet Parameters: Actual dividend payout ratio of 40 percent; assumed payout ratio of **80** percent. Return on beginning equity: **60** percent. Return on beginning equity is currently 59 percent. It has averaged 68 percent the last ten years. As the actual annual dividend is only for background information, and is immaterial to the projection, you may enter an updated value or leave it blank. Earnings growth has averaged 17 percent the last ten years, though it has been volatile. Reasonable, perhaps conservative, growth rates for our spreadsheet: (Years 1-5: **10** percent) (Years 6-10: **10** percent) (Years 11-20: **9** percent) (Years 21-30: **8** percent) (Years 31+: 3 percent).

Sample Spreadsheet Results: At a stock price of **$90**, earnings per share of **$4.70** – implying a current P/E ratio of 19 – and the rest of the parameters as above, the expected return is 12.64 percent a year and the shares look undervalued.

Clorox

Ticker: CLX

Sector: Consumer Staples

Size: Large-cap

Website: http://www.clorox.com

The Business: Clorox makes consumer products, primarily, and professional products. The company splits its business into four segments: Cleaning, Household, Lifestyle, and International. In Cleaning, thirty-two percent of sales, the company sells laundry, home care, and professional products in the U.S. Brands include Clorox, Pine-Sol, Tilex, and Green Works. In Household, also thirty-two percent of sales, the company sells products such as charcoal, cat litter, and plastic bags in the U.S. Brands include Kingsford, Fresh Step, and Glad. In Lifestyle, seventeen percent of sales, the company sells food products, water-filtration systems and filters, and natural personal care products in the U.S. Brands include Hidden Valley, Brita, and Burt's Bees. International, nineteen percent of sales, consists of, wait for it, products sold internationally. Brands include many of the same brands sold in the U.S., but also include specific international brands. The company holds the number one or number two position in several of its brands. Excluding currency effects, the company targets long-term sales growth of 3-5 percent a year. The company operates with low equity and, consequently, high financial leverage. In six of the last ten years, equity has been negative.

Risks: The company has a customer concentration problem: Wal-Mart is responsible for twenty-six percent of sales; Clorox's top five customers, forty-five percent. In the U.S., its primary geography, the markets for its products are mature. Consumers pay up for its brand name. Damage to its brand name will hurt its sales. Presently, mid-2015, the company faces a difficult situation in Argentina – high inflation and price controls – responsible for four percent of sales. Recently, the company left Venezuela, where it faced a similar situation. Private-label products are an ongoing threat. Financial leverage is high. Currency fluctuations are a risk. Commodity costs are another.

The Numbers: Profit margins have averaged ten percent the last ten years. Asset turnover is 1.4. Long-term debt as a percentage of assets is forty-three percent. Financial leverage is remarkable – in a bad way – at 35.3. The descent into high financial leverage began during Fiscal Year 2005, when the company used debt and cash to buy back twenty-nine percent of its shares from a shareholder. Ever since, the company has operated with low, and even negative, equity. With such high leverage, return on equity is meaningless, at four-hundred-and-ninety-two percent.

Dividends and Share Buybacks: In May 2015, the company announced a four percent increase in its annual dividend to $3.08. The dividend payout ratio is sixty-eight percent. The company complements its dividend with a share buyback program that, net, has amounted to 0.7 times what it has paid out in dividends the last ten years. Over the last ten years, the company has retired its shares at a 1.6 percent per year clip.

Spreadsheet Parameters: Actual dividend payout ratio of 60 percent; assumed payout ratio of **80** percent. Return on beginning equity: meaningless, as a huge value is of no help here. Return on beginning equity is currently 377 percent. As the actual annual dividend is only for background information, and is immaterial to the projection, you may enter an updated value or leave it blank. Earnings growth has averaged a paltry 2 percent the last ten years, though this has varied wildly. Dividend growth has averaged 8 percent the last five years and 11 percent the last ten. None of these historical numbers are of much help. Though we can use more sophisticated tricks, we will simply hazard a guess, ideally one that proves somewhat conservative. Using the company's long-term sales growth target of 3-5 percent a year, reasonable growth rates for our spreadsheet: (Years 1-5: **6** percent) (Years 6-10: **6** percent) (Years 11-20: **6** percent) (Years 21-30: **5** percent) (Years 31+: 3 percent).

Sample Spreadsheet Results: At a stock price of **$105**, earnings per share of **$4.70** – implying a current P/E ratio of 22 – and the rest of the parameters as above, the expected return is 8.76 percent a year and the shares look fairly valued.

Colgate-Palmolive

Ticker: CL

Sector: Consumer Staples

Size: Large-cap

Website: http://www.colgatepalmolive.com

The Business: Founded in 1806, Colgate-Palmolive (Colgate) is a leading consumer products company. The company splits its business into four segments: Oral Care, Personal Care, Home Care, and Pet Nutrition. In Oral Care, forty-six percent of sales, the company is the market leader in toothpaste globally, and has leading market share in toothpaste and manual toothbrushes in many parts of the world. Oral Care products include Colgate, Colgate Total, Colgate mouth rinses, and Colgate 360° manual toothbrushes. In the Personal Care market, twenty-one percent of sales, the company has leading market share in liquid hand soap. Personal Care products include Palmolive hand soap, Irish Spring bar soaps, and Speed Stick and Lady Speed Stick deodorants and antiperspirants. In the Home Care market, twenty percent of sales, the company sells products such as Palmolive and Ajax dishwashing liquids, Ajax household cleaners, and Murphy Oil Soap. In Pet Nutrition, thirteen percent of sales, the company sells products under the Hill's Science Diet and Hill's Prescription Diet names. Overall, eighty percent of sales are from outside the U.S. The company is very shareholder-friendly. Long-term investors will do well here. The company has been a steady long-term grower.

Risks: In the developed world, the company's markets are mature. Consumers pay up for its brand name. Damage to its brand name will hurt its sales. Currency fluctuations are another risk. The company maintains pension and other benefit plans with all the financial risks and costs that these plans carry – though U.S. employees no longer earn benefits for future service.

The Numbers: Profit margins are good. They have averaged fourteen percent the last five years and thirteen percent the last ten. Asset turnover is 1.3. Long-term debt as a percentage of assets is forty-two percent.

Financial leverage is 11.8 – much higher than the ten-year average of 5.9 – because of unusual items in its 2014 results. "Normal" financial leverage of close to 6.0 is not problematic for a company such as Colgate with exceptional business stability. Not surprisingly, with strong business credentials and high financial leverage, return on equity is extraordinarily high at one-hundred-and-ninety percent. It has averaged one-hundred-and-three percent the last ten years.

Dividends and Share Buybacks: In February 2015, the company announced a six percent increase in its annual dividend to $1.52. The company has paid dividends without interruption since 1895. The dividend payout ratio is sixty percent, higher than normal because of certain charges that have reduced earnings per share. The ten-year dividend payout average is forty-eight percent. The company complements its dividend with a share buyback program that, net, has amounted to 1.0 times what it has paid out in dividends the last ten years. Over the last ten years, the company has retired its shares at a 1.5 percent a year clip.

Spreadsheet Parameters: Actual dividend payout ratio of 45 percent; assumed payout ratio of **90** percent. Return on beginning equity: **90** percent. Return on beginning equity is currently 95 percent. It has averaged 100 percent the last ten years. As the actual annual dividend is only for background information, and is immaterial to the projection, you may enter an updated value or leave it blank. Earnings growth has averaged 6 percent the last ten years, though this has been prejudiced by occasional accounting charges. Over this period, dividend growth has averaged 12 percent. Reasonable growth rates for our spreadsheet: (Years 1-5: **8** percent) (Years 6-10: **8** percent) (Years 11-20: **7** percent) (Years 21-30: **6** percent) (Years 31+: 3 percent).

Sample Spreadsheet Results: At a stock price of **$65**, earnings per share of **$2.90** – implying a current P/E ratio of 22 – and the rest of the parameters as above, the expected return is 10.61 percent a year and the shares look undervalued.

Donaldson Company

Ticker: DCI

Sector: Industrials

Size: Midcap

Website: http://www.donaldson.com

The Business: Donaldson makes filtration systems and replacement parts. The company operates in two segments: Engine Products (64 percent of sales) and Industrial Products (36 percent). It sells into a broad variety of end markets. Sales are well diversified by geography with forty-one percent from the U.S., thirty percent from Europe, twenty-one percent from Asia Pacific, and eight percent from elsewhere. It is a market leader in many of its product lines. Sales have compounded eight percent a year for twenty-five years. Over the same period, earnings per share has compounded fourteen percent. The company plans to double sales between Fiscal Year 2014 and Fiscal Year 2021. With a difficult Fiscal Year 2015, this goal might prove ambitious. The company is very shareholder-friendly.

Risks: Midcaps are more volatile that large-caps. In addition, the company's business is intrinsically volatile with segments sensitive to cyclical industries such as mining, truck manufacturing, and construction. Likewise, it sells gas turbine products, which because of their large size show sharp changes in activity from year to year. For instance, sales of these products fell sharply, thirty-three percent, in Fiscal Year 2014. Not surprisingly, earnings per share is volatile. In Fiscal Year 2009, earnings per share fell twenty-two percent; in Fiscal Year 2013, earnings per share fell five percent. The company sells hard disk drive filters to the hard disk drive industry, an industry with little growth. The company does slightly less than ten percent of its business with one customer, Caterpillar. Currency fluctuations are another risk. The company lowered earnings expectations for Fiscal Year 2015, ending 31 July 2015. The company maintains pension and healthcare benefit plans with all the financial risks and costs that these plans carry.

The Numbers: Profit margins have averaged nine percent the last ten years. Asset turnover is 1.3. Financial leverage is 1.9. Long-term debt as a percentage of assets is thirteen percent. Return on equity is twenty-six percent. It has averaged twenty-four percent the last ten years.

Dividends and Share Buybacks: In May 2015, the company announced a three percent increase in its annual dividend to 68¢. The company targets a dividend payout ratio of thirty-five to forty-five percent of its average earnings per share over the last three years. The company complements its dividend with a share buyback program that, net, has amounted to 2.5 times what it has paid out in dividends the last ten years. Over the last ten years, the company has retired its shares at a 1.9 percent a year clip.

Spreadsheet Parameters: Actual dividend payout ratio of 35 percent; assumed payout ratio of **65** percent. Return on beginning equity: **25** percent. Return on beginning equity is currently 24 percent. It has averaged 25 percent the last ten years. As the actual annual dividend is only for background information, and is immaterial to the projection, you may enter an updated value or leave it blank. Earnings growth has averaged 11 percent the last ten years. Over the same period, dividend growth has averaged 19 percent. Dividend growth is so much higher than earnings growth because of share buybacks and the recently rising dividend payout ratio. Reasonable growth rates for our spreadsheet, somewhat lower than history to be conservative and to account for business volatility, roughly: (Years 1-5: **9** percent) (Years 6-10: **9** percent) (Years 11-20: **9** percent) (Years 21-30: **8** percent) (Years 31+: 3 percent).

Sample Spreadsheet Results: We have to be careful using our spreadsheet to value stocks with sudden fluctuations in earnings – and Donaldson has had just such sudden fluctuations in the past. Nevertheless, with this caveat, at a stock price of **$35**, earnings per share of **$1.50** – implying a current P/E ratio of 23 – and the rest of the parameters as above, the expected return is 10.01 percent a year and the shares look fairly valued.

Emerson Electric

Ticker: EMR

Sector: Industrials

Size: Large-cap

Website: http://www.emerson.com

The Business: Emerson is a diversified global manufacturing and technology company. It sells a variety of products and services worldwide into industrial, commercial, and consumer markets. The company is organized into five segments: Process Management (36 percent of sales); Industrial Automation (20 percent); Network Power (20 percent); Climate Technologies (16 percent); and Commercial & Residential Solutions (8 percent). Sales are well diversified with forty-six percent from the U.S. and Canada; twenty-two percent from Asia; and thirty-two percent from elsewhere. Acquisitions are an important part of the company's strategy.

Risks: Earnings per share can be volatile. For instance, in the last ten years, earnings per share rose thirty-two percent in Fiscal Year 2006 and fell twenty-six percent in Fiscal Year 2009.

The Numbers: Profit margins have averaged nine percent the last ten years. Asset turnover is 1.0. Financial leverage is 2.4. Long-term debt as a percentage of assets is fifteen percent. Return on equity is twenty-one percent. In the last ten years, return on equity has averaged twenty-two percent.

Dividends and Share Buybacks: In November 2015, the company announced a minuscule one percent increase in its annual dividend to $1.90. The dividend payout ratio is fifty-seven percent. The ten-year average is forty-nine percent. The dividend payout ratio is volatile because earnings per share is volatile. The company complements its dividend with a share buyback program that, net, has amounted to 0.8 times what it has paid out in dividends the last ten years. Over the last ten years, the company has retired its shares at a 1.9 percent a year clip.

Spreadsheet Parameters: Actual dividend payout ratio of 50 percent; assumed payout ratio of **65** percent. Return on beginning equity: **22**

percent. Return on beginning equity is currently 20 percent. It has averaged 23 percent the last ten years. As the actual annual dividend is only for background information, and is immaterial to the projection, you may enter an updated value or leave it blank. Earnings growth has averaged 6 percent the last five years and 7 percent the last ten. Earnings growth has been volatile. Dividend growth has averaged 6 percent the last five years and 8 percent the last ten. Reasonable growth rates for our spreadsheet: (Years 1-5: **7** percent) (Years 6-10: **7** percent) (Years 11-20: **6** percent) (Years 21-30: **6** percent) (Years 31+: 3 percent).

Sample Spreadsheet Results: We have to be careful using our spreadsheet to value stocks with sudden fluctuations in earnings – and Emerson has had just such sudden fluctuations in the past. Nevertheless, with this caveat, at a stock price of **$55**, earnings per share of **$3.45** – implying a current P/E ratio of 16 – and the rest of the parameters as above, the expected return is 9.98 percent a year and the shares look undervalued.

FactSet

Ticker: FDS

Sector: Information Technology

Size: Midcap

Website: http://www.factset.com

The Business: FactSet provides integrated financial information and related analytical tools to investment professionals worldwide. Clients buy subscriptions to the company's products. About five-sixths of annualized subscriptions are from investment manager clients; the rest from investment banking firms doing Merger and Acquisitions work, capital markets services, and equity research. Sixty-eight percent of FactSet's sales are from the U.S.; twenty-four percent from Europe; and eight percent from Asia Pacific. Competitors include Bloomberg, Thomson Reuters, and Standard & Poor's. Bloomberg and Thomson Reuters each have about thirty percent of the overall market; Standard & Poor's between three and five percent, comparable to FactSet's. FactSet has grown sales for thirty-four consecutive years and, according to the company, is one of only three companies to have grown sales and earnings every year for the last eighteen years. The company retains ninety-five percent of its annualized subscriptions each year, thus creating a high level of predictability into next year's sales. The company is very shareholder-friendly.

Risks: Midcaps are more volatile that large-caps. The company must continue to gain market share as its markets are growing very slowly. Results can suffer during prolonged bear markets.

The Numbers: Profit margins have averaged a strong twenty-three percent the last ten years. Asset turnover is 1.4. Financial leverage is 1.3. The company carries no long-term debt. Return on equity is an impressive forty-one percent. Return on equity has averaged thirty-five percent the last five years and thirty-one percent the last ten.

Dividends and Share Buybacks: In May 2015, FactSet announced a thirteen percent increase in its annual dividend to $1.76. The dividend payout ratio is thirty percent. The company complements its dividend with a vigorous share buyback program that, net, has amounted to 3.1 times what it has paid out in dividends the last ten years. Over the last ten years, the company has retired its shares at a 1.3 percent a year clip. Most of this (net) buying has taken place in the last five years. In the last five years, the company has retired its shares at a 2.5 percent a year clip.

Spreadsheet Parameters: Actual dividend payout ratio of 30 percent; assumed payout ratio of **75** percent. Return on beginning equity: **35** percent. Return on beginning equity is currently 39 percent. The ten-year average is 34 percent. As the actual annual dividend is only for background information, and is immaterial to the projection, you may enter an updated value or leave it blank. Earnings growth has averaged 8 percent the last five years and 14 percent the last ten. Dividend growth has averaged 14 percent the last five years and 26 percent the last ten, aided by increases of more than 60 percent in 2007 and 2008. Reasonable growth rates for our spreadsheet: (Years 1-5: **9** percent) (Years 6-10: **9** percent) (Years 11-20: **9** percent) (Years 21-30: **8** percent) (Years 31+: **3** percent).

Sample Spreadsheet Results: At a stock price of **$160**, earnings per share of **$5.90** – implying a current P/E ratio of 27 – and the rest of the parameters as above, the expected return is 9.97 percent a year and the shares look fairly valued (to perhaps slightly overvalued). Currently, mid-2015, FactSet is seeing good business momentum, and in the short term this result may prove conservative.

Genuine Parts

Ticker: GPC

Sector: Consumer Discretionary

Size: Large-cap

Website: http://www.genpt.com

The Business: Genuine Parts distributes automotive replacement parts, primarily under the NAPA brand name (53 percent of sales); industrial replacement parts (31 percent); office products (11 percent); and electrical and electronic materials (5 percent). It operates in the U.S., Canada, Mexico, Australia, and New Zealand. Acquisitions are an important part of the company's strategy. The company is shareholder-friendly. Over the last ten years, return on beginning equity has averaged nineteen percent, just shy of our threshold of twenty percent.

Risks: Earnings per share has fallen in two out of the last ten years. In 2009, earnings per share fell fourteen percent; in 2008, earnings per share fell two percent. In the automotive business, better cars, newer cars, and fewer driven miles negatively impact demand. In the industrial business, lower industrial production and lower capacity utilization negatively impact demand.

The Numbers: As a distributor, profit margins are low. Profit margins have averaged five percent the last ten years. Asset turnover is 1.9. Financial leverage is 2.5. Long-term debt as a percentage of assets is six percent. Return on equity is twenty-one percent. It has averaged nineteen percent the last ten years.

Dividends and Share Buybacks: In February 2015, the company announced a seven percent increase in its annual dividend to $2.46, its 59th consecutive annual increase. The dividend payout ratio is fifty percent. It has averaged fifty-two percent the last ten years. The company complements its dividend with a share buyback program that, net, has amounted to 0.4 times what it has paid out in dividends the last ten years. Over the last ten years, the company has retired its shares at a 1.3 percent a year clip.

Spreadsheet Parameters: Actual dividend payout ratio of 50 percent; assumed payout ratio of **60** percent. Return on beginning equity: **20** percent. Return on beginning equity is currently 21 percent. It has averaged 19 percent the last ten years, just below our comfort level of 20 percent. As the actual annual dividend is only for background information, and is immaterial to the projection, you may enter an updated value or leave it blank. Earnings and dividend growth have averaged 7 percent the last ten years. Earnings growth has been volatile. Over the last ten years, earnings per share growth rate has averaged 8 percent a year. Reasonable growth rates for our spreadsheet: (Years 1-5: **7** percent) (Years 6-10: **7** percent) (Years 11-20: **6** percent) (Years 21-30: **6** percent) (Years 31+: 3 percent).

Sample Spreadsheet Results: We have to be careful using our spreadsheet to value stocks with sudden fluctuations in earnings – and Genuine Parts has had just such sudden fluctuations in the past. Nevertheless, with this caveat, at a stock price of **$85**, earnings per share of **$4.80** – implying a current P/E ratio of 18 – and the rest of the parameters as above, the expected return is 9.04 percent a year and the shares look fairly valued.

Graco

Ticker: GGG

Sector: Industrials

Size: Midcap

Website: http://www.graco.com

The Business: Graco is a global leader in fluid handling. It makes premium equipment to move, measure, control, dispense, and spray fluid and coating materials. The company splits its business into three segments: industrial (59 percent of sales); contractor (31 percent); and lubrication (10 percent). Sales are well-diversified by geography with fifty-six percent from the Americas; twenty-five percent from Europe, Middle East, and Africa; and nineteen percent from Asia Pacific. Acquisitions are an important part of the company's strategy. The company is shareholder-friendly. It has a continuous improvement culture and has been a strong and consistent performer over long periods.

Risks: Midcaps are more volatile that large-caps. The contractor segment depends on a few large customers. A portion of the company's business depends on the cyclical construction and automobile markets. Earnings are volatile. In 2009, earnings per share fell fifty-nine percent; in 2008, earnings per share fell fourteen percent.

The Numbers: Graco prioritizes the use of cash flow as company investments first, acquisitions second, and dividends and share buybacks a joint third. Profit margins have averaged a strong sixteen percent the last ten years. Asset turnover is 0.8. Financial leverage is 2.6. Long-term debt as a percentage of assets has risen from zero percent in 2006 to forty percent in 2014. Return on equity is thirty-eight percent. Over the last ten years, return on equity has fluctuated widely, ranging from a low of twenty-three percent in 2009 to a high of seventy-two percent in 2008. The ten-year average is a healthy forty-three percent.

Dividends and Share Buybacks: In December 2014, Graco announced a nine percent increase in its annual dividend to $1.20. The dividend payout ratio is thirty percent, though this has varied as earnings have fluctuated and the company has managed its dividend payouts. The company targets a dividend payout ratio of twenty-five percent to thirty percent. Graco paid a special dividend of $1.50 in 2004. The company complements its dividend with a share buyback program that, net, varies from robust to moribund. For instance, in 2014, it was robust; in 2012, it was moribund. The company manages its share buybacks and dividend payouts according to the vagaries and priorities of its business. Over the last ten years, the company has retired its shares at a 1.5 percent a year clip.

Spreadsheet Parameters: Actual dividend payout ratio of 30 percent; assumed payout ratio of **65** percent. Return on beginning equity: **40** percent. Return on beginning equity is currently 36 percent. It has averaged 46 percent the last ten years. As the actual annual dividend is only for background information, and is immaterial to the projection, you may enter an updated value or leave it blank. Earnings growth has averaged 16 percent the last ten years. It has been volatile. Dividend growth has averaged 8 percent the last five years and 12 percent the last ten, excluding the special $1.50 dividend in 2004. Reasonable growth rates for our spreadsheet, somewhat lower than history to be conservative and to account for business volatility, roughly: (Years 1-5: **13** percent) (Years 6-10: **13** percent) (Years 11-20: **11** percent) (Years 21-30: **9** percent) (Years 31+: 3 percent).

Sample Spreadsheet Results: This is not an easy stock to model with our spreadsheet because of the volatility in the numbers. We use company guidance and long-term averages and hope for the best. At a stock price of **$65**, earnings per share of **$3.20** – implying a current P/E ratio of 20 – and the rest of the parameters as above, the expected return is 13.14 percent a year and the shares look undervalued.

Honeywell

Ticker: HON

Sector: Industrials

Size: Large-cap

Website: http://www.honeywell.com

The Business: Honeywell is a diversified global technology and manu-facturing company. It sells a variety of products and services worldwide into a variety of markets: homes and buildings, industrial, commercial aerospace, oil and gas, vehicles, defense and space. The company splits its business into three segments: Aerospace; Automation and Control Systems; and Performance Materials and Technologies. In Aerospace, thirty-nine percent of sales, the company supplies a wide variety of me-chanical and electrical products to the aircraft market, both commercial and defense. This segment also includes turbochargers for vehicles. In Automation and Control Systems, thirty-six percent of sales, the com-pany provides environmental and combustion controls, sensing controls, security and life safety products and services, scanning and mobility devices, and building solutions and services. In Performance Materials and Technologies, twenty-five percent of sales, the company produces advanced materials, process technologies, and automation solutions. Forty-five percent of sales are from the U.S., twenty-four percent from Europe, and thirty-one percent from elsewhere. The company expects sales to grow 6-9 percent a year through 2018, including contributions from acquisitions, an important part of the company's strategy. Hon-eywell is not your typical dividend growth stock – its dividend does not always grow. For instance, the dividend remained stagnant between 2000 and 2004. That said, the company has changed for the better since then. Still, likely because of global economic problems in 2009 and 2010, the company did not raise its dividend in 2010.

Risks: Some segments of the company's business are cyclical. Defense and space sales depend on government budgets, which can be fickle. Earnings are volatile. In 2009, earnings per share fell twenty-four percent. In 2010, earnings per share fell nine percent. The company maintains pension and, to a much lesser extent, healthcare benefit plans with all the financial risks and costs that these plans carry. The company has frozen participation in its U.S. pension plans for salaried and non-union hourly employees.

The Numbers: Profit margins have averaged seven percent the last ten years. Asset turnover is 0.9. Financial leverage is 2.6. Long-term debt as a percentage of assets is thirteen percent. Return on equity is twenty-four percent. It has averaged twenty-three percent the last ten years.

Dividends and Share Buybacks: In October 2015, the company announced a fifteen percent increase in its annual dividend to $2.38. The dividend payout ratio is thirty-five percent. The ten-year average is thirty-nine percent. The company complements its dividend with a share buyback program that, net, has amounted to 0.9 times what it has paid out in dividends the last ten years. Over the last ten years, the company has retired its shares at a 0.8 percent a year clip; over the last five years, however, shares have grown at a 0.5 percent a year clip.

Spreadsheet Parameters: Actual dividend payout ratio of 35 percent; assumed payout ratio of **65** percent. Return on beginning equity: **24** percent. Return on beginning equity is currently 24 percent and has also averaged 24 percent the last ten years. As the actual annual dividend is only for background information, and is immaterial to the projection, you may enter an updated value or leave it blank. Earnings growth has averaged 14 percent the last ten years, though it has been volatile. Over the last ten years, dividend growth has averaged 10 percent. Reasonable growth rates for our spreadsheet: (Years 1-5: **9** percent) (Years 6-10: **8** percent) (Years 11-20: **8** percent) (Years 21-30: **7** percent) (Years 31+: **3** percent).

Sample Spreadsheet Results: At a stock price of **$95**, earnings per share of **$6.30** – implying a current P/E ratio of 15 – and the rest of the parameters as above, the expected return is 11.71 percent a year and the shares look undervalued.

Johnson & Johnson

Ticker: JNJ

Sector: Healthcare

Size: Megacap

Website: http://www.jnj.com

The Business: Johnson & Johnson (JNJ), a giant of a company, operates in three areas of healthcare: pharmaceutical (43 percent of sales); medical devices (37 percent); and consumer (20 percent). The company is one of just three industrial companies with a AAA credit rating. JNJ operates on a decentralized basis. More than two-hundred-and-sixty-five worldwide operating companies operate under the JNJ umbrella. Sales by U.S. operating companies account for forty-seven percent of sales; sales by international operating companies, fifty-three percent. Acquisitions are an important part of the company's strategy. JNJ is such a huge company that, in the not-too-distant future, its expected five-year earnings *per share* growth rate may fall below our required minimum of eight percent a year for a dividend growth stock.

Risks: One of JNJ's drugs, REMICADE®, generates nine percent of sales. Ten other drugs each generate sales of more than one-billion dollars annually. As a huge company, size is an impediment to growth, though the company's decentralized operations help alleviate this challenge. Changes in healthcare regulations are a big risk. Currency fluctuations are another risk. The company maintains pension and other benefit plans with all the financial risks and costs that these plans carry.

The Numbers: Profit margins have averaged a strong nineteen percent the last ten years. Asset turnover is 0.6. Financial leverage is 1.9. Long-term debt as a percentage of assets is twelve percent. Return on equity is twenty-three percent. It has averaged an identical twenty-three percent the last ten years.

Dividends and Share Buybacks: In April 2015, JNJ announced a seven percent increase in its annual dividend to $3.00, its 53rd consecutive annual increase. The dividend payout ratio is forty-eight percent. The ten-year average is also forty-eight percent. The company complements its dividend with a share buyback program that, net, has amounted to 0.6 times what it has paid out in dividends the last ten years. Over the last ten years, the company has retired its shares at a 0.7 percent a year clip; over the last five years, however, shares have grown at a 0.2 percent a year clip.

Spreadsheet Parameters: Actual dividend payout ratio of 50 percent; assumed payout ratio of **75** percent. Return on beginning equity: **25** percent. Return on beginning equity is currently 22 percent. The ten-year average is 25 percent. As the actual annual dividend is only for background information, and is immaterial to the projection, you may enter an updated value or leave it blank. Earnings growth has averaged 8 percent the last ten years, though this has been negatively affected by onetime charges. Over the last ten years, dividend growth has averaged 10 percent. Reasonable growth rates for our spreadsheet: (Years 1-5: **7** percent) (Years 6-10: **7** percent) (Years 11-20: **6** percent) (Years 21-30: **6** percent) (Years 31+: 3 percent). (According to our spreadsheet, with these parameters, the average growth rate for Years 1-20 is 7 percent, exceeding the sustainable growth rate of 6 percent. This looks worse than it really is because of rounding. In fact, with an extra digit, the average growth rate for Years 1-20 is 6.5 percent and the sustainable growth rate is 6.3 percent, more than close enough to be acceptable.)

Sample Spreadsheet Results: At a stock price of **$95**, earnings per share of **$6.20** – implying a current P/E ratio of 15 – and the rest of the parameters as above, the expected return is 11.06 percent a year and the shares look undervalued.

McCormick

Ticker: MKC

Sector: Consumer Staples

Size: Large-cap

Website: http://www.mccormickcorporation.com

The Business: McCormick makes, markets, and distributes spices and other flavor-related products to the food industry worldwide. The company operates in two segments, consumer (60 percent of sales) and industrial (40 percent). The consumer segment is the more profitable of the two. In the industrial segment, the company's customers are food manufacturers and food-service companies. Overall, McCormick's two biggest customers are Wal-Mart and PepsiCo, each at eleven percent of sales. The U.S. accounts for fifty-five percent of sales; international, forty-five percent. Acquisitions are an important part of the company's strategy. The company's long-term goal is to increase earnings per share 9-11 percent a year.

Risks: Consumers pay up for its brand name. Any damage to its brand name will hurt its sales. Private-label products are an ongoing threat, though the company itself is a leading supplier. Currency fluctuations are another. The company maintains a pension plan with all the financial risks and costs that this entails.

The Numbers: Profit margins have averaged nine percent the last ten years. Asset turnover is 1.0. Financial leverage is 2.4. Long-term debt as a percentage of assets is twenty-three percent. Return on equity is twenty-four percent. It has averaged twenty-three percent the last ten years. The company's earnings show seasonality with weak first and second quarters offset by a better third quarter and a strong fourth quarter.

Dividends and Share Buybacks: In November 2015, McCormick announced an eight percent increase in its annual dividend to $1.72, its 30th consecutive annual increase. The company has paid dividends since 1925. The dividend payout ratio is forty-five percent. The ten-year average is forty-four percent. The company complements its dividend with a share buyback program that, net, has amounted to 0.6 times what it has paid out in dividends the last ten years. Notably, the company pulled back on share repurchases during the recession-hit fiscal years of 2008 and 2009 when, net, cash spent on share buybacks was actually *negative*. In the last ten years, the company has retired its shares at a 0.6 percent a year clip. Over the last ten years, the company has spent $1.4 billion on acquisitions compared to $0.8 billion, net, on share buybacks.

Spreadsheet Parameters: Actual dividend payout ratio of 45 percent; assumed payout ratio of **65** percent. Return on beginning equity: **22** percent. Return on beginning equity is currently an identical 22 percent. It has averaged 25 percent the last ten years. As the actual annual dividend is only for background information, and is immaterial to the projection, you may enter an updated value or leave it blank. Earnings growth has averaged 8 percent the last ten years. Over the same period, dividend growth has averaged 10 percent. Reasonable growth rates for our spreadsheet: (Years 1-5: **8** percent) (Years 6-10: **8** percent) (Years 11-20: **8** percent) (Years 21-30: **7** percent) (Years 31+: **3** percent).

Sample Spreadsheet Results: At a stock price of **$80**, earnings per share of **$3.50** – implying a current P/E ratio of 23 – and the rest of the parameters as above, the expected return is 9.29 percent a year and the shares look fairly valued.

McDonald's

Ticker: MCD

Sector: Consumer Discretionary

Size: Large-cap

Website: http://www.mcdonalds.com

The Business: McDonald's franchises and operates McDonald's restaurants. About eighty percent of the company's roughly 36,000 restaurants are franchised. Forty percent of sales are from Europe; thirty-two percent from the U.S.; twenty-three percent from Asia Pacific, Middle East, and Africa; and five percent from other countries and through corporate. Just nine countries – U.S., Canada, U.K., France, Russia, Germany, China, Australia, and Japan – account for seventy-five percent of sales. The company targets long-term sales growth of 3-5 percent a year. The company is very shareholder-friendly.

Risks: With such a huge global footprint already, the company must squeeze growth out of its existing store base. Ten commodities make up seventy-five percent of its grocery costs, though the company believes it can control these costs through menu adjustments and promotions. Currency fluctuations are another risk. The stock price reacts to comparable store sales growth data, and rightfully so, because tiny changes here have a significant impact on profit. The public may lose its appetite for fast food.

The Numbers: Profit margins have averaged a strong eighteen percent the last ten years. The company has strong profit margins because it acts primarily as a franchisor. Asset turnover is 0.8. Financial leverage is 2.7. Long-term debt as a percentage of assets is forty-four percent. Return on equity is thirty-seven percent. It has averaged thirty-six percent the last five years and thirty percent the last ten.

Dividends and Share Buybacks: In November 2015, McDonald's announced a five percent increase in its annual dividend to $3.56. The company has paid dividends since 1976 and has raised its dividend every year. The dividend payout ratio is sixty-eight percent. In 2014, the dividend payout ratio jumped because earnings per share fell thirteen

percent. The ten-year average is fifty-two percent. The company complements its dividend with a share buyback program that, net, has amounted
to 1.1 times what it has paid out in dividends the last ten years. Over the
last ten years, the company has retired its shares at a 2.8 percent a year
clip.

Spreadsheet Parameters: Actual dividend payout ratio of 55 percent;
assumed payout ratio of **80** percent. Return on beginning equity: **30**
percent. Return on beginning equity is currently 30 percent and has
averaged 30 percent the last ten years as well. As the actual annual
dividend is only for background information, and is immaterial to the
projection, you may enter an updated value or leave it blank. Earnings
growth has fluctuated the last ten years because of divestitures, other
onetime issues, and recent business weakness. It has averaged 11 percent
the last ten years, but only 1 percent the last five. Dividend growth
has averaged 10 percent the last five years and 20 percent the last ten.
Reasonable growth rates for our spreadsheet: (Years 1-5: **6** percent) (Years
6-10: **6** percent) (Years 11-20: **6** percent) (Years 21-30: **6** percent) (Years
31+: 3 percent).

Sample Spreadsheet Results: At a stock price of **$95**, earnings per share
of **$4.70** – implying a current P/E ratio of 20 – and the rest of the
parameters as above, the expected return is 9.41 percent a year and
the shares look undervalued.

Nike

Ticker: NKE

Sector: Consumer Discretionary

Size: Large-cap

Website: http://www.nike.com

The Business: Nike designs and sells athletic footwear, clothing, equipment, accessories, and services. The company is the largest seller of athletic footwear and clothing in the world. Its key brands are NIKE and Jordan. It also owns Converse and Hurley. The U.S. accounts for forty-six percent of sales; international, fifty-four percent. The company is shareholder-friendly. As large as it is, Nike is still growing well.

Risks: Consumer tastes can be fickle. Any damage to its brand name will hurt its sales. The company must continue to attract athletes as endorsers for its brand. Currency fluctuations are another risk.

The Numbers: Profit margins have averaged nine percent the last ten years. Asset turnover is 1.5. Financial leverage is 1.7. Long-term debt as a percentage of assets is six percent. Return on equity is twenty-five percent. It has averaged twenty-two percent the last ten years. The company carries excess cash and short-term investments on its balance sheet and its "true" return on equity is higher.

Dividends and Share Buybacks: In November 2015, Nike announced a fourteen percent increase in its annual dividend to $1.28. The dividend payout ratio is thirty-one percent. The ten-year average is twenty-seven percent. The company complements its dividend with a share buyback program that, net, has amounted to 2.0 times what it has paid out in dividends the last ten years. Over the last ten years, the company has retired its shares at a 1.9 percent a year clip.

Spreadsheet Parameters: Actual dividend payout ratio of 30 percent; assumed payout ratio of **65** percent. Return on beginning equity: **27** percent, raised slightly to reflect the excess cash and short-term investments on the company's balance sheet. This adjustment is approximate. Return on beginning equity is currently 24 percent. It has averaged 23 percent the last ten years. As the actual annual dividend is only for background information, and is immaterial to the projection, you may enter an updated value or leave it blank. Earnings growth has averaged 12 percent the last ten years. Over the same period, dividend growth has averaged 18 percent. Reasonable growth rates for our spreadsheet: (Years 1-5: **10** percent) (Years 6-10: **10** percent) (Years 11-20: **9** percent) (Years 21-30: **8** percent) (Years 31+: 3 percent). (According to our spreadsheet, with these parameters, the average growth rate for Years 1-20 is 10 percent, exceeding the sustainable growth rate of 9 percent. This looks worse than it really is because of rounding. In fact, with two extra digits, the average growth rate for Years 1-20 is 9.50 percent and the sustainable growth rate is 9.45 percent.)

Sample Spreadsheet Results: At a stock price of **$105**, earnings per share of **$4.10** – implying a current P/E ratio of 26 – and the rest of the parameters as above, the expected return is 9.95 percent a year and the shares look fairly valued. Currently, mid-2015, Nike is seeing strong business momentum, perhaps in part because some of its competitors are struggling. Consequently, this result may prove conservative because near-term earnings per share may rise substantially.

Papa John's

Ticker: PZZA

Sector: Consumer Discretionary

Size: Midcap

Website: http://www.papajohns.com

The Business: Papa John's franchises and operates Papa John's restaurants. About eighty-four percent of the company's roughly 4,700 restaurants are franchised. Although the U.S. market is mature, the company believes it has ample room to grow internationally. In 2015, the company expects three-quarters of its new stores to be opened internationally. The company's competitive selling point is the high quality of its pizzas. As of mid-2015, the company has had eleven consecutive years of positive or flat comparable restaurant sales growth. The company targets steady eps growth, roughly in the mid-teens, amply supported by share buybacks. The company is very shareholder-friendly. It started paying dividends in the third quarter of 2013.

Risks: Midcaps are more volatile that large-caps. The U.S. pizza market is mature, though fragmented. Dramatic increases in cheese prices are a risk – cheese represents 35-40 percent of the company's food costs. Any damage to the company's reputation or the reputation of its founder, John H. Schnatter, the face of the company, will hurt its results. Longer term, the public may lose its appetite for pizzas, or prefer other types of pizza-based concepts such as fast-casual pizzas. Nevertheless, it is hard to see this happening anytime soon, (say) in the next 3-5 years. Moreover, the impact to Papa John's may not be severe, at least initially, as the company's focus has always been on high quality.

The Numbers: Profit margins have averaged five percent the last ten years. Asset turnover is 3.1. Long-term debt has ratcheted up the last two years. This has impacted many financial ratios. Long-term debt as a percentage of assets is forty-five percent. It was twenty percent in 2012. Financial leverage is 5.2. In the eight years prior to and including 2012, it averaged 2.5. Return on equity is seventy-four percent. In the eight years prior to and including 2012, it averaged thirty-one percent.

Dividends and Share Buybacks: In July 2015, the company announced a twenty-five percent increase in its annual dividend to $0.70. The dividend payout ratio is thirty percent. The company complements its dividend with an aggressive share buyback program that, net, amounted to 5.0 times what it paid out in dividends in 2014. The ten-year comparison is not relevant because dividends are recent. Over the last ten years, the company has retired its shares at a robust 4.9 percent a year clip.

Spreadsheet Parameters: Actual dividend payout ratio of 30 percent; assumed payout ratio of **70** percent. Return on beginning equity: **40** percent, somewhat of a guess as we cannot know how much leverage the company intends to hold long term. Return on beginning equity is currently 53 percent. It has averaged 35 percent the last ten years. As the actual annual dividend is only for background information, and is immaterial to the projection, you may enter an updated value or leave it blank. Earnings growth has averaged 5 percent the last five years. The five years prior were too volatile. Dividend growth is not relevant. Reasonable growth rates for our spreadsheet: (Years 1-5: **12** percent) (Years 6-10: **12** percent) (Years 11-20: **10** percent) (Years 21-30: **8** percent) (Years 31+: 3 percent).

Sample Spreadsheet Results: At a stock price of **$65**, earnings per share of **$2.10**, and the rest of the parameters as above, the expected return is 10.43 percent a year and the shares look – at least somewhat – overvalued, not surprising given a current P/E ratio of 31. To be fair, Papa John's has been a strong performer. Moreover, the company's continual and aggressive share buybacks do provide demand for the company's shares. Still, it does appear stretched.

Parker-Hannifin

Ticker: PH

Sector: Industrials

Size: Large-cap

Website: http://www.parker.com

The Business: Parker-Hannifin (Parker) is the global leader in motion and control technologies. The company divides its business into two segments: Diversified Industrial (83 percent) and Aerospace Systems (17 percent). Fifty-six percent of sales are from the U.S.; forty-four percent, internationally. The company is broadly diversified, with roughly 450,000 customers in virtually every significant manufacturing, transportation, and processing industry. Acquisitions are an important part of the company's strategy. The company targets sales growth of twelve percent a year with two-thirds generated organically and one-third from acquisitions. The company is shareholder-friendly.

Risks: Parker is more economically sensitive than a typical dividend growth stock of the same size. In Fiscal Year 2009, earnings per share fell forty-three percent. By contrast, in Fiscal Year 2011, earnings per share rose eighty-seven percent. Currency fluctuations are another risk. The company maintains pension and other benefit plans with all the financial risks and costs that these plans carry.

The Numbers: Profit margins have averaged seven percent the last ten years. Asset turnover is 1.0. Financial leverage is 2.0. Long-term debt as a percentage of assets is eleven percent. Return on equity is sixteen percent. It has averaged eighteen percent the last five years and seventeen percent the last ten.

Dividends and Share Buybacks: In October 2014, the company raised its annual dividend *forty* percent – from the year-earlier dividend – to $2.52. Parker sometimes raises its dividend more than once a year. The dividend payout ratio fluctuates because of earnings volatility. Currently, it is twenty-seven percent. It has risen steadily. The company now targets a dividend payout ratio of thirty percent. The company complements its dividend with a share buyback program that, net, has amounted to 1.6

times what it has paid out in dividends the last ten years. Over the last ten years, the company has retired its shares at a 1.8 percent a year clip. Concurrent with its October 2014 dividend increase, the company announced a share buyback of thirty-five million shares, roughly a quarter of its shares outstanding. The company did not indicate a time frame.

Spreadsheet Parameters: Actual dividend payout ratio of 30 percent; assumed payout ratio of 55 percent. Return on beginning equity: 20 percent. Return on beginning equity is currently 18 percent. It has averaged 19 percent the last five and ten years. As the actual annual dividend is only for background information, and is immaterial to the projection, you may enter an updated value or leave it blank. Earnings growth is distorted because earnings vary so much. Ignoring the more dramatic increases and decreases over the last ten years – although this is not quite kosher – the average is 9 percent. Dividend growth has averaged 14 percent the last five and ten years. Reasonable growth rates for our spreadsheet: (Years 1-5: 9 percent) (Years 6-10: 9 percent) (Years 11-20: 9 percent) (Years 21-30: 8 percent) (Years 31+: 3 percent).

Sample Spreadsheet Results: We have to be careful using our spreadsheet to value stocks with sudden fluctuations in earnings – and Parker has had just such sudden fluctuations in the past. Nevertheless, with this caveat, at a stock price of **$115**, earnings per share of **$7.50** – implying a current P/E ratio of 15 – and the rest of the parameters as above, the expected return is 11.29 percent a year and the shares look undervalued.

Praxair

Ticker: PX

Sector: Materials

Size: Large-cap

Website: http://www.praxair.com

The Business: Praxair is one of the largest suppliers of industrial gases in the world and the largest supplier in North and South America. The company also operates a smaller surface coatings segment. Ninety-four percent of sales are from the industrial gases segment; the remaining six percent, from the surface coatings segment. The company is well-diversified globally with fifty-eight percent of sales from outside the U.S. It serves a broad variety of industries. It conducts most of its business through long-term contracts. Because of these long-term contracts and broad customer base, Praxair is one of the better stocks for long-term investors. The company is shareholder-friendly.

Risks: Company-specific risks are few. As with all companies, it does face general risks, primarily broad economic risks. Its plants constitute large expenditures. The company maintains pension plans with all the financial risks and costs that these plans carry.

The Numbers: Profit margins are good. They have averaged thirteen percent the last ten years. Asset turnover is 0.6. Financial leverage is 3.3. Long-term debt as a percentage of assets is forty-four percent. Return on equity is twenty-eight percent. It has averaged twenty-four percent the last ten years.

Dividends and Share Buybacks: In January 2015, Praxair announced a ten percent increase in its annual dividend to $2.86, its 22nd consecutive annual increase. The dividend payout ratio is forty-five percent. The ten-year average is thirty-nine percent. The company complements its dividend with a share buyback program that, net, has amounted to 0.9 times what it has paid out in dividends the last ten years. Over the last ten years, the company has retired its shares at a 1.1 percent a year clip.

Spreadsheet Parameters: Actual dividend payout ratio of 45 percent; assumed payout ratio of **65** percent. Return on beginning equity: **25**

percent. Return on beginning equity is currently 24 percent. It has averaged 26 percent the last ten years. As the actual annual dividend is only for background information, and is immaterial to the projection, you may enter an updated value or leave it blank. Earnings growth has averaged 7 percent the last five years and 10 percent the last ten, though it has been volatile. Earnings growth has slowed markedly the last three years, averaging 0 percent. Dividend growth has averaged 16 percent the last ten years. Reasonable growth rates for our spreadsheet: (Years 1-5: **9** percent) (Years 6-10: **9** percent) (Years 11-20: **8** percent) (Years 21-30: **8** percent) (Years 31+: 3 percent).

Sample Spreadsheet Results: At a stock price of **$115**, earnings per share of **$6.00** – implying a current P/E ratio of 19 – and the rest of the parameters as above, the expected return is 10.71 percent a year and the shares look undervalued.

Ross Stores

Ticker: ROST

Sector: Consumer Discretionary

Size: Large-cap

Website: http://www.rossstores.com

The Business: Ross Stores operates 1,242 Ross Dress for Less stores and 157 dd's DISCOUNTS stores. Ross Dress for Less is the largest off-price apparel and home fashion chain in the U.S. with stores primarily located in middle-class markets. Ross Dress for Less targets discounts of twenty percent to sixty percent off department store and specialty store regular prices. dd's DISCOUNTS offers lower price points and caters to a younger and lower-income demographic. dd's DISCOUNTS targets discounts of twenty percent to seventy percent off moderate department store and discount store regular prices. The company believes it can grow to 2,000 Ross Dress for Less Stores and 500 dd's DISCOUNTS stores. The company continues to show strong growth. It is very shareholder-friendly.

Risks: Company-specific risks to growth in the next five to ten years are few. Customer traffic may fall during periods of strong economic growth. The stock price reacts to comparable store sales growth data.

The Numbers: Profit margins have averaged six percent the last ten years. Asset turnover is 2.4. Financial leverage is 2.1. Long-term debt as a percentage of assets is eight percent. Return on equity is an impressive forty-one percent. Return on equity has averaged forty-two percent the last five years and thirty-six percent the last ten.

Dividends and Share Buybacks: In February 2015, the company announced an eighteen percent increase in its annual dividend to 47¢ – adjusted for a subsequent stock split in June 2015 – its 21st consecutive annual increase. The dividend payout ratio is eighteen percent. It has averaged sixteen percent the last ten years. The company complements its dividend with a vigorous share buyback program that, net, has amounted to 4.1 times what it has paid out in dividends the last ten years. Over the last ten years, the company has retired its shares at a 3.5 percent a year clip.

These are ongoing and massive long-term buybacks, a rarity in the stock market, and a strong indicator of a healthy and shareholder-friendly company.

Spreadsheet Parameters: Actual dividend payout ratio of 20 percent; assumed payout ratio of **75** percent. Return on beginning equity: **45** percent. Return on beginning equity is currently 46 percent. It has averaged 40 percent the last ten years. As the actual annual dividend is only for background information, and is immaterial to the projection, you may enter an updated value or leave it blank. Earnings growth has averaged 19 percent the last ten years. Over the same period, dividend growth has averaged 26 percent. Reasonable growth rates for our spreadsheet: (Years 1-5: **11** percent) (Years 6-10: **11** percent) (Years 11-20: **10** percent) (Years 21-30: **8** percent) (Years 31+: 3 percent).

Sample Spreadsheet Results: At a stock price of **$50**, earnings per share of **$2.50** – implying a current P/E ratio of 20 – and the rest of the parameters as above, the expected return is 12.73 percent a year and the shares look undervalued.

The TJX Companies

Ticker: TJX

Sector: Consumer Discretionary

Size: Large-cap

Website: http://www.tjx.com

The Business: TJX is the world's leading retailer of off-price apparel and home fashions. It is a bigger, more diversified version of Ross Stores. In addition to apparel stores (where it also sells home merchandise) the company has distinct home stores and has expanded overseas. Currently, it operates 3,395 stores in the U.S., Canada, and Europe. The company's storefronts are T.J. Maxx, Marshalls, HomeGoods, and Sierra Trading Post in the U.S.; Winners, HomeSense, and Marshalls in Canada; and T.K. Maxx and HomeSense in Europe. It also operates three e-commerce sites. The company is growing square footage four percent to five percent a year. Astonishingly, comparable sales have increased thirty-seven of the last thirty-eight years. The company discounts its products twenty percent to sixty percent off department and specialty store regular prices. The company is very shareholder-friendly.

Risks: Company-specific risks to growth in the next five to ten years are few. Customer traffic may fall during periods of strong economic growth. Currency fluctuations are a risk. The stock price reacts to comparable store sales growth data.

The Numbers: Profit margins have averaged six percent the last ten years. Asset turnover is 2.6. Financial leverage is 2.6. Long-term debt as a percentage of assets is fifteen percent. In the last two years, long-term debt has more than doubled as the company has taken advantage of low interest rates. Return on equity is a remarkable fifty-two percent. It has averaged forty-four percent the last ten years.

Dividends and Share Buybacks: In February 2015, TJX announced a twenty percent increase in its annual dividend to 84¢, its 19th consecutive annual increase. The dividend payout ratio is twenty-two percent. The company complements its dividend with a vigorous share buyback program that, net, has amounted to 3.7 times what it has paid out in dividends the last ten years. Over the last ten years, the company has retired its shares at a 3.4 percent a year clip. These are ongoing and massive long-term buybacks, a rarity in the stock market, and a strong indicator of a healthy and shareholder-friendly company.

Spreadsheet Parameters: Actual dividend payout ratio of 20 percent; assumed payout ratio of **80** percent. Return on beginning equity: **50** percent. Return on beginning equity is currently an astonishing 52 percent. It has averaged 48 percent the last ten years. As the actual annual dividend is only for background information, and is immaterial to the projection, you may enter an updated value or leave it blank. Earnings growth has averaged 14 percent the last ten years, though this has been volatile. Dividend growth has averaged 23 percent the last ten years. Reasonable growth rates for our spreadsheet: (Years 1-5: **10** percent) (Years 6-10: **10** percent) (Years 11-20: **9** percent) (Years 21-30: **8** percent) (Years 31+: 3 percent).

Sample Spreadsheet Results: At a stock price of **$70**, earnings per share of **$3.35** – implying a current P/E ratio of 21 – and the rest of the parameters as above, the expected return is 12.11 percent a year and the shares look undervalued.

United Technologies

Ticker: UTX

Sector: Industrials

Size: Large-cap

Website: http://www.utc.com

The Business: United Technologies provides a broad range of high-tech products and services to the building systems and aerospace industries. The company splits its business into five segments: Otis (elevators, escalators, and moving walkways – 20 percent of total segment sales); UTC Climate, Controls and Security (a wide variety of products related to heating, ventilation, air-conditioning, refrigeration, building controls, and so on – 25 percent); Pratt & Whitney (primarily aircraft engines and related – 22 percent); UTC Aerospace Systems (aerospace products and related – 22 percent); and Sikorsky (primarily helicopters – 11 percent). Forty-five percent of sales are from commercial and industrial markets; thirty-five percent from commercial aerospace; and twenty percent from military aerospace and space. Overall, sixty-two percent of sales are from outside the U.S. Acquisitions are an important part of the company's strategy. In 2012, the company bought Goodrich. The company is shareholder-friendly. In July 2015, the company announced the sale of its Sikorsky division to Lockheed Martin. Currently, the company is experiencing difficulties: In November 2014, the company's long-term CEO abruptly resigned. In July 2015, after the company's second quarter earnings report, the stock price fell seven percent in one day, a substantial drop for the quintessential blue-chip stock.

Risks: Building systems are sensitive to building activity and remodeling. Aerospace is cyclical. In 2009, earnings per share fell sixteen percent. In 2012, the company experienced no organic growth and earnings per share was essentially flat. The company provides financing and other commitments to its commercial aerospace customers. Currency fluctuations are another risk. Government budgets can be fickle. The company maintains pension and other benefit plans with all the financial risks and costs that these plans carry.

The Numbers: Profit margins have averaged eight percent the last ten years. Asset turnover is 0.7. Financial leverage is 2.8. Long-term debt as a percentage of assets is twenty percent. Return on equity is nineteen percent. The ten-year average is twenty percent.

Dividends and Share Buybacks: In February 2015, the company announced an eight percent increase in its annual dividend to $2.56. The company raises its dividend at extended intervals, rarely every four quarters in recent years, usually every five or six. The company has paid dividends since 1936. The dividend payout ratio is thirty-five percent. The ten-year average is thirty-three percent. The company complements its dividend with a share buyback program that, net, has amounted to 0.9 times what it has paid out in dividends the last ten years. Over the last ten years, the company has retired its shares at a 1.2 percent a year clip.

Spreadsheet Parameters: Actual dividend payout ratio of 35 percent; assumed payout ratio of **50** percent. Return on beginning equity: **20** percent. Return on beginning equity is currently 19 percent. It has averaged 21 percent the last ten years. As the actual annual dividend is only for background information, and is immaterial to the projection, you may enter an updated value or leave it blank. Earnings growth has averaged 9 percent the last ten years. Over the same period, dividend growth has averaged 13 percent. Reasonable growth rates for our spreadsheet: (Years 1-5: **9** percent) (Years 6-10: **9** percent) (Years 11-20: **9** percent) (Years 21-30: **8** percent) (Years 31+: 3 percent).

Sample Spreadsheet Results: At a stock price of **$100**, earnings per share of **$6.40** – implying a current P/E ratio of 16 – and the rest of the parameters as above, the expected return is 10.68 percent a year and the shares look fairly valued. These results implicitly include Sikorsky.

Valspar

Ticker: VAL

Sector: Materials

Size: Large-cap

Website: http://www.valspar.com

The Business: Founded in 1806, Valspar is a global leader in the paint and coatings industry. Coatings generate fifty-six percent of sales; paints, forty percent; "other," the remaining four percent. The company operates in more than twenty-five countries. Sales are well diversified with sixty percent from the Americas; twenty-two percent from Asia Pacific; and eighteen percent from Europe. Acquisitions are an important part of the company's strategy. Valspar has acquired more than fifty businesses since 1980. The company is very shareholder-friendly.

Risks: Valspar has a customer concentration problem in its paints segment: The top five customers in this segment account for fifty-five percent of paint segment sales. Lowe's accounts for more than ten percent of company-wide sales. More troublesome, Lowe's has started selling Sherwin-Williams' paint. Earnings per share growth is noisy because the company takes frequent accounting charges. In three of the last ten years, earnings per share has fallen. In Fiscal Year 2011, earnings per share was negative as the company took a large accounting charge.

The Numbers: Profit margins have averaged five percent the last ten years. Asset turnover is 1.1. Long-term debt as a percentage of assets is twenty-four percent. Financial leverage is 4.0, as the company has aggressively bought back shares in recent years, thus lowering equity, and increasing debt, relative to assets. Return on equity is thirty-four percent. It has increased sharply the last three years, when it has averaged twenty-eight percent. In the six years prior to Fiscal Year 2011, when earnings per share turned negative, return on equity averaged just thirteen percent.

Dividends and Share Buybacks: In November 2015, Valspar announced a ten percent increase in its annual dividend to $1.32, its 38th consecutive annual increase. The dividend payout ratio is twenty-six percent.

Excluding Fiscal Year 2011, when the company reported a loss, the dividend payout ratio has averaged thirty-one percent over the other nine of the last ten years. The company targets a dividend payout ratio of twenty-five percent to thirty-five percent. The company complements its dividend with a share buyback program that, net, has amounted to 2.1 times what it has paid out in dividends the last ten years. Over the last five years, the company has retired its shares at a rapid 3.8 percent a year clip. This rapid pace is a recent phenomenon. Over the five years prior, the company had retired its shares at a more modest 0.5 percent a year clip. Over the entire ten years, the company has retired its shares at a 2.2 percent a year clip.

Spreadsheet Parameters: Actual dividend payout ratio of 30 percent; assumed payout ratio of **65** percent. Return on beginning equity: **25** percent. Return on beginning equity is currently 31 percent. Excluding Fiscal Year 2011, when the company reported a loss, return on beginning equity has averaged 23 percent over the other four of the last five years. As with return on equity, return on beginning equity has increased sharply the last three years. As the actual annual dividend is only for background information, and is immaterial to the projection, you may enter an updated value or leave it blank. Earnings growth has been haphazard. Over the last ten years, dividend growth has averaged 11 percent. This is probably a better indicator of the "true" earnings growth rate, though this has to be marked down for share buybacks. Reasonable growth rates for our spreadsheet: (Years 1-5: **9** percent) (Years 6-10: **9** percent) (Years 11-20: **8** percent) (Years 21-30: **7** percent) (Years 31+: 3 percent).

Sample Spreadsheet Results: At a stock price of **$80**, earnings per share of **$4.50** – implying a current P/E ratio of 18 – and the rest of the parameters as above, the expected return is 10.95 percent a year and the shares look undervalued.

Bonus: Starbucks

Ticker: SBUX

Sector: Consumer Discretionary

Size: Large-cap

Website: http://www.starbucks.com

The Business: Starbucks sells coffee, primarily, as well as tea and food items in sixty-five countries. It operates 21,366 stores with half owned by the company and half licensed. Company-owned stores generate seventy-nine percent of sales with almost three-quarters from beverages. Licensed stores generate ten percent of sales; packaged goods, eight percent; foodservice, three percent. The company divides its business into five segments with seventy-three percent of sales from the Americas; eight percent from Europe, Middle East, and Africa; seven percent from China and Asia Pacific; nine percent through outlets such as grocery stores; and three percent from other areas. As large as Starbucks is, it is still growing exceptionally well – a rarity for a company of this size. In fact, with earnings per share growth rates in the high teens – or even low twenties, recently – and similar earnings per share growth rates expected in the next five years, Starbucks is more of an aggressive growth or even large-cap speculative stock than a dividend growth stock. Invest in it only if you can accept more volatility than a comparable dividend growth stock of the same size. Starbucks started paying dividends in Fiscal Year 2010. I only consider data from that year on.

Risks: When the economy is bad, customers reduce their purchases or choose other options. Customers pay up for its brand name. Damage to its brand name will hurt its sales. The company's growth depends on its performance in China and Asia Pacific. Commodity costs are a risk, especially the price of arabica coffee beans. In bear markets, investors punish stocks with high P/E multiples. At some point, company growth will slow and the P/E multiple will adjust.

The Numbers: Profit margins are good. They have averaged eleven percent the last five years. Asset turnover is 1.5. Financial leverage is 2.0. Long-term debt as a percentage of assets is nineteen percent. Return on equity is an impressive thirty-nine percent. It has averaged thirty-two percent the last five years.

Dividends and Share Buybacks: In October 2015, Starbucks announced a twenty-five percent increase in its annual dividend to $0.80. The dividend payout ratio is forty-one percent. The five-year average is thirty-seven percent. The company complements its dividend with a share buyback program that, net, has amounted to 0.7 times what it has paid out in dividends the last five years. Over the last five years, despite the share buybacks, shares have grown at a 0.2 percent a year clip.

Spreadsheet Parameters: Actual dividend payout ratio of 40 percent; assumed payout ratio of **50** percent. Return on beginning equity: **35** percent. Return on beginning equity is currently 46 percent. It has averaged 35 percent the last five years. As the actual annual dividend is only for background information, and is immaterial to the projection, you may enter an updated value or leave it blank. Ignoring Fiscal Year 2010 which saw a huge earnings increase from a depressed Fiscal Year 2009, earnings growth has averaged 22 percent the last four years. Ignoring Fiscal Years 2010 and 2011 – because the company started paying dividends in Fiscal Year 2010 and paid only three quarterly dividends that fiscal year – dividend growth has averaged 25 percent the last three years. Reasonable growth rates for our spreadsheet – indicative of an aggressive growth or even large-cap speculative stock rather than a dividend growth stock, and likely too optimistic longer term for a company this size: (Years 1-5: **20** percent) (Years 6-10: **16** percent) (Years 11-20: **14** percent) (Years 21-30: **10** percent) (Years 31+: 3 percent).

Sample Spreadsheet Results: At a stock price of **$60**, earnings per share of **$1.80**, and the rest of the parameters as above, the expected return is 12.24 percent a year and the shares look overvalued, perhaps not surprising given a current P/E ratio of 33. Companies that grow so robustly, and consistently, tend to have high P/E ratios as investors continue to pile in. The company will have to continue to surpass expectations, a likely scenario, on average, over the next few years as business momentum looks good. Further out, it probably will be difficult.

Tables 11.2 and 11.3 provide an abbreviated, mostly numerical, summary of our twenty dividend growth stocks. These tables do not include dividend yield. Dividend yield is only part of a stock's expected return, and for our dividend growth stocks, not the biggest part.

Ticker	Sector	Size	Dividend Payout Ratio	Assumed Payout Ratio	Return on Beginning Equity	Earnings Growth Rate
ACN	IT	L	40	80	60	10
CLX	CS	L	60	80	NM	6
CL	CS	L	45	90	90	8
DCI	IND	M	35	65	25	9
EMR	IND	L	50	65	22	7
FDS	IT	M	30	75	35	9
GPC	CD	L	50	60	20	7
GGG	IND	M	30	65	40	13
HON	IND	L	35	65	24	9
JNJ	H	MG	50	75	25	7
MKC	CS	L	45	65	22	8
MCD	CD	L	55	80	30	6
NKE	CD	L	30	65	27	10
PZZA	CD	M	30	70	40	12
PH	IND	L	30	55	20	9
PX	MAT	L	45	65	25	9
ROST	CD	L	20	75	45	11
TJX	CD	L	20	80	50	10
UTX	IND	L	35	50	20	9
VAL	MAT	L	30	65	25	9
Average:	-	-	38	70	34	9

Table 11.2. Summary of our Twenty Dividend Growth Stocks – Part I. For sector, the abbreviations are as follows: CD – Consumer Discretionary, CS – Consumer Staples, H – Healthcare, IND – Industrials, IT – Information Technology, and MAT – Materials. For size, the abbreviations are as follows: MG – Megacap, L – Large-cap, and M – Midcap. All numbers are in percent. Earnings growth rate is the average *earnings* growth rate for the next ten years. Earnings growth rate is not on a per share basis. It is not the earnings per share growth rate. NM stands for not meaningful.

Ticker	Stock Price	EPS	Current P/E Ratio	Expected Return	Valuation Comment
ACN	90	4.70	19	12.64	U
CLX	105	4.70	22	8.76	FV
CL	65	2.90	22	10.61	U
DCI	35	1.50	23	10.01	FV
EMR	55	3.45	16	9.98	U
FDS	160	5.90	27	9.97	FV
GPC	85	4.80	18	9.04	FV
GGG	65	3.20	20	13.14	U
HON	95	6.30	15	11.71	U
JNJ	95	6.20	15	11.06	U
MKC	80	3.50	23	9.29	FV
MCD	95	4.70	20	9.41	U
NKE	105	4.10	26	9.95	FV
PZZA	65	2.10	31	10.43	O
PH	115	7.50	15	11.29	U
PX	115	6.00	19	10.71	U
ROST	50	2.50	20	12.73	U
TJX	70	3.35	21	12.11	U
UTX	100	6.40	16	10.68	FV
VAL	80	4.50	18	10.95	U
Average:	86	-	20	10.72	-

Table 11.3. Summary of our Twenty Dividend Growth Stocks – Part II. EPS is earnings per share six months in the past plus six months in the future. Current P/E ratio is share price divided by EPS. Expected return is a long-term expectation, in percent. For the valuation comment, the abbreviations are as follows: U – Undervalued, FV – Fairly Valued, and O – Overvalued. The valuation comment is a rough indication of risk-adjusted return.

Of these *businesses*, that is, putting aside the question of valuation, of the large-caps and one megacap, as of mid-2015, Colgate-Palmolive, Honeywell, Nike, Praxair, Ross Stores, and the TJX Companies stand out. Likewise, of the midcaps, all four – Donaldson Company, FactSet, Graco, and Papa John's – stand out. I believe a portfolio of these ten stocks (bought regularly, for instance, to even out the effect of growth rate in P/E ratio on return) beats the market over the long term – with less risk. For our purposes, over the long term means a period of ten years.

Realistically, check your stocks regularly to determine that underlying business fundamentals remain sound. Likewise, our list needs to be revisited every five years or so as business conditions and opportunities do change.

Now it's your turn. Here are 12 stocks (with tickers) that may qualify as dividend growth stocks. Have they reached the age and maturity to be considered dividend growth stocks? Is long-term return on beginning equity 20 percent or more? Is expected five-year earnings per share growth rate within the expected range for our dividend growth stocks: 8-12 percent for a large-cap and 8-16 percent for a midcap?

After you have winnowed down the list, determine which companies meet the remaining guidelines listed at the end of Chapter 9. Analyze those that do. Next, run our spreadsheet. Finally, as we have done, create a two-page summary for each stock. Include sections about the business; risks; the numbers; dividends and share buybacks; spreadsheet parameters; and spreadsheet results.

- Abbott (ABT)

- Air Products and Chemicals (APD)

- Becton Dickinson (BDX)

- Church & Dwight (CHD)

- Diageo (DEO)

- General Electric (GE)

- General Mills (GIS)

- Linear Technology (LLTC)

- Nestlé (NSRGY)

- Paccar (PCAR)

- Procter & Gamble (PG)

- T. Rowe Price (TROW)

Some investors dislike owning individual stocks directly. It makes them uncomfortable. They'd rather be surfing. They prefer funds.

If you are one of these mavericks, you will find the next chapter on dividend growth mutual funds and ETFs more entertaining. Aloha. ♣

Chapter 12

Dividend Growth Mutual Funds and ETFs

"Simplify, simplify." Henry David Thoreau

FUNDS differ in their interpretation of dividend growth. Some accept any level of dividend growth, however minimal. Others insist on consecutive years of dividend growth. Some take a purely mechanical approach. Others take a more holistic view.

Funds differ in other, more general, ways too. Some follow a passive approach while others take an active approach. Some permit nondiversified portfolios while most insist on diversification. Some focus entirely on U.S. stocks while others invest globally.

You may not see dividends per share rise with dividend growth funds. This happens, for instance, when a fund replaces a higher-yielding stock with a lower-yielding one; or when it increases its stake in lower-yielding assets, for instance, cash as of mid-2015. Slightly more treacherously, it also happens when fund expenses take a bigger bite out of dividends that the fund receives – thus leaving a smaller dividend for fund holders. In these cases, among others, the fund's dividends per share growth rate slows – or even turns negative. In the latter case, dividends per share falls.

Mutual Funds

"The last ever dolphin message was misinterpreted as a surprisingly sophisticated attempt to do a double-backward somersault through a hoop while whistling the Star-Spangled Banner, but in fact the message was this: So long and thanks for all the fish." Douglas Adams (The Hitchhiker's Guide to the Galaxy)

Holders of mutual funds face a bewildering array of costs:

- *Purchase-related fees* take the form of purchase fees and front-end loads.

- *Ongoing expenses* pay for things such as management fees, distribution fees, administrative costs, and shareholder services. Ongoing expenses include the much maligned 12b-1 fee, a distribution fee. A fund's *expense ratio* equals ongoing expenses divided by assets, expressed as a percentage. **Like a silent thief, a mutual fund's expense ratio is a hidden cost. You never see it explicitly; yet it eats away at your returns.** Though some expenses are understandable, expense ratios should not be too high. Expense ratios vary by mutual fund category. Index mutual funds have relatively low expense ratios. By contrast, small-cap and international mutual fund categories have high expense ratios – expense ratios of more than one-and-a-half percent are not uncommon. Nevertheless, as a general rule, view any expense ratio of more than one percent with caution. Mutual funds with high expense ratios have a high burden to cross.

- *Redemption-related fees* take the form of redemption fees and back-end loads.

- *Miscellaneous fees* include, for instance, account fees that funds charge investors with small balances.

Owning individual stocks can be cheaper than owning mutual funds, especially as your assets increase. As your assets increase, the costs of

Ongoing costs, in *dollars*, of owning mutual funds and stocks			
	Mutual Funds		Stocks – low turnover
	Expense Ratio		Traditional
Assets	0.50%	1.00%	Brokerage
$1,000	**$5**	$10	$40
$5,000	**$25**	$50	$40
$10,000	$50	$100	**$40**
$25,000	$125	$250	**$40**
$50,000	$250	$500	**$40**
$100,000	$500	$1,000	**$40**

Table 12.1. *Ongoing* costs, in *dollars*, of owning mutual funds and stocks. The two mutual funds have expense ratios of (a) 0.50% and (b) 1.00%. The stocks are part of a long-term portfolio with low turnover, for instance, a typical dividend growth portfolio. The costs for the traditional brokerage account assume transaction costs of $10 a trade and four transactions a year, one a quarter (low turnover again). Realistically, you will place more trades than this initially – but these are *onetime* costs to establish the portfolio. If you were to establish a portfolio of ten stocks, for instance, you would add $100 in onetime costs. The cheapest costs are shown in **bold**.

owning stocks stay roughly the same or increase only slightly – costs depend on transaction costs, which are typically flat rates, and account fees, which are often zero (and, in any case, should never be accepted as a percentage of your assets). *By contrast, with mutual funds, as your assets increase, your costs increase because the mutual fund levies expenses – for instance, the expense ratio – as a percentage of your assets.* For an illustration of the difference in costs between owning stocks and owning mutual funds, see Tables 12.1 and 12.2. In these tables, the stocks are part of a long-term portfolio with low turnover, for instance, a typical dividend growth portfolio.

Some mutual funds sell various flavors, or *classes* of shares, each with a different cost structure. The classes are standardized, usually A, B, C, and others. For instance, Class A shares, the most popular, have

	Mutual Funds Expense Ratio		Stocks – low turnover Traditional Brokerage
Ongoing costs, as a *percentage* of assets, of owning mutual funds and stocks			
Assets	0.50%	1.00%	
$1,000	**0.50%**	1.00%	4.00%
$5,000	**0.50%**	1.00%	0.80%
$10,000	0.50%	1.00%	**0.40%**
$25,000	0.50%	1.00%	**0.16%**
$50,000	0.50%	1.00%	**0.08%**
$100,000	0.50%	1.00%	**0.04%**

Table 12.2. *Ongoing* costs, as a *percentage* of assets, of owning mutual funds and stocks. The assumptions are the same as those of Table 12.1. The cheapest costs are shown in **bold**.

sizable front-end loads but compensate with relatively moderate expense ratios and no back-end loads. The longer you hold on to your Class A shares, the less costly the impact of the front-end load on your returns – like a bad memory, with time, it fades away. Funds sometimes lower the front-end load when you invest more. These reductions are not always advertised. You have to ask.

Mutual fund names can be misleading. For instance, a dividend *growth* mutual fund may actually favor dividend yield. Other funds may allow fund managers wide discretion, for instance, allowing them to buy more than just dividend growth stocks. Look for clues such as these to ensure that you are buying a dividend growth fund and not a dividend-yield-focused or other fund:

- Check the fund's ten largest holdings. These should be moderate growers with reasonable yields; not lethargic growers with high yields or momentum stocks or anything else.

- Check the fund's *investment style*. It should tilt toward "large blend." On the other hand, if it tilts toward "large value," for instance, then the fund, if it focuses on dividends, is more likely a dividend-yield-focused fund and not a dividend growth fund.

Prefer big funds with low expenses and low turnover from reputable fund families. All else equal, prefer a no-load fund. Look for expense ratios of one percent or less. Even better is half-percent or less. Prefer low turnover. Low turnover is twenty percent or less. Reputable fund families include Vanguard and T. Rowe Price.

In the following list, I describe four dividend growth mutual funds. The first three funds are no-load funds. The fourth is a load fund. All have low turnover. Holdings, sector (or industry) information, and five- and ten-year returns are as of 31 December 2014. Expense ratio, fees, and turnover are from the most recent prospectuses. To gauge downside risk, I include returns for the fourth quarter of 2008 and all of 2008. To put these returns into perspective, Vanguard Total Stock Market Index Fund Investor Shares, VTSMX, returned -22.7% in the fourth quarter of 2008 and -37.0% in 2008.

Vanguard Dividend Appreciation Index Fund Investor Shares (VDAIX)

VDAIX tracks the performance of the NASDAQ US Dividend Achievers^{TM} Select Index. This is an index of companies that have a record of increasing dividends at least ten consecutive years, but excluding REITs and companies that might have low potential for dividend growth.

- Ten largest holdings: Wal-Mart, Johnson & Johnson, Coca-Cola, Pepsico, QUALCOMM, Exxon Mobil, CVS Health, IBM, 3M, United Technologies

- Percentage of net assets in ten largest holdings: 36%

- Three largest sectors: Industrials, Consumer Goods, Consumer Services

- Percentage of net assets in three largest sectors: 59%

- Expense ratio: 0.20%

- Fees:

    No purchase fee, no front-end load

    No redemption fee, no back-end load

    An account service fee of $20 a year for account balances below $10,000, unless exempt

- Turnover: 3% (exceptional)

- 2008 Fourth Quarter return: -15.3%

- 2008 return: -26.6%

- Five-year average annual return: 13.9%

- Ten-year average annual return: n.a.

Vanguard Dividend Growth Fund (VDIGX)

VDIGX focuses on high-quality companies that are typically large-cap and undervalued and have the potential to pay increasing dividends over time. The fund is actively managed and tries to be diversified.

- Ten largest holdings: UPS, The TJX Companies, UnitedHealth, Lockheed Martin, ACE Limited, Wal-Mart, Cardinal Health, Praxair, Accenture, Nike

- Percentage of net assets in ten largest holdings: 26%

- Three largest sectors: Healthcare, Industrials, Consumer Staples

- Percentage of net assets in three largest sectors: 49%

- Expense ratio: 0.31%

- Fees:

    No purchase fee, no front-end load

    No redemption fee, no back-end load

    An account service fee of $20 a year for account balances below $10,000, unless exempt

- Turnover: 18%

- 2008 Fourth Quarter return: -17.1%

- 2008 return: -25.6%

- Five-year average annual return: 14.6%

- Ten-year average annual return: 9.1%

T. Rowe Price Dividend Growth Fund (PRDGX)

PRDGX focuses on stocks that have a strong track record of paying dividends or that are expected to increase dividends over time. The fund is actively managed.

- Ten largest holdings (in alphabetical order): Danaher, JPMorgan Chase, McKesson, PepsiCo, Pfizer, State Street, United Technologies, United-Health, Visa, Wells Fargo

- Percentage of net assets in ten largest holdings: 18%

- Three largest sectors: Financials; Healthcare; Industrials and Business Services

- Percentage of net assets in three largest sectors: 50%

- Expense ratio: 0.66%

- Fees:

  No purchase fee, no front-end load

  No redemption fee, no back-end load

  An account service fee of $20 a year for account balances below $10,000, unless exempt

- Turnover: 13%

- 2008 Fourth Quarter return: -20.6%

- 2008 return: -33.3%

- Five-year average annual return: 14.6%

- Ten-year average annual return: 7.9%

Franklin Rising Dividends Fund (Class A Shares) (FRDPX)

FRDPX buys companies that have consistently and substantially grown their dividends the last ten years. It imposes strict criteria including, for example, that companies must have raised their dividends eight of the last ten years, without a decrease, and that the dividend must have doubled, at least, over those ten years. The fund sells classes of shares. The information here pertains to the Class A shares. These shares have a front-end load. Expenses include a 12b-1 fee. The fund has a higher expense ratio than the previous three funds.

- Ten largest holdings: Johnson & Johnson, Roper, United Technologies, Medtronic, Praxair, Air Products and Chemicals, Pentair, Bunge, Honeywell, Archer-Daniels-Midland

- Percentage of net assets in ten largest holdings: 30%

- Three largest industries (FRDPX does not use sectors): Capital Goods, Healthcare Equipment and Services, Materials

- Percentage of net assets in three largest industries: 39%

- Expense ratio: 0.94%

- Fees:

  5.75% front-end load

  No back-end load

- Turnover: 4% (exceptional)

- 2008 Fourth Quarter return: -15.7%

- 2008 return: -27.2%

- Five-year average annual return: 13.5% with the front-end load; 14.8% without

- Ten-year average annual return: 6.5% with the front-end load; 7.1% without

ETFs

"Simplicity and charm." Horace

ETFs, or exchange-traded funds, differ from mutual funds in subtle but important ways:

- ETFs trade throughout the market day.

- ETFs can be sold short.

- ETFs are marginable.

- ETFs generally have lower expense ratios than equivalent mutual funds.

- ETFs have the potential for lower capital gains.

ETFs can be passively managed or actively managed. Passively managed ETFs track the performance of an index. In this regard, they are similar to index mutual funds. Actively managed ETFs are similar to actively managed mutual funds, fund managers choosing what and when to buy and sell. Passively managed ETFs were the only ETFs allowed until early 2008, when the SEC allowed actively managed ETFs.

You buy and sell ETFs in the same way that you buy and sell stocks. This means you typically pay commissions – though certain brokerages let you trade specific ETFs for free. For instance, Vanguard, quite naturally, lets you trade their ETFs for free in a Vanguard brokerage account. In fact, when combined with the low expense ratios typical of ETFs, free trades with ETFs are a tough act to beat. In terms of costs, they beat most mutual funds and virtually all small and moderately sized portfolios of individual stocks, assuming a reasonable number of trades. In effect, you get to keep your cake and eat it too – a ready-made portfolio at a reasonable cost with no time spent to analyze individual stocks. *If you prefer not to pick stocks, ETFs with free trades are the way to go.*

In the following list, I describe two ETFs, VIG and PFM. Holdings and sector information are as of 31 December 2014 for VIG and 3

February 2015 for PFM. For both, five- and ten-year returns are as of 31 December 2014. Expense ratio and turnover are from the most recent prospectuses. To gauge downside risk, I include returns for the fourth quarter of 2008 and all of 2008. To put these returns into perspective, Vanguard Total Stock Market ETF, VTI, returned -22.8% in the fourth quarter of 2008 and -36.8% in 2008.

Vanguard Dividend Appreciation ETF (VIG)

VIG tracks the performance of the NASDAQ US Dividend Achievers™ Select Index. This is an index of companies that have a record of increasing dividends at least ten consecutive years, but excluding REITs and companies that might have low potential for dividend growth. VIG is the ETF clone of the Vanguard Dividend Appreciation Index fund Investor Shares (VDAIX) mutual fund.

- Ten largest holdings: Wal-Mart, Johnson & Johnson, Coca-Cola, Pepsico, QUALCOMM, Exxon Mobil, CVS Health, IBM, 3M, United Technologies

- Percentage of net assets in ten largest holdings: 36%

- Three largest sectors: Industrials, Consumer Goods, Consumer Services

- Percentage of net assets in three largest sectors: 59%

- Expense ratio: 0.10%

- Turnover: 3% (exceptional)

- 2008 Fourth Quarter return: -15.4%

- 2008 return: -26.4%

- Five-year average annual return: 14.1%

- Ten-year average annual return: n.a.

PowerShares Dividend Achievers™ Portfolio (PFM)

PFM tracks the NASDAQ US Broad Dividend Achievers™ Index. This is an index of companies that have raised their dividends at least ten consecutive years.

- Ten largest holdings: Exxon Mobil, Wal-Mart, Procter & Gamble, Johnson & Johnson, Chevron, Coca-Cola, AT&T, Intel, IBM, PepsiCo

- Percentage of net assets in ten largest holdings: 34%

- Three largest sectors: Consumer Staples, Energy, Industrials

- Percentage of net assets in three largest sectors: 53%

- Expense ratio: 0.55%

- Turnover: 21%

- 2008 Fourth Quarter return: -19.2%

- 2008 return: -29.5%

- Five-year average annual return: 14.2%

- Ten-year average annual return: n.a.

The following three dividend growth ETFs are of a more recent vintage:

- ProShares S&P 500® Aristocrats ETF (NOBL), which started in October 2013 and tracks the performance of the S&P 500® Dividend Aristocrats® Index.

- WisdomTree U.S. Dividend Growth Fund (DGRW), which started in May 2013 and tracks the performance of the WisdomTree U.S. Dividend Growth Index.

- iShares Core Dividend Growth ETF (DGRO), which started in June 2014 and tracks the performance of the Morningstar® U.S. Dividend Growth Index.

Two other ETFs with a slightly different take include:

- PowerShares *International* Dividend Achievers™ Portfolio (PID), which tracks the NASDAQ International Dividend Achievers™ Index.

- PowerShares *Buyback* Achievers™ Portfolio (PKW), which tracks the NASDAQ US BuyBack Achievers™ Index.

We're almost there. In the next and final chapter, we draw to a close this season of *All My (Dividend Growth) Children* with a discussion of portfolios – including examples of five dividend growth portfolios – and a few other odds and ends. ♣

CHAPTER 13

Putting It All Together

"Patience, and shuffle the cards." Miguel de Cervantes (Don Quixote)

T HE importance of diversification stands as one of the crowning achievements of Modern Portfolio Theory. By systematically removing risks that the market does not reward, the proper portfolio for *all* investors becomes the market, the so-called *market portfolio*. Investors hold a blend of the market portfolio and cash in proportion to their tolerance of risk.

The market portfolio consists of all stocks from all sectors of the market. Investors hold each stock in proportion to its market value, that is, its market capitalization. In essence, they are fully diversified. The largest sector receives the most money.

And in this little detail arises the first of two principal problems with diversification and the market portfolio: *Sometimes the largest sector is also the most overvalued.* In the late 1990s, Information Technology went berserk. In the mid-2000s, Financials boiled out of control. If you held the market portfolio at these times, your largest positions were in the most overvalued and dangerous sectors – just as the market collapsed. Instead of scaling out of risk, you went down with the ship.

Valuation and rationality never matter to the market portfolio. The advocates of Modern Portfolio Theory believe that everything is correctly priced at all times. Never mind that, to any rational long-term investor – who performs even a basic valuation – risks are sometimes massive because share prices make no sense.

The market portfolio eliminates company-specific risks. Moreover, because of the braiding of risk and return, it eliminates company-specific returns. Does this mean the market portfolio returns nothing? No. Instead, it returns whatever remains as the benefit of holding the remaining risk that cannot be diversified away. In fact, putting aside events such as weather and war, the factors that ultimately drive the market portfolio's return (and risk) are broad economic factors such as economic growth and interest rates.

And in this little detail arises the second principal problem with diversification and the market portfolio: *Few investors understand these economic factors; even fewer can predict them.* Therefore, when they own the market portfolio, investors unwittingly own something they do not understand. They invest on faith. They hope history repeats – but they have no guarantees here. For instance, the aging and shrinking of the population in many developed countries poses a challenge to long-term domestic economic growth.

Moreover, investors face an understated risk when they own the market portfolio and do not understand the economy: When times turn bad, when stock prices collapse, they panic. In a burst of fear, they sell at the low, almost surely eviscerating their returns.

Instead of worrying about complex economic factors, the intelligent investor worries about his or her *companies.* Why panic when you own a Johnson & Johnson or a Clorox, each selling at a reasonable valuation? *With high-quality companies, you understand what you own. You react better to market collapses. Perhaps you buy more when prices fall, thus boosting your returns.*

Admittedly, economic forces still matter, as they always do – but they are not the only driver. Moreover, understanding straightforward businesses is *much* simpler than understanding and predicting the economy.

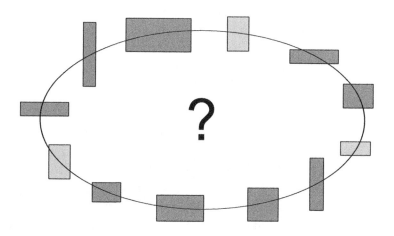

Figure 13.1. For individual investors, owning too many stocks results in a cacophony of confusion – hard to track, difficult to understand, and impossible to follow.

Warren Buffett scoffs at the dogma of wide diversification and, by extension, the market portfolio. According to Buffett, "wide diversification is only required when investors do not understand what they are doing." His answer to the question of what to buy is not in the nuances of the economy or the market portfolio, but in the simplicity of Coca-Cola. Though Buffett does use cash to buffer risk, his approach to investing makes a mockery of the mantra of diversification and the market portfolio:

- Buffett does not diversify. He concentrates on a few businesses.

- Buffett does not hold stocks in proportion to their market values – or anything else.

- Buffett does not mechanically rebalance his portfolio.

- Buffett accepts short-term volatility for long-term gain.

- Buffett keeps selling to a minimum.

Buffett invests with an eye toward fundamentals and valuation. His portfolio provides a wealth of lessons for the dividend growth investor:

- *Do not own tens of stocks.* Do not get carried away with diversification, especially if you are a long-term investor, in particular, a dividend growth investor. For individual investors, owning too many stocks results in a cacophony of confusion (Figure 13.1) – hard to track, difficult to understand, and impossible to follow. Buffett's enormous portfolio, larger than all but a handful of funds, focuses on a few core holdings. Similarly, as a dividend growth investor, *focus on ten to fifteen stocks in five or more sectors*. That should be plenty. In truth, with dividend growth stocks, you cannot build a diversified portfolio because just five of the ten market's sectors *broadly* qualify for dividend growth: Consumer Discretionary, Consumer Staples, Financials, Healthcare, and Industrials (Table 13.1). On the other hand, if you feel you must have broader diversification, use Vanguard's Sector ETFs (Table 13.2) to fill in the gaps of your dividend growth portfolio.

- *Keep position sizes simple.* For instance, hold large-caps and megacaps in equal proportions. Hold a midcap at (say) one-third to one-half the size of a large-cap or megacap.

- *Only balance your positions when they begin to "own" you.* Give your companies room to grow. Balancing too often chops the legs off your stocks. When you sell infrequently, you pay less in trading costs, pay less in taxes, keep more of your money working for you, and make fewer decisions – all are essential to earning a good long-term return. Reduce the size of a position when the stock begins to "own" you – for instance, when you worry about the stock excessively or you cannot sleep because you think about it or you need to constantly review its stock price. Alternatively, if you want a mechanical rule, create something simple. For instance, reduce the size of a position in a large-cap or megacap when it grows to 15.0 percent of your portfolio and a midcap when it grows to 7.5 percent.

- *Take the long-term view.* Give your companies time to grow. Look at what Buffett has done. He has held some stocks seemingly

Sector	Suitability for dividend growth
Consumer Discretionary	Diverse sector, some too volatile, many are suitable
Consumer Staples	Stable and suitable, though growth can be slow
Energy	Generally volatile, though many pay rising dividends
Financials	Many areas are leveraged, a few are suitable
Healthcare	Regulatory risk, but many are suitable
Industrials	Big and diversified, many are suitable
Information Technology	Young sector, early payers may be suitable
Materials	Generally volatile, some are suitable
Telecommunication Services	Generally not suitable, growth is anemic
Utilities	Generally not suitable, growth is anemic

Table 13.1. *Broad*-brush sector suitability for dividend growth. Of course, exceptions exist. In our list from Chapter 11, for instance, we had Information Technology and Materials stocks – and no Financials.

Sector	Vanguard Sector ETF
Consumer Discretionary	VCR
Consumer Staples	VDC
Energy	VDE
Financials	VFH
Healthcare	VHT
Industrials	VIS
Information Technology	VGT
Materials	VAW
Telecommunication Services	VOX
Utilities	VPU

Table 13.2. Vanguard Sector ETFs.

forever, holding companies such as GEICO for more than a generation. Taking the long-term view results in less work, less worry, and, very likely, higher returns.

With wide diversification, the economy molds your returns, your companies disappearing into the fog of what everyone else is doing. You buy everything with passing regard to quality. To long-term investors who take the time to understand their investments – *and accept the company-specific risks that they are taking* – this makes little sense. It is the complete opposite of what the intelligent investor should do.

First Things First – You Must Save

Investors climb the slippery rungs of risk when they do not save enough. They buy the riskiest of stocks, hoping that their picks one day pay off. After all, low savings do not matter if returns are high enough.

But our intrepid investors soon learn that the chances of extraordinary success are remote. They eventually realize that the highest risks do not necessarily translate into the highest returns. In fact, the highest risks just as readily translate into the highest losses. *Even worse, over a long enough horizon, the highest risks often translate into complete failure.*

Eventually, our investors learn that when excessive risk-taking persists for too long, instead of doing much better than the market, they do much worse.

You can reduce this problem, if not eliminate it, if you save more. *When you save more, your psychology changes. Your investment strategy gravitates toward taking no more than* **reasonable risk***. You think, "safety first."* And, ironically, mainly because your stocks collapse less, chances are you will become wealthier more quickly than if you had embraced greater risk.

Estimating how much to save can be complex. As a rough guide, however, **start by saving at least ten percent of your income. Eventually, aim for fifteen percent**. Save early, save often – but do not be frugal as this defeats the purpose of money. Think of any 401(k) matches or other employer contributions as bonuses. Do not include these in the ten or fifteen percent.

Put your savings on autopilot. Electronically deposit part of your income in pre-tax and taxable savings accounts. That way, you do not see the money. You do not crave it. **Build a spending plan only after you have accounted for your savings**. That way, you become used to how much you can spend. As your income rises, let your savings rise faster.

Savings postpone the gratification of spending; but you cannot become rich unless you sufficiently save. Once you are saving enough, you are ready to invest.

When to Buy and When to Sell

"Look at market fluctuations as your friend rather than your enemy; profit from folly rather than participate in it." Warren Buffett

Some investors wait until the market collapses before they buy. With dividend growth stocks, this is not necessary, or even prudent. After all, you must eventually sell to prepare for the next market collapse. This may work but is not easy because market timing is not easy. Moreover, this is generally *not* the way to get long-term compounding to work for you. After all, with constant buying and selling, even if you are right, you take one step back – because of taxes and the loss of tax deferral – for every two or three steps forward. Your after-tax returns fall. And, over a long enough period, as we've seen, even a small reduction in after-tax returns leads to a big reduction in long-term wealth.

Instead, only one primary, and obvious, buying rule matters to the long-term dividend growth investor: Buy when valuations are attractive. This gets you the return you were hoping for – or more, if you valued your stocks conservatively. To this primary rule, add any other you find attractive or that you learn through experience. For instance, you can place a standing order to buy at ten percent below the current stock price, if the current stock price looks reasonable and you have confidence in the company.[1] You can also buy on technical trading rules or on market overreaction to earnings or on signs of continued momentum or, as long as prices are fair, even randomly – in fact, dividend reinvestment is random buying.

Selling is more difficult than buying. Selling is more sudden. As a long-term investor, you will usually be selling a larger amount than when you were buying – or, at least, that's the hope anyway.

Many sell during the terrifying panic of sharp falls during a bear market. This is precisely the wrong time to sell. As a long-term investor, you want to be buying during a bear market, not selling. Warren Buffett has minted fortunes buying when the market has cratered.

As with buying, our primary rule for selling is simple: Consider selling your high-quality dividend growth stocks when they have become overvalued, resulting in low expected returns for the risks that you are taking. Consider why you would hold a stock with an expected return of

---

[1]Sometimes, stock prices fall so rapidly you end up owning the stock at a much lower price than you had anticipated because the stock price gaps below the price of your standing order. Inevitably, the news causing such collapses is dreadful. In situations such as these, you need to have confidence in what you own. Imagine placing an order to buy Lehman at ten percent below its current price during the first two weeks of September 2008.

nine percent if another were available with an expected return of eleven percent with equal or lower risk.

That said, do not let moderate overvaluation concern you. Even in normal markets, stocks fluctuate around a reasonable valuation range, which, for large high-quality dividend growth stocks, is probably ten or so percentage points around a "normal value" – whatever the market deems that to be.

When you sell, accept that you cannot be right all the time. It can be painful to watch a stock continue to rise after you have sold – but that's just the way it is. Learn from experience. Understand what works, why it works, and what does not. Understand how psychology affects your selling.

Always watch for dangerously overvalued markets. In these markets, the public has become enamored of stocks and overconfident. Signs of overconfidence include articles that proclaim "this time is different" and "Dow XX,XXX;" a general feeling of euphoria; a sense that everyone wants a piece of the action; and, most directly, a *parabolic* increase in one or more of the market's riskier indexes, for instance, the NASDAQ.

Parabolic increases signal the last move in a major bull market. Stocks race ahead in the last few frenetic weeks. New money, eager to join in the frenzy, rushes in. Short-sellers turn desperate – and cover. The force with which all this money hits the market causes it to surge. Market returns during this period can be intoxicating, twenty to thirty percent or more. You look at your portfolio daily or even hourly. You want the good times to continue.

But the bull market is on its last legs. The crowd is mad. Value your stocks. You will find few long-term buys. Trim your positions. Depending on how mad the market is, move seventy-five percent or more of your portfolio into cash. You will regret it immediately. A year or two later, you will be relieved.

If you prefer simple rules – with one exception noted in the next paragraph – consider taking a profit in your high-quality dividend growth stock after it has had a big one-year return, (say) thirty to fifty percent or more. Nine times out of ten, the stock is overvalued – and in any case, after such a big move, the stock will typically consolidate or lose value the following year. Value it. Usually, analysts have revised earnings upward. Check that the higher level of earnings is justified – and sustainable. Compare the stock's expected return before and after the run.

The one exception is in the aftermath of panic-related falls when valuations collapse. Gains for one or two years after these periods can be huge – but only because stocks are recovering from world-is-ending type valuations to more normal valuations.

Finally, as noted earlier, reduce the size of a position when the stock begins to "own" you – for instance, when you worry about the stock excessively or you cannot sleep because you think about it or you need to constantly review its stock price. You may forfeit a higher return. You gain with peace of mind.

Account Choices

"Advice to persons about to marry. — Don't." Punch

You can buy and sell dividend growth stocks and funds through four basic types of firms or plans:

- Mutual fund, and related, firms.

- Traditional brokerage firms.

- Dividend reinvestment, and related, plans.

- Specialized brokerage firms with fixed monthly fee plans.

At mutual fund, and related, firms, you typically pay no commissions to buy and sell the firm's ETFs and mutual funds. As always, check fund costs and realize that, at least with mutual funds, the funds themselves may charge a redemption fee if you sell too soon.

Traditional brokerage firms, both discount and full-service, can be appropriate. Some let you trade a restricted set of ETFs and mutual funds for free. As above, check fund costs including redemption fees. You can use traditional brokerage firms to buy stocks regularly, but, in general, only if you trade infrequently; otherwise, you end up paying too much in commissions. For instance, suppose a trade costs $10 and you buy five stocks a month. These cost $50 a month or $600 a year. Using one percent as a benchmark ongoing cost, you need at least $60,000 in assets for these costs to equal one percent or less of your assets. To reduce costs, pool your funds and buy less frequently. For instance, if you buy one stock a month, your costs drop to $120 a year. In this case, you need a much lower $12,000 in assets for these costs to equal one percent of your assets. Pooling works but it limits choice. Some full-service brokerage firms charge an account fee.

If you want to *regularly* invest *fixed dollar amounts* in stocks, you face two other problems with traditional brokerage firms:

- You typically cannot buy fractional shares except through dividend reinvestment. These firms operate on the principle of share-based trades, not dollar-based trades.

- You typically do not have the option of using a recurring investment plan. Instead, like scenes from a bad movie, you have to enter your buy orders every time. (Some firms let you save orders, which you can then reuse.)

Your next choice includes Dividend Reinvestment Plans (DRIPs), and related plans – such as Direct Stock Purchase Plans (DSPPs). DRIPs let you reinvest your dividends. DSPPs let you buy shares. Typically, you must own at least one share in your name before you can enroll in a DRIP. By contrast, DSPPs let you buy your first share. Plans can combine DRIPs and DSPPs. For instance, IBM's plan includes both. Because these plans offer dollar-based trades and recurring investment plans, they solve the two problems noted above with traditional brokerage firms.

With these plans, you make onetime buys and recurring buys. Costs are usually higher for onetime buys. IBM's plan typically charges $5 for a onetime buy and $1 for a recurring buy. There is an additional $10 charge if you are not a shareholder of record and you are making your first buy. You sell shares either at market or batched. IBM's plan charges $25 plus 10¢ a share for market sales. Batch sales are pooled by the plan administrator and sold according to plan guidelines. For batch sales, the plan charges $10 less. Dividend reinvestment is routine, though not always free. IBM's plan charges two percent of the amount reinvested, not to exceed $3.

In fact, not much is free with these plans these days. The labyrinth fee structure can be confusing. Some plans have an initial setup fee. IBM's plan charges $10. Read the plan prospectus carefully.

Dividend growth investors face four other problems with these plans:

- Not all companies offer DRIPs and DSPPs. If you want to invest in a company, but it does not offer a plan, you are out of luck.

- Some plans make their recurring buys once a month. Having the choice to buy more frequently, (say) weekly, is better.

- The recurring investment minimum, though normally fair (IBM's plan requires $50), nevertheless constrains choice.

- Multiple accounts can be a nuisance. For instance, you have to open ten accounts for ten stocks. That said, you should be able to consolidate accounts across a plan administrator.

Check a company's investor relations website to see if it offers a dividend reinvestment, or related, plan. As of mid-2015, of the stocks to consider in Chapter 11, Clorox, Colgate-Palmolive, Donaldson Company, Emerson Electric, Genuine Parts, Honeywell, Johnson & Johnson, McCormick, McDonald's, Nike, Parker-Hannifin, Praxair, United Technologies, and Valspar offer dividend reinvestment, or related, plans. (Also, our bonus stock, Starbucks, offers a dividend reinvestment, or related, plan.) Accenture, FactSet, Graco, Papa John's, Ross Stores, and the TJX Companies do not. Thus, fourteen of the twenty, and Starbucks, do and six of the twenty do not.

Your final choice is an account at a specialized brokerage firm that offers a fixed monthly fee plan. With these plans, you build a portfolio, typically, by making so-called window trades each month. Window trades take place on specified days – within one or more specific periods called windows. With window trades, you exchange the immediacy of a market trade for a typically lower cost per trade (if you trade enough times a month). Ideally, brokerages place these trades at least somewhat randomly during the day so that other market participants do not take advantage of the rush of money coming in. In any case, you should have the option of market buys and sells, though typically for a higher fee.

Fixed monthly fee plans address the four problems noted above with DRIPs and DSPPs:

- You can invest in a wider range of stocks.

- You can trade weekly. With some firms, you can trade daily.

- The firms do not require high minimum trading amounts.

- You do not need to open separate accounts to trade each stock.

Unfortunately, these plans are going the way of hairlines. ShareBuilder used to offer a $12-a-month plan that included twelve window buys a month. ShareBuilder has discontinued this plan – though you can still place window buys. As of mid-2015, each window buy costs $3.95. Window buys take place on Tuesdays. All sales are real time and cost $6.95. Thus, if you place ten window buys a year and make two sales a year, you pay $53.40 a year. Folio*fn* Investments, as a recognized larger name, continues to offer fixed monthly fee plans. It offers a basic plan and an unlimited plan. The basic plan is more cost effective if you trade a few times a month. It costs $4 per security per window. Windows are available twice daily on all trading days. However, the basic plan charges an inactivity fee of $15 a quarter if you make three or fewer trades a quarter. Thus, if you trade four times a quarter (to avoid the inactivity fee), you pay $64 a year – for sixteen trades. The unlimited plan is more flexible – you can place a mind-boggling two-thousand trades a month – but more expensive at $29 a month or $290 a year.

You have tradeoffs when costs are involved, so compare the advantages and disadvantages of the four basic types of firms or plans carefully. The best choice is not always the cheapest.

Whichever choice you make, try to eventually bring your costs down to one percent, or less, of your assets. Even better is half-percent or less. Your percentage costs will typically start out higher; but, as your account balance gets larger, your costs will fall, ideally, to well below one percent in 5-10 years.

Finally, it is worth pointing out that many brokerages have recently come under fire for directing their customers' trades to certain pools in exchange for fees. This so-called payment for order flow is a hidden cost. What customers gain with low flat rates they potentially lose with higher overall costs.

Building a Dividend Growth Portfolio

"Please accept my resignation. I don't care to belong to any club that will accept me as a member." Groucho Marx

You build a dividend growth portfolio in three basic ways:

- With a dividend growth mutual fund or ETF. Take this diversified approach if you do not have the time – or inclination – to research and own stocks. You do not need to buy more than one fund. One is enough.

- With dividend growth stocks. *Buy ten to fifteen stocks in five or more sectors.* You will not be diversified but you will better understand what you own. If you choose to ignore the ten to fifteen suggestion, try to in any case limit your picks to (say) twenty. At that point, it becomes burdensome to track so many. If you are cautious, focus primarily on large-caps and megacaps. If you are more aggressive, include midcaps. Table 13.3 is a conservative portfolio of ten dividend growth stocks based on our twenty and data from Chapter 11. It includes nine large-caps and one megacap. The stocks represent five sectors. Likewise, Table 13.4 is a more aggressive portfolio of twelve dividend growth stocks again based on our twenty and data from Chapter 11. This portfolio consists

Stock	Ticker	Sector	Size	Return on Beginning Equity	Earnings Growth Rate
Clorox	CLX	CS	L	NM	6
Colgate-Palmolive	CL	CS	L	90	8
Honeywell	HON	IND	L	24	9
Johnson & Johnson	JNJ	H	MG	25	7
McCormick	MKC	CS	L	22	8
McDonald's	MCD	CD	L	30	6
Praxair	PX	MAT	L	25	9
The TJX Companies	TJX	CD	L	50	10
United Technologies	UTX	IND	L	20	9
Valspar	VAL	MAT	L	25	9

Table 13.3. A conservative portfolio of ten dividend growth stocks. The data come from Chapter 11. For sector, the abbreviations are as follows: CD – Consumer Discretionary, CS – Consumer Staples, H – Healthcare, IND – Industrials, and MAT – Materials. For size, the abbreviations are as follows: MG – Megacap and L – Large-cap. Both numbers are in percent. Earnings growth rate is the average *earnings* growth rate for the next ten years. It is not on a per share basis. It is not the earnings per share growth rate. NM stands for not meaningful. One caveat: Any stock becomes risky if you pay too much. Always pay attention to valuation. In this table, I assume prices paid are reasonable.

of eight large-caps and four midcaps. The stocks represent five sectors. Just because a portfolio is more aggressive does not mean every stock within it must be aggressive. A portfolio is more than the sum of its parts. Always include some conservative choices in your portfolio, regardless of posture. (You can own fewer stocks than ten to fifteen, (say) just five to seven, though this can be risky. If you choose this route, I encourage you to pick from (say) four or more sectors and I strongly encourage you to keep your picks on the conservative side of even our relatively conservative dividend growth stock spectrum. See Table 13.5. Having such a few positions in conservative stocks may not be as aggressive as

Stock	Ticker	Sector	Size	Return on Beginning Equity	Earnings Growth Rate
Accenture	ACN	IT	L	60	10
Clorox	CLX	CS	L	NM	6
Colgate-Palmolive	CL	CS	L	90	8
Donaldson Company	DCI	IND	M	25	9
FactSet	FDS	IT	M	35	9
Graco	GGG	IND	M	40	13
Honeywell	HON	IND	L	24	9
Nike	NKE	CD	L	27	10
Papa John's	PZZA	CD	M	40	11
Ross Stores	ROST	CD	L	45	11
The TJX Companies	TJX	CD	L	50	10
Valspar	VAL	MAT	L	25	9

Table 13.4. A more aggressive portfolio of twelve dividend growth stocks. The data come from Chapter 11. For sector, the abbreviations are as follows: CD – Consumer Discretionary, CS – Consumer Staples, IND – Industrials, IT – Information Technology, and MAT – Materials. For size, the abbreviations are as follows: L – Large-cap and M – Midcap. Both numbers are in percent. Earnings growth rate is the average *earnings* growth rate for the next ten years. It is not on a per share basis. It is not the earnings per share growth rate. Just because a portfolio is more aggressive does not mean every stock within it must be aggressive. A portfolio is more than the sum of its parts. Always include some conservative choices in your portfolio, regardless of posture. NM stands for not meaningful. One caveat: Any stock becomes risky if you pay too much. Always pay attention to valuation. In this table, I assume prices paid are reasonable.

Stock	Ticker	Sector	Size	Return on Beginning Equity	Earnings Growth Rate
Clorox	CLX	CS	L	NM	6
Colgate-Palmolive	CL	CS	L	90	8
Honeywell	HON	IND	L	24	9
Johnson & Johnson	JNJ	H	MG	25	7
Praxair	PX	MAT	L	25	9

Table 13.5. A portfolio of five dividend growth stocks. Owning such a few stocks can be risky. If you choose this route, I encourage you to pick from (say) four or more sectors and I strongly encourage you to keep your picks on the conservative side of even our relatively conservative dividend growth stock spectrum. The data come from Chapter 11. For sector, the abbreviations are as follows: CS – Consumer Staples, H – Healthcare, IND – Industrials, and MAT – Materials. For size, the abbreviations are as follows: MG – Megacap and L – Large-cap. Both numbers are in percent. Earnings growth rate is the average *earnings* growth rate for the next ten years. It is not on a per share basis. It is not the earnings per share growth rate. NM stands for not meaningful. One caveat: Any stock becomes risky if you pay too much. Always pay attention to valuation. In this table, I assume prices paid are reasonable.

it sounds. Only rarely does the stock market push valuations of conservative stocks to extreme levels. Still, this approach requires a certain iron will and iron stomach. Be prepared for an increase in volatility – though the reason I advise conservative picks is precisely to avoid too much volatility.)

- Combine both approaches. Own dividend growth stocks and a dividend growth fund. The portion you own in dividend growth stocks depends on your appetite for owning individual stocks and your acceptance of company-specific risk. You could, for instance, choose to own a few stocks that you like or understand and put the rest in a dividend growth fund. With this approach, you do not need to own ten to fifteen stocks. You can own fewer because the dividend growth fund adds an element of conservatism. You

Stock	Ticker	Sector	Size	Return on Beginning Equity	Earnings Growth Rate
Colgate-Palmolive	CL	CS	L	90	8
Honeywell	HON	IND	L	24	9
Johnson & Johnson	JNJ	H	MG	25	7

plus

a larger position in a dividend growth fund, such as a mutual fund, VDAIX, or an ETF, VIG.

Table 13.6. A conservative portfolio of three dividend growth stocks plus a dividend growth fund. The data come from Chapter 11. Sector and size are for information only. They are not as big a concern for this portfolio as they are for an all-stock portfolio. For sector, the abbreviations are as follows: CS – Consumer Staples, H – Healthcare, and IND – Industrials. For size, the abbreviations are as follows: MG – Megacap and L – Large-cap. Both numbers are in percent. Earnings growth rate is the average *earnings* growth rate for the next ten years. It is not on a per share basis. It is not the earnings per share growth rate. Fewer stocks are needed here compared to an all-stock portfolio because the dividend growth fund adds an element of conservatism. One caveat: Any stock becomes risky if you pay too much. Always pay attention to valuation. In this table, I assume prices paid are reasonable.

also do not have to worry too much about sectors or other forms of diversification. Just remember to balance your risks by putting much more in the dividend growth fund. As before, you do not need to buy more than one fund. One is enough. Table 13.6 is a conservative portfolio of three dividend growth stocks, based on our twenty and data from Chapter 11, plus a dividend growth fund. Likewise, Table 13.7 is a more aggressive portfolio of seven dividend growth stocks, again based on our twenty and data from Chapter 11, plus a dividend growth fund. As before, consider including some conservative choices in your portfolio, regardless of posture, though the dividend growth fund adds a sizable element

Stock	Ticker	Sector	Size	Return on Beginning Equity	Earnings Growth Rate
Colgate-Palmolive	CL	CS	L	90	8
FactSet	FDS	IT	M	35	9
Graco	GGG	IND	M	40	13
Nike	NKE	CD	L	27	10
Papa John's	PZZA	CD	M	40	11
Ross Stores	ROST	CD	L	45	11
The TJX Companies	TJX	CD	L	50	10

plus

a larger position in a dividend growth fund, such as a mutual fund, VDAIX, or an ETF, VIG.

Table 13.7. A more aggressive portfolio of seven dividend growth stocks plus a dividend growth fund. The data come from Chapter 11. Sector and size are for information only. They are not as big a concern for this portfolio as they are for an all-stock portfolio. For sector, the abbreviations are as follows: CD – Consumer Discretionary, CS – Consumer Staples, IND – Industrials, and IT – Information Technology. For size, the abbreviations are as follows: L – Large-cap and M – Midcap. Both numbers are in percent. Earnings growth rate is the average *earnings* growth rate for the next ten years. It is not on a per share basis. It is not the earnings per share growth rate. Just because a portfolio is more aggressive does not mean every stock within it must be aggressive. A portfolio is more than the sum of its parts. Consider including some conservative choices in your portfolio, regardless of posture, though the dividend growth fund adds a sizable element of conservatism. Fewer stocks are needed here compared to an all-stock portfolio because the dividend growth fund adds an element of conservatism. One caveat: Any stock becomes risky if you pay too much. Always pay attention to valuation. In this table, I assume prices paid are reasonable.

of conservatism.

You may take portfolios and diversification – if you believe in its importance – several steps further, though some of these steps are complex. For instance, you may want to hold stocks other than dividend growth stocks (you may include, for instance, higher-yielding stocks, growth stocks, or even a relatively few speculative stocks, depending on your goals and tolerance of risk). Or you may want to diversify with respect to world stocks or world investments (Vanguard has inexpensive world mutual funds and ETFs). Or you may want to study mathematically how diversification affects your portfolio's risk and return profile and investigate what happens when you add or remove stocks or funds from your portfolio (the mathematics can be tricky and this relies mostly on history, something that does not always extrapolate well for financial variables). Or you may want to use options and other derivatives (unless you are careful, usually a bad idea, and best left to professionals). Or you may want to see how your portfolio meshes with your human assets (your job primarily). Or you may want to consider how bonds and other fixed income assets mesh with your overall portfolio (bonds look expensive these days, mid-2015). Or you may want to build positions in alternative assets (expensive, but takes diversification further).

Calculating Your Portfolio's Return

"What, me worry?" Alfred E. Neuman (Mad Magazine)

"Our favorite holding period is forever." Warren Buffett

Use a spreadsheet to properly calculate your portfolio's return. In Excel 2007, here's how to do it (for a complete example, and to follow along, see Figure 13.2):

1. Determine the period over which you are calculating your portfolio's return.

	A	B	C	D	E	F	G	H	I	J
1										
2										
3	Beginning ->		12/31/2013	27,235.00						
4	Ending ->		11/22/2014	(35,498.00)		XIRR	15.9%			
5	Deposits and Withdrawals ->		1/10/2014	7,500.00		Formula	=XIRR(D3:D7,C3:C7,0.1)			
6			7/17/2014	(7,254.00)						
7			10/16/2014	3,500.00						
8										
9										

Figure 13.2. Calculating your portfolio's return in Excel 2007 – a complete example that you can follow along. Record the beginning date and balance, followed by the ending date and balance, and dates and balances of all deposits and withdrawals. Record the ending balance as a *negative* of what it is. Record deposits as positive numbers. Record withdrawals as negative numbers. Thus the ending balance of $35,498 is recorded as a negative number; the deposit of $7,500 is recorded as a positive number; the withdrawal of $7,254 is recorded as a negative number; and the deposit of $3,500 is recorded as a positive number. Calculate the portfolio's return using the XIRR function. The answer in this case is 15.9 percent. *This is an **annual** return.* The formula used is shown. The 0.1 in the XIRR function is a guess to help Excel along. If you do not get an answer, or if you get an answer that looks obviously wrong, say a 0 or a #NUM! error, try -0.1. I usually find that one of these two guesses gets Excel to the right answer. You may need to try other guesses if your true return turns out to be very high or very low. This is a quirk in the algorithms that Excel uses to converge to the true return. In certain cases, a true return may not exist. This is a function of the mathematics.

2. Record your portfolio's beginning date and beginning balance in a row on the spreadsheet. If your beginning balance is 0, enter a nominal value such as 0.01. If you wish to include your entire account history and your beginning balance includes a deposit, enter a nominal value of 0.01 at a date one date earlier than the opening date of your account. In tests, I had to implement these workarounds to ensure Excel does not generate an artificial – and almost always wrong – 0.0% return.

3. Below the row in Step Two, record your portfolio's ending date and ending balance in another row. Record the ending balance as a *negative* of what it is.

4. Note every deposit and withdrawal *after the beginning date and before and including the ending date.* This assumes account balances

are calculated at the end of each day. Thus, we exclude transactions on the beginning date because they do not have a bearing on return; and we include transactions on the ending date because they do have a bearing on return.

5. Below the row in Step Three, record the dates and amounts of these deposits and withdrawals, one transaction per row. Record deposits as positive numbers. Record withdrawals as negative numbers. Ideally, your brokerage account lets you download these transactions, in which case it is a relatively painless copy and paste.

6. Use Excel's XIRR function on the sequence of values and dates entered in Steps Two, Three, and Five to calculate your portfolio's so-called internal rate of return. This internal rate of return is your portfolio's return. *Excel 2007 calculates this as an **annual** return*. In Figure 13.2, the 0.1 in the XIRR function is a guess to help Excel along. If you do not get an answer, or if you get an answer that looks obviously wrong, say a 0 or a #NUM! error, try -0.1.[2] I usually find that one of these two guesses gets Excel to the right answer. You may need to try other guesses if your true return turns out to be very high or very low. This is a quirk in the algorithms that Excel uses to converge to the true return. In certain cases, a true return may not exist. This is a function of the mathematics.

If you are willing to accept a loss of accuracy – and sometimes a *huge* loss of accuracy, so be careful – you can skip the spreadsheet and the recording of every deposit and withdrawal. Here's a *rough* – and sometimes *very* rough, so again be careful – answer to your *portfolio's return*:

---

[2]One way to check Excel's answer, and thus also notice if things are obviously incorrect, is to do the following (refer to Figure 13.2): (1) In cell E3, enter =D3*(1+G4)^((C4-C3)/365.25). (2) Copy this to cells E4 to E7. (3) In cell E2, enter =SUM(E3:E7). If Excel gets the right answer, the value in cell E2 should be tiny relative to the balances and transactions. Ideally, it is zero, but that is rare. For the example in the figure, I get a sum of *minus* 3.31. This is tiny relative to the thousands in the balances and transactions. The formula to calculate the return worked. What these calculations do is check that the equation Excel uses to calculate the answer evaluates to zero (or close enough) at the ending date using Excel's purported answer. Actually, it does not matter which date we use. We just happen to use the ending date.

	Description	Formula	Result
(A)	Portfolio beginning value on 09/15/2013		52,000
(B)	Portfolio ending value on 07/15/2015		65,000
(C)	Deposits		5,000
(D)	Withdrawals		400
(E)	Net deposits	(C) - (D)	4,600
(F)	Overall portfolio gain	(B) - (A) - (E)	8,400
(G)	Average assets	(A) + (E)/2	54,300
(H)	Rough return	(F)/(G)	15.5%

Table 13.8. Calculating your portfolio's rough return.

$$\frac{(Ending\ Value - Beginning\ Value - Net\ Deposits)}{Beginning\ Value + \frac{Net\ Deposits}{2}}$$

where:

$$Net\ Deposits = Deposits - Withdrawals$$

The beginning and ending values are your portfolio's values at the beginning and ending dates of the period over which you are calculating your return. Net deposits are deposits minus withdrawals, with both deposits and withdrawals included *after the beginning date and before and including the ending date.* As before, this assumes account balances are calculated at the end of each day. Refer to your brokerage account statements for the four items that you need: beginning account balance, ending account balance, deposits, and withdrawals.

In this formula, think of the numerator as your portfolio's overall gain. Think of the denominator as the *rough* value of your portfolio's *average* assets. Thus the formula sensibly calculates your portfolio's return by dividing overall gain by average assets. For an example, see Table 13.8. Unlike the spreadsheet method which calculates an annual return, this return will *not* be an annual return if you calculate the return over a period other than a year.

Generally, use the spreadsheet method. Use this rough method only if you want a back-of-the-envelope result. If you get a result that feels too good to be true, check your result against the spreadsheet method.

Keep track of your portfolio's return. Calculate it every year. ♣ ♣

A Summary: Part III

"Someone's sitting in the shade today because someone planted a tree a long time ago." Warren Buffett

Here are the more important points from this part of the book:

- When you search for your long-term investment ideas, read, watch, and listen – but focus on those who ask the right questions. Prefer long-term insight and careful analysis. Tune out the noise.

- Holdings of appropriate mutual funds, ETFs, and indexes afford us a wealth of dividend growth investment ideas. Use them.

- Stock screeners are another way to find dividend growth stocks – though they require more work and are not foolproof.

- Finviz (a favorite) and Google Finance provide two of the more capable free stock screeners. Value Line also has a good stock screener.

- We considered the following twenty dividend growth stocks: Accenture, Clorox, Colgate-Palmolive, Donaldson Company, Emerson Electric, FactSet, Genuine Parts, Graco, Honeywell, Johnson & Johnson, McCormick, McDonald's, Nike, Papa John's, Parker-Hannifin, Praxair, Ross Stores, The TJX Companies, United Technologies, and Valspar.

- Of these businesses, that is, putting aside the question of valuation, of the large-caps and one megacap, as of mid-2015, Colgate-Palmolive, Honeywell, Nike, Praxair, Ross Stores, and the TJX Companies stand out. Likewise, of the midcaps, all four – Donaldson Company, FactSet, Graco, and Papa John's – stand out.

- For amusement – and to pay homage to the Peppermint Mocha – we also considered Starbucks, currently, mid-2015, more of an aggressive growth stock or large-cap speculative stock rather than a dividend growth stock.

- Owning individual stocks can be cheaper than owning mutual funds, especially as your assets increase.

- Prefer big funds with low expenses and low turnover from reputable fund families. All else equal, prefer a no-load fund. Look for expense ratios of one percent or less. Even better is half-percent or less. Prefer low turnover. Low turnover is twenty percent or less. Reputable fund families include Vanguard and T. Rowe Price.

- Two good dividend growth mutual funds to consider – with good performance and low fees – are Vanguard Dividend Appreciation Index Fund Investor Shares (VDAIX) and Vanguard Dividend Growth Fund (VDIGX).

- ETFs have lower expense ratios than equivalent mutual funds. They also have the potential for lower capital gains.

- You buy and sell ETFs in the same way that you buy and sell stocks. This means you typically pay commissions – though certain brokerages let you trade specific ETFs for free. For instance, Vanguard, quite naturally, lets you trade their ETFs for free in a Vanguard brokerage account.

- If you prefer not to pick stocks, ETFs with free trades are the way to go.

- Vanguard Dividend Appreciation ETF (VIG) is a good dividend growth ETF to consider. Its expense ratio is a stingy 0.10 percent.

- Understand what you own.

- Do not get carried away with diversification, especially if you are a long-term investor, in particular, a dividend growth investor. Do not own tens of stocks. Focus on ten to fifteen stocks in five or more sectors.

- Keep position sizes simple.

- Only balance your positions when they begin to "own" you. Give your companies room to grow.

- Take the long-term view. Give your companies time to grow.

- Over a long enough horizon, the highest risks often translate into complete failure. When excessive risk-taking persists for too long, instead of doing much better than the market, investors do much worse.

- Start by saving at least ten percent of your income. Eventually, aim for fifteen percent.

- Build a spending plan only after you have accounted for your savings.

- Savings postpone the gratification of spending; but you cannot become rich unless you sufficiently save. Once you are saving enough, you are ready to invest.

- Only one primary, and obvious, buying rule matters to the long-term dividend growth investor: Buy when valuations are attractive.

- Selling is more difficult than buying.

- As with buying, the primary rule for selling is simple: Consider selling your high-quality dividend growth stocks when they have become overvalued, resulting in low expected returns for the risks that you are taking. That said, do not let moderate overvaluation concern you.

- Always watch for dangerously overvalued markets.

- Parabolic increases signal the last move in a major bull market.

- Depending on how mad the market is, move seventy-five percent or more of your portfolio into cash.

- Not much is free with DRIPs and DSPPs these days. Read the plan prospectus carefully.

- Whichever account choice you make, try to eventually bring your costs down to one percent, or less, of your assets. Even better is half-percent or less.

- You can build a dividend growth portfolio with funds only, stocks only, or a combination of stocks and funds.

- If your dividend growth portfolio is funds only, you do not need to buy more than one dividend growth fund. One is enough.

- With dividend growth stocks, you can build a conservative portfolio or a more aggressive portfolio.

- Always include some conservative choices in your portfolio, regardless of posture. Always include conservative choices, maybe *only* conservative choices, if you own just a few stocks.

- If your dividend growth portfolio is stocks only, buy ten to fifteen stocks in five or more sectors. (You can own fewer stocks than ten to fifteen, (say) just five to seven, though this can be risky. If you choose this route, I encourage you to pick from (say) four or more sectors and I strongly encourage you to keep your picks on the conservative side of even our relatively conservative dividend growth stock spectrum. Having such a few positions in conservative stocks may not be as aggressive as it sounds. Only rarely does the stock market push valuations of conservative stocks to extreme levels. Still, this approach requires a certain iron will and iron stomach. Be prepared for an increase in volatility, though the reason I advise conservative picks is precisely to avoid too much volatility.)

- If your dividend portfolio is a combination of stocks and funds, you do not need to own ten to fifteen stocks. You can own fewer because the dividend growth fund adds an element of conservatism. Just remember to balance your risks by putting much more in the dividend growth fund. You do not need to buy more than one dividend growth fund. One is enough.

- Keep track of your portfolio's return. Calculate it every year. Use the spreadsheet method described in this chapter to calculate your portfolio's return. ♣ ♣ ♣

Conclusion

"No thing great is created suddenly, any more than a bunch of grapes or a fig. If you tell me that you desire a fig, I answer you that there must be time. Let it first blossom, then bear fruit, then ripen." Epictetus

"Time is the friend of the wonderful company, the enemy of the mediocre." Warren Buffett

P ATIENCE does wonders for your high-quality investments. When you are patient, you give your investments time to grow. Over long enough periods, this results in staggering wealth (Figure 1). See what some of the greatest investors have to say about patience:

- "Only buy something that you'd be perfectly happy to hold if the market shut down for 10 years." Warren Buffett

- "One, which I mention several times elsewhere, is the need for patience if big profits are to be made from investment. Put another way, it is often easier to tell what will happen to the price of a stock than how much time will elapse before it happens." Philip A. Fisher (*Common Stocks and Uncommon Profits*)

317

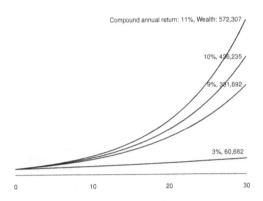

Compound annual return: 11%, Wealth: 572,307

10%, 436,235

9%, 331,692

3%, 60,682

0   10   20   30

Figure 1. Wealth after thirty years starting with $25,000 given equity-like compound annual returns. At nine percent, the long-term return of a good stock mutual fund minus one percentage point in expenses, wealth reaches $331,692. At ten percent, the long-term return of the stock market with no expenses, wealth soars to $436,235. At eleven percent, admittedly a challenging return to maintain over thirty years, wealth reaches $572,307. For comparison, the figure includes wealth after inflation only: At three percent, roughly the average rate of inflation, the original investment grows to $60,682.

- "It takes remarkable patience to hold on to a stock in a company that excites you, but which everybody else seems to ignore. You begin to think everybody else is right and you are wrong. But where the fundamentals are promising, patience is often rewarded … " Peter Lynch (*One Up on Wall Street*)

Patience is your one true advantage over the stock market. Perhaps, for the non-professional, the individual investor, your only advantage. If you are impatient, the market wins.

And when you are patient, sometimes you get lucky. Two of the twenty stocks I initially had penciled in, and analyzed, and written up, for Chapter 11 were acquired before I finished the book: PetSmart and Sigma-Aldrich. In September 2014, Merck KGaA offered to buy

Figure 2. Basis of dividend growth investing: dividends, dividend reinvestment, and dividend growth.

Sigma-Aldrich for $140 a share. In December 2014, a group of private equity investors offered to buy PetSmart for $83 a share. Subsequently, I replaced these stocks with others. Although typical large-cap and all megacap dividend growth stocks are too large to be acquired, the smaller large-cap and midcap dividend growth stocks make excellent acquisition candidates.

In general, try to act like Buffett: (1) Think of ten years as the right time frame for your stocks; (2) take advantage of the stock market's regular fits of regurgitation; (3) remain committed.

To be a successful investor requires that you be an optimist, not an overzealous one, just a well-reasoned, quiet, and self-assured one – someone who knows that given enough time great companies selling at fair prices produce great results. The occasional bad years are not of concern. For both the investor and company, they are the pauses that rest, the crises that strengthen, the lessons that teach.

By following the investment approach in this book, you are investing with a long-term view in high-quality dividend growth stocks. Dividends, dividend reinvestment, and dividend growth form the basis of dividend growth investing (Figure 2). For dividend growth stocks, the dividend provides an element of conservatism; dividend growth provides the right amount of aggressiveness; dividend reinvestment is always a form of savings.

The business underlies the numbers. If you ignore this, all else is lost. For your long-term investments, always invest in companies with good long-term internal returns. Internal returns form the basis of shareholder returns. Return on beginning equity is an investment return within the company, an internal return. A long-run return on beginning equity average of twenty percent or more is a good internal return. It allows a company to grow at a sensible and sustainable pace yet pay a reasonable share of its earnings as dividends. It signals both maturity and high quality.

Financial leverage magnifies internal returns – which eventually translates into higher dividends and higher returns. For dividend growth stocks, the ability to comfortably take on higher financial leverage than an equivalent company without as stable a business is a genuine benefit – and an understated one. Nevertheless, as always, even for dividend growth stocks, financial leverage should not be taken too far.

Always consider the risks. For stocks, risk comes in two primary flavors: business risk and valuation risk. For dividend growth stocks, business risk is relatively low. This is risk *within* the company. A good understanding of the company's business and a check of its earnings history will give you a good assessment of business risk. The business should be simple and stable with a high return on equity and no more than a comfortable level of debt. Earnings history should show steady growth with few, if any, negative surprises. As with all stocks, valuation risk is low, reasonable, or high. This is stock price risk, risk *external* to the company. Essentially, P/E ratio is the ultimate arbiter of valuation risk.

We created a spreadsheet model to value our dividend growth stocks. Our model depends on just three factors: assumed payout ratio, growth rates (of earnings), and current P/E ratio.

Over the long term with dividend growth stocks – and admittedly contrary to Modern Portfolio Theory – your annual returns should exceed that of the market with less risk, and certainly much less anguish. I believe you will do better than the market if you buy reasonably valued, or better, high-quality dividend growth stocks growing at reasonable rates *and* are patient.

In *Stocks for the Long Run*, fifth edition, Jeremy Siegel lists twenty stocks with the highest returns of the original five hundred in the 1957 S&P 500®. Of the top ten, eight are consumer staples stocks. Boring is not just good. Over the long term, it can help you become rich.

And probably even more so because investors are more likely to hold on to these stocks for the long term; whereas with more volatile stocks they usually sell too quickly when stocks rise or panic and sell desperately when stocks fall. This is essentially no different from what we noted at the beginning of this book, that investors in 401(k) plans who time the market perform worse than those who do nothing – and also perform worse than the funds themselves.

I suspect greater damage has been caused to portfolios by impatience more than anything else. Be patient with your good companies. Unlike those who trade in speculative stocks, for instance, you do not have to regularly buy and sell. In the end, you will almost certainly be better off.

The stock market's long-term returns of ten percent or so incorporate multiple panics, recessions, and wars. As long as your companies continue to earn a good internal return – with enough opportunities for growth – and valuations are reasonable or better, stock prices will rise and you will do just fine.

As a dividend growth investor, very often you will find that you have nothing to do. When you hold *high-quality* stocks, especially high-quality *stable* stocks, you win when you are lazy. You gain when you trade less; you gain when you put aside your stocks and forget about them, ideally, for a long, long time.

Let the long-term compounding of earnings and dividends work their magic for you. In time, your wealth will soar. You succeed when you devote most of your effort to finding the right stocks. Value them. Buy them. Monitor them. Monitor the market. Be wary of overvalued stocks. Be wary of overvalued markets. But, mostly, leave your high-quality dividend growth stocks alone. ♣ ♣ ♣ ♣

Tickers

These are current as of mid-2015.

3M	MMM
Abbott	ABT
ABM Industries	ABM
Accenture	ACN
ACE Limited	ACE
Aflac	AFL
Air Products and Chemicals	APD
Albemarle	ALB
Alcatel-Lucent	ALU
Alcoa	AA
Alphabet	GOOG, GOOGL
Apple	AAPL
Archer-Daniels-Midland	ADM
AT&T	T
Bank of America	BAC
Becton Dickinson	BDX
Bemis	BMS
Berkshire Hathaway	BRK-A, BRK-B
Brady	BRC
Bunge	BG

Cardinal Health	CAH
Carlisle	CSL
Chevron	CVX
Chubb	CB
Church & Dwight	CHD
Cintas	CTAS
Cisco	CSCO
Clorox	CLX
Coca-Cola	KO
Colgate-Palmolive	CL
CVS Health	CVS

Danaher	DHR
Diageo	DEO
Donaldson Company	DCI
Dover	DOV

Ecolab	ECL
Emerson Electric	EMR
EOG Resources	EOG
Exxon Mobil	XOM

Fannie Mae	FNMA
First Solar	FSLR
Franklin Rising Dividends Fund (Class A Shares)	FRDPX
Freddie Mac	FMCC

General Dynamics	GD
General Electric	GE
General Growth Properties	GGP
General Mills	GIS
Genuine Parts	GPC
Google (now part of Alphabet)	GOOG, GOOGL
Graco	GGG
Grainger (W. W.)	GWW

Honeywell	HON

IBM	IBM

Intel	INTC
iShares Core Dividend Growth ETF	DGRO
John Wiley & Sons	JW-A, JW-B
Johnson & Johnson	JNJ
Jones Soda	JSDA
JPMorgan Chase	JPM
Las Vegas Sands	LVS
Linear Technology	LLTC
Lockheed Martin	LMT
Matthews	MATW
McCormick	MKC
McDonald's	MCD
McKesson	MCK
Medtronic	MDT
Merck	MRK
Microsoft	MSFT
Nestlé	NSRGY
Netflix	NFLX
Nike	NKE
Nucor	NUE
Occidental Petroleum	OXY
Oracle	ORCL
Paccar	PCAR
Papa John's	PZZA
Parker-Hannifin	PH
Pentair	PNR
PepsiCo	PEP
Pfizer	PFE
PowerShares Buyback Achievers™ Portfolio	PKW
PowerShares Dividend Achievers™ Portfolio	PFM
PowerShares International Dividend Achievers™ Portfolio	PID
Praxair	PX
Procter & Gamble	PG
ProShares S&P 500˚ Aristocrats ETF	NOBL

QUALCOMM	QCOM
RLI	RLI
Roper	ROP
Ross Stores	ROST
Starbucks	SBUX
State Street	STT
Stryker	SYK
T. Rowe Price	TROW
T. Rowe Price Dividend Growth Fund	PRDGX
Target	TGT
Texas Instruments	TXN
The TJX Companies	TJX
United Technologies	UTX
UnitedHealth	UNH
UPS	UPS
Valspar	VAL
Vanguard Consumer Discretionary ETF	VCR
Vanguard Consumer Staples ETF	VDC
Vanguard Dividend Appreciation ETF	VIG
Vanguard Dividend Appreciation Index Fund Investor Shares	VDAIX
Vanguard Dividend Growth Fund	VDIGX
Vanguard Energy ETF	VDE
Vanguard Financials ETF	VFH
Vanguard Health Care ETF	VHT
Vanguard Industrials ETF	VIS
Vanguard Information Technology ETF	VGT
Vanguard Materials ETF	VAW
Vanguard Telecommunication Services ETF	VOX
Vanguard Total Stock Market ETF	VTI
Vanguard Total Stock Market Index Fund Investor Shares	VTSMX
Vanguard Utilities ETF	VPU
Vanguard Wellington Fund Investor Shares	VWELX
Visa	V

Walgreens Boots Alliance	WBA
Wal-Mart	WMT
Wells Fargo	WFC
West Pharmaceutical Services	WST
WisdomTree U.S. Dividend Growth Fund	DGRW

Index

do not part with their money for promises, 23

early, in successful companies, 108

expect future earnings to drive gains in expensive markets, 138

few understand economic factors, 288

for long-term, bear markets are the wrong time to sell, 294

for long-term, important to know company's internal return, 127

for long-term, moderate growth brackets ideal range, 112

get punished with faddish stocks, 12

greatest, say about patience, 317–318

higher yields seduce, 34

hold more in mutual funds, 40

holding stable vs. volatile stocks, 81

homemade dividends, 22

in the stock market are not as rich as they think they are, 74

individual, *see* individual investors

information spigot and long-term, 207

intelligent, 288

interplay between stock market, company, and, 141–143

knowing sustainable growth rate, crucial to long-term, 140

many are too cautious, 16, 75

many emphasize yield over growth, 71

more likely to hold boring stocks for the long term, 321

most interested in dividends *per share*, 148

often compare dividend yields to interest rates, 35

often guess growth rates, 175

one obvious buying rule for dividend growth, 294

only buy undervalued or very undervalued stocks, 222

per Modern Portfolio Theory, proper portfolio for all, 287

portfolios, debt and equity, 140

prefer certainty of dividends in inexpensive markets, 139

prefer the dividend payout ratio to dividend to cash flow ratios, 137

problems with DRIPs and related plans for dividend growth, 298

risk, 11–14

savings must come first, 292–293

some consider return on invested capital, economic returns, 128

some wait for market collapse, 293

sometimes consider long-term debt instead of all debt, 123

success, 319

taxes, 39, 40, 46

understand that stocks are riskier than bonds, 34

view dividends as something *real*, 47

want their dividends, 22

wanted their money back, 3

wide diversification makes little sense to long-term, 292

wide diversification not required when you know what you are doing, 289

with small account balances, miscellaneous fees, 274

without dividends, have to believe in the sanctity of the stock market, 22

worry about dividend cuts, 137

Swanson, Robert H., 54

T. Rowe Price, 29, 272, 277
Target, 211
taxes, 10, 36–44, 119, 124, 222, 294
　3.8 percent surtax, 36
　avoid, (legally), 63
　benefits of debt, for companies,
　　53
　cash used for buybacks only once
　　subject to, 46
　dividends and buybacks as rear-
　　rangements of blocks, 50–52
　effects related to stock options, 55,
　　144
　investment accounts, comparison
　　of (figure), 38
　on dividends, then company fails,
　　67
　rates, REITs and MLPs, 25
　return after, 10
　some companies pay lower, 121
　some companies prefer buybacks
　　for lower, 114
　spreadsheet model, 176
　the fall in share price and, 29–33
　the reinvestment factor and, 63–
　　65
　to the government similar to div-
　　idend to shareholders, 23
　trading, 81, 290
telecommunication services, see under
　sectors
Texas Instruments, 211
Thoreau, Henry David, 4, 273
time
　as requirement for success, 4, 5
　benefits of exponential growth with,
　　62
　give companies, 290
　given enough, not reinvesting vs.
　　reinvesting, 58
　given enough, simple vs. com-
　　pound interest, 58
　passage of, Linear Technology, 54

trade off a lower return for longer,
　62
TJX Companies, The, 55, 133, 260–261,
　269–271, 279, 298, 301, 302,
　305
　dividend and shareholder yields
　　(table), 56
　dividend payout ratio comparisons
　　(figure), 134
traders
　holding or playing with more volatile
　　stocks, 81
　many decisions, 90, 91
　need right mindset and resources,
　　4
　overall, do worse than the market,
　　4
Treasuries, 34, 35, 127, 128, 167
turnover, 40, 208, 209, 275, 277, 283

United Technologies, 208, 209, 211, 262–
　263, 269, 270, 278, 280, 281,
　284, 298, 301
UnitedHealth, 279, 280
UPS, 279
utilities
　Gordon Model, 158
　sector, see under sectors

Valspar, 107, 264–265, 269, 270, 298, 301,
　302
valuation, 151–196
　Buffett, eye toward fundamentals
　　and, 290
　buy when attractive, 294
　collapses in aftermath of panic-
　　related falls, 296
　comes after screening, 218
　comment, in commentaries, 221,
　　222
　higher dividend yield *can* suggest
　　attractive, 25
　must be reasonable or better for
　　success, 4, 321
　never matters to market portfolio,
　　288

Made in the USA
Coppell, TX
03 September 2024

36784201R00215